SHORT TRIPS
in the
Hill Country

Dear Dr. Grissom,

Thank you for your support & guidance.
I have enjoyed working for you! May the
future bring you peace & happiness!

Sincerely,

Trinity University
Bookstore

Laura Trim

LDT Press
2400 Rio Grande Blvd NW, Suite 233
Albuquerque, New Mexico, 87104.

Printed by Thomson-Shore, Inc.
Dexter, Michigan.

Cover: Art United Methodist Church.

CONTENTS

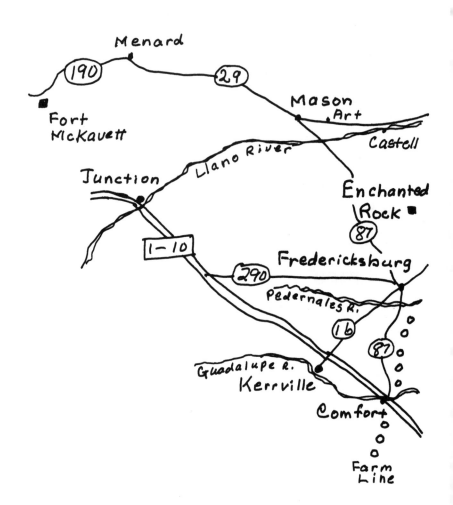

The Hill Country

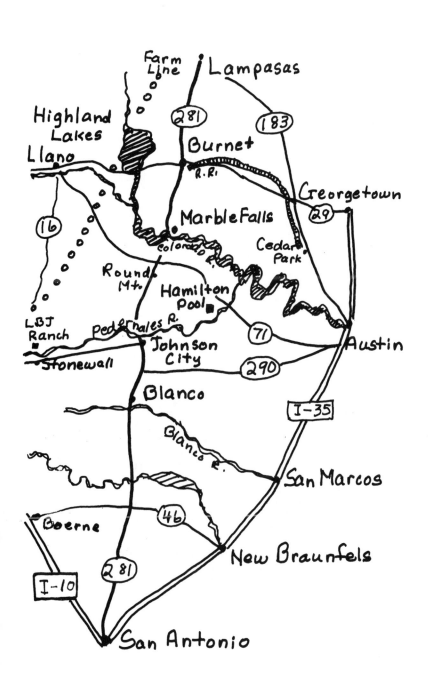

About the artists

Several artists drew pictures for this book. My daughter, Heather Trim, sketched the Johnson Settlement in Johnson City and the emblem of the Buffalo Soldiers in connection with Fort Mason. Patty Huddleston of East Texas drew the White Elephant Saloon in Fredericksburg, the picnickers in Blanco, the rocking chair and the tube ladies in New Braunfels.

Laverne Lee of Mason made the drawings of the houses and barns and churches of Fredericksburg, Mason, and Art. Her illustration of the church at Art is on the cover.

Cassandra Black of Dallas drew portraits, gravestones, statues, trains, Christmas wreaths, eagles, cafes, bakeries, and peach stands. She was the all-purpose artist. The guard dog with the sheep is hers, as well as the waterfalls at Hamilton Pool and the dance hall at Gruene.

Phylis Burke of Dallas helped me put the book together. We designed the cover, decided on the format, and then worked at reducing the drawings to the appropriate sizes. Phylis produced all of the calligraphy. She also pasted up the pages.

My thanks to all of these artists, and also to others who accompanied me on my trips. There was much help and many a kind word of encouragement along the way.

Introduction

The Hill Country is a special place in the limestone region west of Austin. Steep ridges and deep valleys and low-water concrete bridges characterize this country. Decreasing rainfall marks it from east to west. Deer abound. Birds twitter in the early mornings. Wildflowers spread a blanket of blues and yellows and whites and fushias in early spring. Many call the Hill Country a kind of paradise.

For the richest experiences you need to drive occasionally out on county roads, in remote sections. Here you find deer leaping fences, armadillos creeping

along creek bottoms, jack rabbits with long ears pointed up, crouched in fields, staring at the passers-by, but hoping the visitors won't see them. Sometimes, you need to stay in a country cottage, with only the sounds of the birds and a distant rumble on the highway for company. And, sometimes, you need to visit a country church, with

1

an "Up, Up, Up He Arose" on Easter mornings or a throwing open of ancient wooden shutters to reveal the stained-glass windows behind.

The Hill Country will not disclose her deepest secrets easily. You have to stay for awhile, savor what she has to offer. Then you may join the legions who declare this hilly region casts a bit of a spell.

East Meets West

The rugged hills west of Austin and New Braunfels mark the beginning of the Hill Country, a place where the East meets the West, a transition zone.

The shift here is abrupt, unlike areas in North Texas, and indeed up the prairies to Canada, where the change is marked by the passage from forests to prairies to stunted woodlands and then out to the plains - all the while registering the drop in annual rainfall. At this divide, the Balcones Escarpment or fault zone, the shift from East to West takes place quickly, not slowly as you drift over prairies and through bands of stunted woods. Here the flora and fauna are taken somewhat by surprise. As a consequence, you will find the eastern and western birds living together in this transition zone, the eastern crested blue jays near the western scrub jays. If you descend into special pockets of the Hill Country, into canyons or grottoes, you will encounter cypress trees and ferns, columbines or palmettos, while above the land may support only cactus and mesquite and scrub oak.

These special pockets exist because the Hill Country is the crumbling edge of a vast slab of limestone, the Edwards Plateau, which was laid down in the Cretaceous Period about 100 million years ago, was then "uplifted" about 10 million years ago, but is now slowly eroding. The plateau itself, rising in undeformed layers to the height of 2000 feet, stretches almost to the Big Bend. It is barren territory, home of sheep and goats, the principal area, in fact, of wool and mohair production in the United States. The topsoil here is thin, maybe only two inches at highway cuts, maybe only six inches in a field where soil has washed down. The vegetation includes lots of cedar trees - and cedar is what you see in the famed decorations of a Fredericksburg Christmas.

Northeast of the Edwards Plateau lies an extraordinary geological region: the Llano Uplift, the site of an ancient mountain range, a place where some of the world's oldest rocks have been uplifted and exposed. A billion years ago conditions were such that a huge batholith of molten rock emerged from deep within the earth. This magma, or molten rock did not reach the surface, as does lava in a volcano, but stayed below and gradually cooled into granite. The heat from this intrusion changed the other rocks that were present (from 1 to 3 billion years old) into gneiss and schists and other forms. This process of metamorphosis, or "cooking," changes limestone into marble, graphite into diamonds. This section of Texas, the Central Mineral District, a 30-mile radius around Llano, contains many rare minerals in small quantities as well as large supplies of graphite and unlimited amounts of granite that is suitable for building materials. The state capitol in Austin was constructed in the 1880s from the pink stone at Granite Mountain in Marble Falls.

East of the Llano Uplift, heading back towards Austin, we encounter another boundary between East and West, the long, sinuous Highway 281 that stretches all the way from the southern tip of Texas to the Canadian border. All along its enormous length this highway parallels roughly the limit of traditional agriculture, the 98th meridian. East of the marker 30 inches or more annual rainfall support subsistence farming. West of the boundary, where the rainfall slackens, the land was traditionally used for grazing. Beyond 21 inches, even this was difficult before the era of deep wells. American pioneers turned to ranching.

3

Up and down Highway 281, at Lampasas, Burnet, Marble Falls, Johnson City, and Blanco, the annual rainfall registers around 30 inches. At Llano, it drops to 26 inches. Eastern Mason County get 24 inches, but the western part of that county is lucky to get 22. True desert begins west of the Edwards Plateau at the Devil's River.

The map shows an 1850 Farm Line, a more accurate estimate of the limits of subsistence farming here. It cuts down from Fort Worth, passes just east of Llano, swings down to Fredericksburg, passes through Medina County west of San Antonio, and then makes a sharp turn to Corpus Christi. The fabulous ranches of South Texas lie outside its scope, but you can see on the map that the LBJ Ranch lies just within it.

The rivers in this region - the Guadalupe, the Pedernales, the Blanco, the Llano and others - flow off from the great bench formed by the Edwards Plateau. Many originate near Eldorado, the highest point at 2000 feet. But, as well as streams above ground, this area is characterized by acquifers, or underground rivers, which crawl back hundreds of miles beneath the plateau. These erupt in springs in many places. Fort Mason was built near a large springs. Lampasas was known for its sulphur springs with medical qualities. Others erupt where the eastward flow of the aquifers is interrupted by the broken crust at the Balcones Fault Zone. The springs and short Comal River are counted among the natural treasures of the state.

There is much to see and study here: special pockets in the opening folds of the Hill Country, especially Westcave Preserve and Hamilton Pool, the beautiful picnic spot on the river at Blanco, the seven falls in the river at Pedernales State Park, and the wonders of the Llano Uplift, including, of course, the fabled Enchanted Rock. The Plains Indians knew the locations of all the oases, the springs and watering holes in this dry land, but certain landmarks they revered. Enchanted Rock was such a place. We still keep the Indian name for the huge granite knob rearing off the plain because we, too, find this place infinitely fascinating.

Historical Framework

When the line of the Southern frontier moved across Texas in the middle of the nineteenth-century, it halted for a long time in the the Hill Country. Here were problems not encountered back in East Texas or on the broad central prairies. Here the rain stopped. Here men had to learn to manage cattle on horseback. And, most important, here were the Plains Indians en masse. West Texas was their hunting ground, the site of their trade routes to Mexico, their ancestral home. It was generally understood by all that the land west of the Balcones Fault was their territory.

When Austin was set up as the capital of the Republic of Texas in 1839, it teetered right at the edge of the Anglo-Saxon frontier. A tall wooden stockade surrounded its log buildings. Danger was ever present. The capital was not definitely set at Austin until 1872, the year the railroad arrived and also the same time that the Indian threat was ended.

Texas had inherited a war with the Plains Indians when it became a Republic in 1836, when it became independent from Mexico. This battle with the Plains Indians was to drag on for another forty years. Overshadowed by the Mexican War, the Civil War, the coming of the Industrial Age, the Indian War nevertheless continued unabated in the West. Not until the last of the Kiowas and Comanches in West Texas were sent to reservations in Oklahoma in 1875 did settlers in Central Texas feel completely safe from attack.

There were lulls during the seiges, however, and, during these, white pioneers ventured out. Some went out to check on land grants awarded them for service in the Texas Revolutionary War in 1836. One of these, Mathew

Moss, received a large spread south of the present Llano, but he did not make a permanent settlement there until the 1850s.

The first group to actually establish a center out in the hills was a colony of German immigrants. They made their way out to set up a way station on the route to a land grant they claimed north of the Llano River. They were warned by the Governor of Texas not to proceed, warned that he could not protect them, but the intrepid Germans not only succeeded in founding the village of Fredericksburg and maintaining it, but also in making a peace treaty with some of the Comanche chiefs.

These Germans went out in 1846 during the Mexican War. Not long afterwards they received substantial reinforcement. With the peace treaty of 1848 Texas became a state in the Union and the U. S. government guaranteed to protect its borders. The first of a chain of forts was built at Fredericksburg. It was followed by others at the present Burnet and Gatesville. Fort Worth was another; it started in 1849 with a log fort down by the river.

Pioneers began to settle many parts of the Hill Country in the 1850s. German farmers pushed north to the Llano River. Southerners arrived from the east. The line of forts was pushed farther west. Fort Mason and Fort McKavett were part of this new chain which extended from the Rio Grande to the Red River. New counties were formed in this ranching country: Llano in 1856, Jack in 1856, Mason and Brown in 1858.

The Civil War came as a terrible shock, and most of the western counties voted against it. Cattlemen out on the range were loath to see the federal troops depart. Texas had been the largest stronghold of the U.S. army before the war. There had been twenty forts, 2500 men, large caches of arms and equipment. Leaders such as Robert E. Lee played a part. The army, learning to fight the Indians on horseback, was generally more effective here in the 1850s than is generally recognized.

With the federal force gone, the Confederate state legislature set up a Frontier Regiment in November, 1861, and ran a line of camps from Archer County (Graham) down through the counties of Brown, San Saba, Mason, Gillespie, and Kerr. Later, this Frontier Regiment was transferred into the Confederate Army, and the legislature set up a Home Guard in seventeen counties from Cooke County south through Lampasas, Burnet, and Blanco. Significant was how far back east the line was drawn this time. The frontier had receded as much as two hundred miles.

After the Confederate draft law of 1862, the loyalty of many persons was suspect and many were killed by Confederate sympathizers. All men of fighting age had to decide what to do. The clever ones had left early, men like Noah Smithwick of Burnet County who had owned two slaves but opposed the war and left for California as soon as the conflict began. Others who waited ran into trouble. John Scott, the first chief justice of Burnet County, born in New York State, reared in New Jersey, opposed to the war though his four sons served in the Confederate Army,

tried too late to flee to Mexico. He was murdered by bushwhackers on his way out of the county.

With the end of the war, the Home Guard was disbanded in the western counties, the federal forts were reestablished, and the Plains Indians were finally subdued and banished to reservations in Oklahoma. The last significant incident in the Hill Country was at Pack Saddle Mountain near Llano in 1875.

Meanwhile, ranchers were driving large herds of cattle to the new railheads in Kansas. Among the first to head out were Damon Slator and Crockett Riley from Llano County in 1868. The Johnson brothers in Blanco County, Lyndon Johnson's grandfather and great uncle, were enormously successful driving cattle to Kansas between 1868 and 1871. There were others, too: George Littlefield in Austin, the Oatmans in Llano County, John Gamel and Anna Martin in Mason County. From the cattle trade sprang many a fortune.

Finally, the 1880s ushered in an era of peace and prosperity. The wars were over, the Indians were gone. The industrial revolution was bringing drilled wells, barbed wire, and railroads. Cotton, first introduced in Blanco County in 1870, did well at first. Two-story stone buildings sprang up around courthouse squares. The last of the frontier cabins was gone from the Llano square in 1883.

It was an era of emerging banks, hotels, mercantile establishments, larger homes, new courthouses and jails. A full measure of civilization had arrived. Much of this development is what we still see today in the Hill Country.

Railroads came to New Braunfels in 1880, to Burnet in 1882, to Brady (north of Mason) in 1886 and to Comfort (south of Fredericksburg) in 1887. The line to Burnet faltered until the state legislature voted to use the granite at Granite Mountain for the new state capitol and to build a connecting line from Burnet to the quarry. It was only one mile from Granite Mountain to the future site of Marble Falls, and that town began and remained for several decades the work of a developer, Adam Johnson, who had come back blinded from the Civil War, worked as a land agent, and waited until he could clear the titles to this land. North Llano also was built up by outside

8

promoters, but it was a rail line from Burnet in 1892 that put Llano at the center of the granite industry.

By the 1920s, the early bloom and years of promise were long past. The land here had worn out. Soil that was always thin had washed away when plowed. Wind erosion played a part, too. Cedar and mesquite and other brush had crept up from ravines and covered mile after mile, choking out what grasses might have remained and sending down long roots that dried up the springs. Now much of the land was so poor that neither crops nor grazing was possible.

It was then, 1920 to 1922, that Sam Johnson, Lyndon Johnson's father, tried cotton farming on the old family place and lost everything he owned. This was the era when Lyndon and other young people like him wanted out, out of the Hill Country, away from little towns like his that did not have paved streets or electricity.

In any case, the frontier had moved on, south towards the valley or up to the far northwest, where deep wells, irrigation, fertilizers and heavy machinery had paved the way for the major cash crops of the twentieth century.

The cars and trucks of the 1920s facilitated moving, and there was little to hold them here. It must have stung to hear reports of an oil boom at Jacksboro, due north on Highway 281, in 1926. Down in the Hill Country there was no oil.

But it was the same Lyndon Johnson, the young man who wanted out in the 1920s, who came back a decade later to lead efforts towards restoration of the range. Government programs paid ranchers $5 per acre to clear the cedar from their land, to coax back the grass and the natural springs. Young Congressman Johnson also led efforts to build dams on the Colorado and to form the Pedernales Electricity Cooperative that would provide power for his home town and other rural areas.

Between 1929 and 1951 five dams were completed on the Colorado River, reaching fifty miles up from Austin. The lakes nestled in the hills behind these dams attracted vacationers and the retired. Demand for property was such that ranchers - some of the oldest families here - sold off their properties to be subdivided into small plots. The area came to be called the Highland Lakes.

In 1951, the same year the dams were completed, Lyndon Johnson bought his aunt's run-down ranch on the Pedernales River at Stonewall. Lady Bird Johnson protested at first. This wasn't her country - the lush meadows and forests of East Texas - but soon she became enthusiastic about the hills and mesas and wildflowers. The Johnsons, as "gentleman ranchers" with outside money, built dams, put in irrigation systems, erected fine fences and barns, and bought registered cattle. Soon theirs was a showplace.

Even before Johnson was president there was a parade of visitors to his ranch and always these visitors were taken to see nearby Fredericksburg. The little town began to stir, to pull itself up, to spruce up its celebrations, to revive its customs. A paved highway had come in the mid-30s, and an historical association had been formed then, but now the town leaders were buying an ancient cottage for the local museum. The newly formed Episcopal Church bought another one. The old Nimitz Hotel was closed, with plans laid for a museum to honor Admiral Nimitz and all who served in the Pacific War.

New Braunfels, too, thrived in those years. A group of citizens had banded together to form a museum honoring their German heritage in 1933, but, beginning in 1961, town leaders here held a big annual celebration, the Wurstfest, that brought in lots of money and enabled them to make many civic improvements.

The Hill Country blossomed in other directions as well. In Blanco a rancher spearheaded efforts to restore the beautiful park on the river there and reinstate it as one of the gems of the state parks system. Folks in Mason began to appreciate their town built almost entirely of Pre-Cambrian sandstone and erected an attractive new library from an abandoned stone fence found out in the

countryside. Burnet languished until an excursion train
from Austin arrived in 1992, and then that town came
alive.

And so it was throughout the Hill Country. The
communities began to prosper. Tourists came. Bed-and-
breakfasts opened. Llano became the "Barbecue Capital of
Central Texas." Wonderful restaurants opened in Marble
Falls.

LBJ wrapped up and delivered a remarkable package of
Johnson family sites to the National Park Service in
November, 1972, just two months before he died. The
Johnson family saga curiously reflects the different eras
here - from early cattle drives to town building to efforts in
the 1930s to lift this area up to the preservation concerns
of the 1960s. The stories of eight members of this family
mirror the events of 150 years, almost all the developments
back to the beginning.

Why Germans Came to Texas

Steeped as we are in British history, we often fail to
grasp how close the Germans are to their feudal past, to
kingdoms and duchies, castles, and serfs who belonged to
the land. As late as 1800 these institutions were intact
throughout the area that now constitutes modern
Germany.

Oddly, changes occurred because the French, under
Napoleon, occupied first the southern and then all of the
German states between 1801 and 1813. The French,
imbued with their ideals of liberty, equality, and fraternity,
espoused by their revolution of 1789, decreed German serfs
free from bondage, towns free from their owners (who had
been appointed by the nobility), the middle classes free to
buy property, and the general citizenry free to change
vocations or locations if so desired.

These developments, of course, stirred up all Germany. But after the defeat of Napoleon, after the German states had settled back into their habitual regimes, these notions of liberty and equality were harshly repressed, thrown out with the French. Life continued as before for the average German. Not only was he denied representative government and trial by jury, he was restricted in his choice of vocation, his ability to move away from his place of origin, even in his freedom to hunt game in the forests. That latter privilege was reserved strictly for the nobles, the kings, the dukes and barons who ruled the thirty-nine

different states of the Germans. Only four of these - the so-called Free Cities of Hamburg, Bremen, Lubeck, and Frankfurt - were not constitutional monarchies.

But the French had left their mark. In 1813, for the first time, a German ruler had appealed to the spirit of nationality in his efforts to rally his people in the campaign against the French. King Friedrich Wilhelm III of Prussia had uttered an appeal to "My People."

For scholars and the educated classes the burning question of the nineteenth century was could the German states unite and could they form under a constitutional democracy? From the Congress of Vienna in 1815 to German unification in 1871, debates flared, insurrections erupted, and governments clamped down again. Finally, with the formation of the German Empire, these issues were settled. The German states, without Austria, would unite, but they would shun a republican form of government. Germany at that time could not sustain both nationalism and liberalism, the twin offspring of the French Revolution.

Throughout the volatile decades that followed the Congress of Vienna, political refugees fled Germany, and some even made their way to Texas. Ferdinand Lindheimer, one of the principal figures in the early days of New Braunfels, escaped the Frankfurt Putsch in 1833. Then, later, after the failed revolution in 1848, so many dissidents came that they were called as a group, "the Forty-Eighters." Since these political rebels were usually university graduates, they brought a range of talents that was unknown on the frontier. Several of them became the famous doctors of San Antonio, Fredericksburg, and New Braunfels.

Others sought acreage in Texas, the rich soils, the mild climate. Some came for religious freedom. Still others, like the Sangers of Dallas, came to avoid military conscription, the constant snatching of the flower of young manhood for Europe's ceaseless wars. As each of the six sons reached the age of sixteen, he left for Texas.

From these examples, we can see that many chose to escape Germany for greater freedoms of one kind or another, whether political, economic, or religious. Certainly most came for the opportunity to acquire a piece of land, coming as they did from overcrowed conditions in Europe at the beginning of the modern population explosion. Others wished to leave a restrictive society with firmly drawn class line, where one could not rise above one's station in life, and where the average person could not even hunt. Why, in America, any man could hunt and even a servant girl could aspire to rise to the top of society.

But there was another, and less obvious, reason why some fled Germany and other increasingly industrialized countries of Western Europe. These people had been forced out of their jobs by the Industrial Revolution. Because of this, cabinetmakers, brewers, and tanners sought special areas along the Western frontier - not too close to wild Indians - to follow their traditional trades. A place like Texas offered a window of opportunity for several decades. A wagonmaker could set up shop in the 1840s and do very well until the railroads of the 1870s brought in manufactured goods. An interesting example of this is the cabinetmaker Jahn in New Braunfels, whose handcrafted furniture lost favor to "knocked down" factory tables and chairs from New York.

German emigrants of the 1830s and 1840s seeking locations near the frontier in America considered Ohio, Illinois, Wisconsin, Iowa, Missouri, and Texas. The last two were the only Southern states that still offered desirable, unoccupied land.

Texas - as Republic or state in the Union - would qualify. Various tracts about Texas were already circulating in the Germany of 1830. The "Texas myth" in the European mind had begun, even then. That the writers of these books had seen only East Texas, the land of adequate rainfall, did not cross the mind of would-be pioneers ready for adventure. Friedrich Ernst, writing a letter from east of Austin in 1831, stated: "Climate like that of Italy. The soil needs no fertilizer. No winter, almost like March in Germany. Bees, birds, butterflies the whole winter through. A cow with a calf costs ten dollars. Planters who have seven hundred head of cattle are common. . . Vegetables of all kind, peaches in great quantity grow wild in the woods, mulberries, many kinds of walnuts, wild plums, persimmons as sweet as honey . . . deer, bears, raccoons, wild turkeys, geesed . . . Free hunting and fishing." In short, Ernst made Texas sound like the Garden of Eden.

And so the pioneers started across, first in small groups and later by the thousands. The clipper ships of the 1830s and 1840s took up to twelve weeks to cross from Bremen to Galveston. Conditions in these boats were appalling, but by the 1850s modern steam ships made the trip in less than two weeks. At first the immigrants spread out in farming communities in East Texas, joining Anglo-Americans and learning many agricultural and building techniques from them.

But, later, beginning in 1844, large groups came under the auspices of a German emigration company sponsored by a group of noblemen. These settlers formed a German town at New Braunfels, at the edge of the Hill Country and on the fringe of "civilized" Texas. Then, bravely, they blazed new trails farther west in order to settle a claim north of the Llano River. This was well beyond the "pacified" areas. Indeed, this was in the heart of the Comanche territory and one of the Indians' favorite hunting grounds. Even though the Governor of Texas sent a cautionary message, the heedless Germans formed another village at Fredericksburg and then proceeded north to make a peace agreement with the Comanches and to plant several settlements on the north bank of the Llano River, in the "promised land."

Of course, to blaze new trails, to settle out in a semi-arid section with rattlesnakes and wild Indians close by, was not the original intent of the stolid German peasants who had only wanted to find a safe place in America. But so it was in Texas.

Although the nobleman's experiment lasted only a few years, its promotion included advertisements in newspapers across Germany. Thousands sailed under its auspices between 1844 and 1847. Even after its demise, waves of emigrants descended on the ports of Texas. German farmers filled up the interfluvial areas of East Texas. German ranchers bought territory in the west. Merchants settled in Houston and Galveston. Doctors, lawyers, and professional men flocked to San Antonio.

By 1850, German settlers constituted twenty percent of the white population of Texas. Eventually their colonies spread through Central Texas, out towards Fredericksburg and Kerrville and up towards Mason. The Hill Country became a bastion of their culture.

During the last half of the nineteenth century, German emigration closely followed political and economic events here and abroad. During the American Civil War, emigration to Texas ebbed because the ports were blocked. Some Texas Germans, persecuted for their abolitionist views, escaped to Mexico, moved north, or even fled back to Germany. After the war, emigration resumed, even reached a peak in the 1880s, but then slowed towards the end of the century as a united Germany surged ahead as the greatest industrial power in Europe.

By 1900, a transfer from Germany to America was from one modern nation to another. Little seemed to be gained from this move. The special opportunities available on the last frontiers, those out in far West Texas or down in the Rio Grande delta, were apparent to only a few. And, for these last frontiers, the pioneer needed money and experience. The British and many Yankees invested in ranches in far West Texas, but generally the Germans did not invest there nor try their luck in Texas after 1890.

Emigration from Germany virtually ceased, but the beachhead was established. Descendants of the mass of German settlers who arrived in the nineteenth century still form the largest European minority in the state.

German Colonies in Texas

In the mid-1840s, just as Texas was becoming a state in the Union, the pattern of German emigration changed. Up to this time, individual families had made their way to

Texas, one family encouraging another, and the Germans in East Texas had mixed readily with other Texans.

But, in 1842, a group of German noblemen met to form the Society for the Protection of German Immigrants to Texas, the Mainser Adelsverein, or more simply the Verein, an organization intended to found a colony in what was then the Republic of Texas. Part of the motivation of this group was to help the poorer classes escape to America, but part was also aimed at financial gain, at acquiring large spreads of land for themselves.

The Verein dispatched several emissaries over the next few years, the most prominent of whom was Prince Carl of Solms-Braunfels. He landed in Galveston in July, 1844, with the understanding that he would inspect several land deals offered to the Verein. But in late August he learned that the Society had put down money on a contract that gave German settlers the "rights to settle" on a huge tract north of the Llano River. This Fisher-Miller Grant had previously been made by the State of Texas to Henry Francis Fisher and Burchard Miller, two Germans who had lived in Texas long enough to establish themselves as land dealers and to change their names from Heinrich Franz Fischer and Brukart Mueller.

Prince Solms took this news in stride, but then began to worry about how he would settle the hundreds of German immigrants who would soon arrive on the coast. The Fisher-Miller Grant, located between the Llano and Colorado Rivers, lay about a hundred miles west of the Texas line of settlement, smack in the middle of Comanche hunting grounds. That no Germans had ever laid eyes on the property did not seem to figure in the calculations.

Solms was advised by Colonel Jack Hays of the Texas Rangers that he should consider a "way station" to the grant, a first colony that could serve as a staging area. The prince thought this a good idea and bought what everyone called a "beautiful" spot on the Guadalupe River, about 20 miles north of San Antonio. He purchased it from its Spanish owners, the Veramendis of San Antonio.

17

Then he named it after his ancestral castle in Germany. Thus we have the beginnings of New Braunfels.

His was a distinctly German undertaking. The Prince even devised a separate way for these pioneers to proceed north from Galveston. Instead of leading them through Houston, Cat Spring, and Industry on the main road to Central Texas, he established a port at Indianola, shuttled his followers there, and then blazed a new trail along the Guadalupe River to New Braunfels. He wanted his settlers to avoid "rough, uncultured Americans," to maintain their language and their customs. And certainly to retain their German names.

Already Prince Solms had revealed himself as a medieval dandy in his travels and inquiries throughout the region. Attired in the military uniform of the Austrian army, he rode about with a retinue of followers fitted up in velveteen blouses and broad black hats sporting rooster feathers. It was like a fairy tale to have royalty such as this roaming about in the wilds of Texas. But, in any case, the prince did not stay long. By May of 1845, only two months after founding New Braunfels, he was on his way back to Europe. He had run up a great many debts and had failed to even keep a record of them.

His replacement was a better man, trained in finance, but he found trouble here. Baron Otfried Hans von Meusebach (plain John O. Meusebach as soon as he reached Texas soil) found debts on every side, an indifferent military man in charge of the books, and an administration that had little interest in the running of the colony and considerably more in training of the "troops" - organizing practice in horsemanship and marksmanship.

Meusebach said the "troops" would now be a work force. And then he set about to determine the amount of the debts, approximately $20,000. He found his position very difficult because the colony was set up as a commune. In the spirit of the 1840's, with its ideals of communal living and socialistic utopian experiments, the Verein had

18

promised to provide transportation from the coast, food until the first harvest, housing, tools, seeds and livestock, as well as doctors, education, and religious facilities. As director of the society, he was obliged to continue with these responsibilities.

Meusebach appealed for more funds, but money was not forthcoming. Initially capitalized at only $80.000, the Verein was now bankrupt, and its officers were loathe to assess the members for more cash. Instead they announced they were sending four thousand more emigrants. Having advertised in German newpapers, they had found many who were willing to come to America under the "protection" of the noblemens' group.

The result, of course, was disaster. Meusebach could fit few more into the New Braunfels tract, which by now held about four hundred and fifty settlers. Instead, he looked to the Fisher-Miller Grant, hapless proposition as that was. In May, 1846, he established another way station at Fredericksburg, and then he bravely went north to make a treaty with the Comanche Indians. This trip north is the stuff of legends, and nobody tells the story better than a young geologist, Ferdinand Roemer, who was sent to Texas to make surveys by the Berlin Academy of Sciences. He tells of accompanying Meusebach to the Indians' hunting grounds. In his book, *Texas*, he tells of accompanying Meusebach to the Indians' hunting grounds. He relates how his group was approached by an advance guard who asked what the Germans were doing there. Meusebach responded, through an interpreter, that he wanted to meet with the Indians. And meet they did. At the advice of his interpreter, a Mexican who was a former captive of the Comanches, Meusebach rode into the center of the gathering, pointed his pistol up and discharged all his ammunition. This was his signal of friendly relations, of trust that they would not harm him. The Comanches then took Meusebach's group into council and said they would meet with them again shortly, when their head chiefs could be present. When the gathering reconvened, they made a pact which was honored on both sides for several years, long enough to give the Germans access to their grant.

Meusebach lost no time establishing four small settlements on the north bank of the Llano River. One of these was Bettina, a commune founded by forty young intellectuals whom Prince Solms had rallied at the Universities of Heidelberg and Giessen and at the industrial school in Darmstadt on his return. This communal experiment lasted only a year, only as long as the Verein sent provisions, but the young men had a "glorious time" and most of them stayed in Texas to add their considerable talents to the local scene. Their group included lawyers, doctors, foresters, carpenters, architects, mechanics, as well as a butcher, a brewer, a miller, and a theologian. None were farmers, and none spoke fluent English.

But what of the four thousand emigrants who landed on the coast in the winter of 1846? Meusebach's endeavors in western Texas did not provide for many settlers, so what happened to the four thousand languishing on the coast? Some, indeed, followed the Verein to New Braunfels, Fredericksburg, and even up to the Llano River. Others lingered along the Guadalupe River on the way to New Braunfels. Still others stayed in Galveston or Houston, or moved to San Antonio or Austin. Many disassociated themselves from the Verein upon arrival. Families like the Fuchs of Cat Spring broke off from the Society in Galveston upon landing. They later said their frail mother's life would never have been spared otherwise. But, sad to relate, a great many immigrants perished at Indianola - perhaps a thousand. Housed in dug-outs or tents, ill-fed, and prey to diseases, they fell by the score. Hundreds more died as they staggered north. The officials of the Verein did not provide wagons as they had promised. In the spring of 1846, officials in the Mexican War had commandeered what transportation Meusebach had managed to garner.

In July, 1847, Meusebach resigned as the head of the Verein in Texas. He had fulfilled his obligations to open the Fisher-Miller Grant after he had achieved a treaty with the Comanches. He left the organization $120,000 in debt. More funds had arrived, but never enough.

Meusebach never doubted the validity of settling the grant north of the Llano River, but others, even those on the fabled trip north with him, differed in their estimations of the situation. The geologist, Roemer, points out in his book that the soil in the grant was "thin", as well as sandy and not as fertile as in other parts of Texas. He argues that the distance from the coast was too far. And he adds that the Comanches, while maybe "not dangerous" would be "at least very annoying" - they tended to steal small articles. He thought a better arrangement would have been to buy fertile stretches between New Braunfels and San Antonio, or areas around the Colorado River in the vicinity of Little River or the San Gabriel. He points out that land was still cheap and large areas available. He recommended abandoning the grant between the Llano and the Colorado, leaving it to the Indians, who indeed did hold sway there until the 1870's.

But the settlements on the Llano River did persist for a few years and settlers there were eventually given deeds to lands in the Fisher-Miller Grant by the State of Texas in 1850's. The Verein disintegrated a few years after Meusebach's resignation, but German settlers had by then put down roots, spread out from New Braunfels and Fredericksburg.

The first wave of immigrants was joined by the political refugees of 1848, the Forty-Eighters, who established a colony at Sisterdale on the Guadalupe in the present Kendall County. One of the newcomers here was the brother-in-law of Karl Marx, the Baron von Westphal. Karl Marx himself fled Germany for London in 1848. With the trend begun, more emigrants arrived from Germany. They filled the valleys of the Hill Country.

It was these political rebels in the Hill Country, the Forty-Eighters, most of them not citizens of the United States, who turned the tide against all Germans in Texas in 1854. At a meeting of the German singing societies in San Antonio, they inserted an abolitionist plank in a platform that was adopted by the general assembly. These views were by no means held by all Germans, but, regardless, Anglo-Texas was outraged. From that date Germans in the Hill Country were suspect.

During the secessionist vote in 1861, most of the counties with German majorities voted against separation. Although many Germans served in the Confederate Army Meusebach's three brothers-in-law and many others from New Braunfels - others ducked service in one way or another. They dressed as women in the fields, hid in the woods, fled to the North, to Mexico, or back to Germany.

In the western sections, some joined the Home Guard, but, when they were suspected of treason, a small band of this militia attempted to escape to Mexico. They were

intercepted and many were killed at the so-called Battle of the Nueces. A monument to these fallen young men, with an inscription reading "Treue der Union" stands in the town of Comfort. This is the only monument to Union sympathizers in the South.

After the war, German settlers in the Hill Country prospered. Some were busy supplying the federal forts on the frontier or the drovers on the cattle trails. By the 1880s, German ranchers were acquiring thousands of acres.

Many of the old hurts had healed by the time of the First World War. But 1917, the year America entered the conflict, marked a turning against "foreign elements," against instruction in the German language in the schools, church services in the German language, German family names, streets names, town names. The German communities in the Hill Country were jolted.

During the Depression of the 1930s, descendants of the original pioneers began to achieve a greater degree of cultural integration. But then came the great war with Nazi Germany, when German-Americans were again suspect.

At the conclusion of this war, Admiral Chester Nimitz, Fleet Commander of the Pacific, came home to tumultous celebrations. This son of the Hill Country, scion of two prominent families in Fredericksburg, rode in triumphant parades throughout the nation. Pride began to swell in old customs and folkways, in ancient cottages and stone churches, in bakeries and meat markets.

Then, in 1951, Senator Lyndon Johnson bought his aunt's ranch in Stonewall and Lady Bird Johnson led him to Episcopalian services in a tiny half-timbered cottage in nearby Fredericksburg. They always took their visitors to see the town. In 1961, when Konrad Adenauer, West Germany's first Chancellor, came to visit then Vice-President Johnson, he delivered a speech in German to a crowd of 5000 in Fredericksburg. His untranslated remarks were widely understood. He was charmed. The town was equally delighted in him.

So we can see that the Germans of the Hill Country have come full circle. Arriving from a war-torn, fractured Europe, they expected to find a land of milk and honey . . . and peace. Instead they found hostile Indians, rattlesnakes, and a country fighting over the issue of slavery. The Mexican War hampered their transportation

west. The long struggle with the Plains Indians evolved
into an undeclared war that lasted for thirty years. The
Civil War ushered in an era of great turmoil on the Indian
frontier. World War I meant curtailment of certain rights
and privileges that had been taken for granted, and World
War II brought more suspicion. Finally, after this last
conflict, with Admiral Nimitz a great war hero and one of
theirs, the Germans of the Hill Country were able to thrust
aside the mantle of persecution and to rise up in a great
flowering of appreciation for their culture and traditions.
Even so, this reawakening was slow in coming. It may be
hard to realize this now when you visit Fredericksburg,
but in the late 1950s it was a very quiet place, little given to
self-promotion.

New Braunfels

INTRODUCTION TO NEW BRAUNFELS

New Braunfels stole my heart years and years ago. I first came with my husband on his parents' recommendation - Grandma and Grandpa Trim loved this place. We stayed at their favorite river camp, the old Camp Warnecke, in a very rustic cabin that had only screens for walls and one bare light bulb, hanging down from the middle of the ceiling. This was probably in the early 1960s, not so many years after the Second World War, when Texans found many uses for barracks-like housing.

About ten years later I came again, this time to The Other Place (river cabins next door, the "other place" as distinguished from Camp Warnecke), comfortable cottages that also faced the river. I arrived with Grandma Trim and

our son, Jeff, and the three of us had a fine time tubing on the Comal River, the principal amusement here. We had trouble getting Grandma into her tube, but once we had her installed, we were on our way. In those days, visitors could make a simple loop around Camp Warnecke and The Other Place. This we did, again and again. That trip Jeff and I will never forget.

Still later, we came again to The Other Place. This time we found the rustic cabins at Camp Warnecke entirely gone. In their stead were motel units strung along the edge of the river. We could not make the simple loop around the old river camps because the exit at Camp Warnecke was closed, but by then a much longer tube ride was available. The Other Place ran a shuttle up to the new Chute in Prince Solms Park. Tubers could then take a leisurely float all the way down to the concrete steps of The Other Place.

So, back we have come through the years, always staying at The Other Place, always beguiled by the river, always sensing that this must be a small piece of paradise. Once an owl drifted off in his morning sleep a few feet from our balcony. Often we see turtles out for a morning's swim. The water is so clear that we easily see the bottom of the river.

But there is another side to New Braunfels, and at first we didn't see it. Though enchanted by the river and by a venerable bakery downtown, we failed to realize that New Braunfels was the seat of much German culture. Such things were not celebrated then as now. But, gradually, as I began to do research, I discovered what a treasure trove lay hidden here behind the facades of what appeared to be a fairly typical small Texas town. And as I began to walk the streets by the river, I found my way to the houses of the original settlers, homes of the 1840s on their original sites - not ancient cabins tucked in among city skyscrapers like John Neeley Bryan's log house in downtown Dallas.

Walking. New Braunfels is for walking. We go everywhere afoot: up the river as far as possible, through

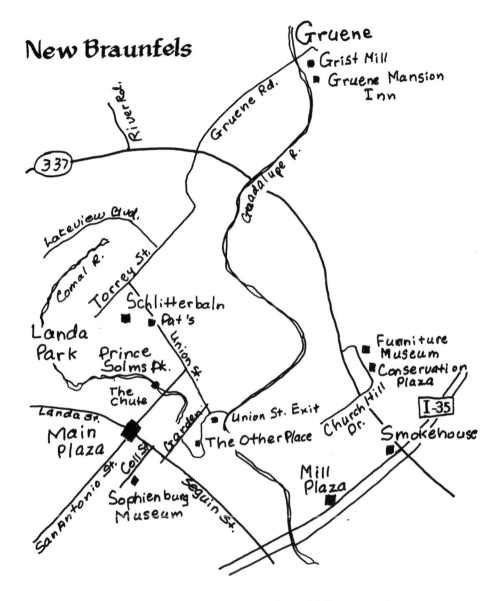

New Braunfels

Gruene
- Grist Mill
- Gruene Mansion Inn

337

River Rd.
Gruene Rd.
Guadalupe R.

Lakeview Blvd.
Comal R.
Torrey St.

Schlitterbaln
Pat's

Landa Park
Prince Solms Pk.
Union St.

The Chute

Landa St.
Main Plaza
Coll St.
Bardea

Furniture Museum
Conservation Plaza
Church Hill Dr.
I-35
Smokehouse

Union St. Exit
The Other Place

San Antonio St.
Seguin St.
Sophienburg Museum

Mill Plaza

Comal and Mill Streets to peer at the old houses, to museums, to the bakery, to glorious Landa Park, to the wonderful festival, the Wurstfest, at the beginning of November.

There are changes, of course, since our first visits in the 1960s and 70s. The old mill store out on I-35 is now the anchor for a shopping mall of 50 stores. An amusement park, the Schlitterbaln, is a major attraction. It now even owns the old Camp Warnecke. The Smokehouse Restaurant out on the highway has expanded and expanded, has even added a grape arbor for outdoor breakfasts. And now so many people come. Sometimes the crowds are immense.

But the spirit here remains the same. New Braunfels is still a delightful place of cool running rivers, overhanging cypress trees, cypress "knees" entangled along the banks, twenty turtles sunning on a log, and old-fashioned bridges arching over these scenes. Since the beginning, when the Spanish named it Las Fontanas for its springs and the Germans declared it "beautiful," everyone has thought it special. The first Germans were fortunate to find this spot in all of Texas. And we were lucky, long ago, to hear word of it from Grandma and Grandpa Trim.

EARLY YEARS: 1845-1850

New Braunfels was set up as a commune when such utopian experiments were not uncommon in America. Another of that era was Brook Farm, 1841-1847, established nine miles west of Boston by a Unitarian minister and supported by the intellectuals of that time and place: Ralph Waldo Emerson, Bronson Alcott, and Nathaniel Hawthorne. Yet another was New Harmony, Indiana, founded in 1814, where the German followers of George Rapp built a prosperous community that sold its produce and manufactured products up and down the Ohio River.

In setting up the framework of New Braunfels, Prince Solms followed the guidelines of the German Immigration Society, known as the Verein or the Society. All operations would be controlled from the center, the administrative headquarters with its ample warehouses and barns. Food would be doled out until the first crops were in. Oxen or cattle would be slaughtered on a regular basis by the

Verein butchers. The society would provide everything needed for agriculture, including seeds, tools, work animals. Further, the commune would provide doctors, druggists, churches, and schools.

To administer this bureaucracy, the prince appointed a Council of Five, with himself as director, a trusted retired lieutenant, Jean Jacques von Coll, as bookkeeper, and another military man, Nicolaus Zink, as civil engineer. Next, he found a doctor, Theodore Koester, but it was not until Prince Solms reached Texas that he found his minister of the gospel. Louis Ervendberg had organized Protestant congregations in East Texas, at Cat Spring and neighboring communities. The prince met him through the botanist and scout, Ferdinand Lindheimer. Prince Solms hired both of them, the minister and the botanist, to lead his first group of two hundred colonists from the coast to the site of the present New Braunfels.

After arrival on March 21, 1845, the first settlers set up camp along the river bank. But before a month passed, Engineer Zink had laid out a neat German town of thirty-six blocks, with two central plazas and wide streets connecting the parts. (The plaza remains exactly the same today and you can examine Zink's surveying tools in the Sophienburg Museum.) The settlers drew lots by choosing numbered pieces of paper from a hat. They wasted little time before they cut logs and erected their first crude shelters. Each plot was large - one-half acre - because Zink had laid out a typical German farming town. The idea was that the settlers would keep a garden and animals in town, but would drive out to a farm of ten acres a few miles away.

While the colonists were erecting their own homes, Prince Solms engaged a contractor from Seguin to construct the Society headquarters. At the dedication of its cornerstone in April, he strung up the orange and black colors of the Austrian flag, but he was not to be outdone by the colonists, who raised a homemade version of the Texas flag in the main plaza.

29

Solms, however, was soon gone. Leaving a trail of debts behind him. His replacement was a more capable administrator. But Meusebach was resented throughout his tenure. He could not make restitution on all of Solms' debts, deliver everything Santa Claus had promised.

One issue that Prince Solms left unresolved was the delicate issue of religious worship. Would Lutherans and Roman Catholics gather in a community church under one pastor? Though Solms, a Catholic, had requested a priest from the diocese of Baltimore, he had actually hired a Protestant. The first services, therefore, were Protestant. The combination church and school, dedicated in January, 1846, was also considered Protestant. Not much time elapsed, however, before a Catholic monsignor came calling on Director Meusebach. In November, 1846, he asked for a donation of lots from the colony, promising to raise the building funds himself. Meusebach complied. Soon Catholic services were held under a tree on the property. In 1849, the first Catholic church (on the present site) was completed.

Just at this point, in January 1846 when the various religious groups were deciding how to array themselves, along came a delightful young man who has left us a marvelous picture of the colony, Ferdinand Roemer. He was sent by the Berlin Academy of Science (at Prince Solms instigation - he did continue an interest in "the Texas experiment") to see what was what and, fortunately for us, he made notes. In the tiny houses, which often held several families, he noted that "unpacked chests and boxes often looked like the steerage of an immigrant ship." He was amazed that Doctor Koester could function as a druggist as well as a doctor. Such an arrangement was unheard of in Germany, where guilds regulated all the trades and no one was allowed to follow more than one. He relished the experience of a German count who opened a tavern and "did a thriving business." This count had started out with only "a barrel of whiskey which he bought in San Antonio and ladled out under a tent." But in time he grew prosperous, and by Roemer's arrival he was serving one and all in his tavern. It was startling to Roemer to find a situation where "the humblest worker, ordering a glass of whiskey, was served by the count in person. One had to conclude that here, indeed was the land of perfect equality and brotherhood."

The count was not the only German colonist to start out with little capital. Others did, as well. Also, Germans were not alone in early New Braunfels. Anglo-Americans had been involved from the beginning. Prince Solms had engaged the trading firm, the Torrey Brothers of Houston, to supply wagons and teams to bring the colonists up from the coast. He had also bought guns from them, and swords for his mounted retinue. John Torrey, a Connecticut Yankee, accompanied the group and soon established a trading post here, as well as a grinding mill for the first corn crop. Later, in 1848, he entered into an agreement with the Verein whereby he would build a grist and saw mill on the river at the foot of Mill Street. (In recent years the stone ruin of his mill became The Chute for tubers.)

Another mill, built by William Merriweather of Tennessee in 1847, was acquired twelve years later by the German Landas. It is this property that forms the core of the magnificent city park today - Landa Park- the jewel of New Braunfels, the site of the Wurstfest, the giant swimming pools, the toy train, the paddle boats, the magic of summer evenings.

By 1850 mills hummed on the river, and stores and shops of many artisans lined Seguin Street. New Braunfels was known for its excellent wagons, its saddles, its fine furniture, its beer. The census of 1850 showed New Braunfels the fourth largest town in the state - after Galveston, Houston, and San Antonio.

Nevertheless, there were empty houses in New Braunfels. Why would this be? During the first years the farmers had begun to move out, down the Comal Creek towards San Antonio, west into the Hill Country. Even

31

Meusebach encouraged the families to spread out. He said the old ways wouldn't work here. Much later, after the Civil War, he settled his family in Loyal Valley, halfway between Fredericksburg and Mason

This commune, like others, didn't last, but it is important to know of it because the town is essentially as Zink laid it out - his wide streets, his half-acre lots, and in many cases, the cottages of the original colonists. New Braunfels is consequently a fascinating place to explore.

THREE PROFILES

We continue the story of New Braunfels with tales of some of the principal figures. Ferdinand Lindheimer, an intellectual and a revolutionary leader in Germany, was a botanist and a newspaper editor. Johann Jahn was a cabinetmaker whose furniture is among the finest ever made in Texas. Joseph and Harry Landa were storekeepers, millers, and the first industrialists in New Braunfels.

Lindheimer's house and many of his possessions mark his legacy here. Jahn's furniture is displayed in three local museums. Landa Park is the enduring gift of the Landas.

FERDINAND LINDHEIMER (1801-1879) was the son of a wealthy merchant, a university graduate, a college teacher, and a younger cousin of Goethe. He taught botany at the Bunsen Institute and was a close friend of the Bunsens, known for their Bunsen burner. But after he was implicated in the Frankfurt Putsch in April, 1833, he left Germany quickly, never to return. He lived for a time in Illinois, but later he set out to join the revolutionaries in Texas. He arrived one day too late to join Sam Houston at San Jacinto. After a few years in East Texas, he returned to St. Louis to discuss with his friend, Georg Engelmann of the Botanical Garden, his plans for a botanical survey in Texas. It was agreed that Lindheimer would send specimens back to Engelmann and also to Asa Gray at Harvard University in Massachusetts.

Back in Texas, he set out in a two-wheeled Mexican cart, took some silk pressing papers, sugar, coffee, salt, and two dogs. He must have seemed an oddity scouring the countryside, digging up plants here and there. The Comanche Indians noticed him, but they left him alone because they thought anyone that interested in plants must be a medicine man.

It was while he was on these journeys that he met Louis Ervendberg, the first German Protestant pastor in Texas. Prince Solms engaged Ervendberg as the first pastor of his colony and asked Lindheimer to act as guide for the first group coming up from the coast. Lindheimer not only accepted, but he put down roots in the new community. He took up land on the Comal River, built a tiny log cabin, and soon married one of the young women among the immigrants, Eleonore Reinarz, who helped press and prepare his specimens for shipment.

He finished his project, the first classification of Texas flora, in 1851. Then Lindheimer built a new house for his growing family - the same house that you see today - and launched into a new career. He started the first local newspaper, thinking of it as a public service. His opinion was that freedom of the press was necessary if a populace was to be enlightened and informed about their rights and duties. But his leadership of the paper thrust him into the storm preceding the Civil War, when the German community was deeply divided.

Through his role as editor of the *Neu-Braunsfelzer Zeitung* , Lindheimer became the leader of those German Texans who favored standing by Texas and supporting the Confederacy. Revolutionary as a young man, Lindheimer now counseled moderation. He feared his fellow German-Americans would lose their political rights if they did not "fall into step." Therefore, he fought the Prohibitionist Plank of the Manifesto approved by the singing society in San Antonio in 1854. He feared reprisals by Anglo-Americans, feared the suspect Germans would be denied their rights.

Not all agreed with his ideas. Some threw his printing press into the river. (He fished it out.) The Forty-Eighters accused him of selling out to the South.

Lindheimer continued as editor of his paper until 1872, when he was ready to retire. He died seven years later, but his descendants kept the family home. In the 1960s a grandaughter presented it to the Conservation Society and it is open for regular tours. Here you see evidences of all the skeins of Lindheimer's life: mementos of Germany, botanical specimens, the type face of his newspaper. Outside, you behold his beloved garden, still a beautiful spot overlooking the Comal River.

JOHANN MICHAEL JAHN (1816-1883) arrived as a master craftsman, a cabinetmaker, who had served a lengthy apprenticeship in Prague and who had then worked as a journeyman in Switzerland. He came to America because he did not see opportunities for a skilled cabinetmaker in the Europe of the Machine Age. He did not come, in all probability, to avoid military draft, because, while he was an apprentice, his instructor had thrown a tool which struck him in the hip and crippled him for life.

Jahn, like Lindheimer, arrived with the founding group at New Braunfels. He drew Lot 177 on Sequin Street (at Butcher) and lost little time erecting his first shop. He also helped his shipmate, Stephan Klein, build his small cottage. (The Klein House still stands at 131 S. Seguin.) Within a few years, Jahn married the Klein's daughter, Anna Marie, whose first husband, Carl Belmer, had died in 1850. Anna Marie and Johann Michael became the parents of Carl Andreas (1851) and Emma Marie (1853).

Jahn prospered along with perhaps fifteen other cabinetmakers in the New Braunfels of the 1850s. He advertised in Lindheimer's newspaper, and Lindheimer in turn supported the handmade versus the mass-produced. Even during the Civil War there was money for furniture. For the cotton that still found its way down to Mexico, payment was in gold.

But, immediately after the war, in 1866, Jahn ordered his first knocked-down furniture from a company in New York. This was furniture shipped in parts and then assembled at its destination. Jahn's shipment came by boat to Indianola and then overland by wagon. In the same year, Jahn and his son constructed a two-story workshop and store where they could assemble factory-made parts, do repairs, and also continue to work on handmade pieces.

By the time the International and Great Northern Railroad reached New Braunfels in 1880, Jahn had a thriving trade, but much of this was factory furniture he merely assembled. He lived only a few years longer, until 1883, but his son and two grandsons continued the business until 1944. Little handmade furniture was made after his time, however.

The era of handcrafted furniture lasted only a brief time, from 1845 to 1865 and a few years beyond. And, of course, it is these pieces that we want to see: cabinets with carefully-matched grained woods, chairs made on the model of the Greek Klismos (see one at Winedale), sofas with a bit of restrained carving, chests with inlaid bone or brass escutcheons with keys instead of knobs or drawer pulls - the classic, unadorned Biedermeier style that was passing from favor in Germany by the time of the Amercan Civil War.

Jahn constructed his pieces with mortise-and-tendon, butt, or dovetailed joints, but he never used pegs unless to make a repair. He used woods that were locally available, mainly black walnut, but also mesquite and cherry and imported mahagony. Pine and oak were used only as secondary woods. Some of his tools were from Germany, some he made.

He didn't sign his handcrafted pieces; only the factory furniture took his initials, J J, on the bottom. We know the origin of the handcrafted pieces by details of their craftsmanship and by their associations. Much of Jahn's work descended in his family and in that of the Verein

35

bookkeeper, Jean Jacques von Coll. The extraordinary rocking chair displayed in the Lindheimer House belonged to his grandson, Paul. A matching child's rocker, now at the Sophienburg Museum, was made for his daughter, Emma. The veneered corner cupboard at the Museum of Handmade Furniture belonged to the family of his brother-in-law, Joseph Klein.

Although Jahn was only one of many fine cabinetmakers here, his work is now the best known, the most revered. He stands as an emblem for all the craftsmen of superior skills in the Hill Country who brought their talents from the Old World to enrich the new.

JOSEPH LANDA (1810-1896) came from Germany to Texas in 1844, but by an entirely different route from Lindheimer or Jahn. Not a political dissident like Lindheimer nor a craftsman who joined the Verein like Jahn, Joseph Landa was a religious refugee. His parents wanted him to become a rabbi. Young Landa balked at this and ran away. He boarded a ship for America in England, but in the steerage he was the only Jew and he was considered unlucky when the ship encountered a storm. Superstitious Irish tried to throw him overboard, but the captain intervened and hid him in another part of the ship. Landa arrived in New York with only a British half crown, a pair of trousers, and a navy pea jacket.

Fortunately for him, friends from home took him in hand, but Landa did not stay long in New York. He acquired a spring wagon and a horse and traveled south with a load of goods which he peddled as he went along. When he reached San Antonio, he stopped. Here he set up a shop, only the second store manned by a white in San Antonio. This was 1844, the year before the German colonists settled New Braunfels.

Three years later he rode his mule up to look at what was called a "prosperous little German settlement." His son relates in an extraordinary autobiography, *As I*

36

Remember (1945), that his father liked what he saw. He was intrigued by the beautiful surroundings, especially the Comal River and springs. Landa decided to pull up stakes in San Antonio. He loaded everything on four prairie schooners and went up to New Braunfels, where he became the leading merchant. He took annual buying trips to New York, as arduous as it was to travel then, and on one of these he met his future wife. He and Helena Friedlander were wed in 1851 by the noted Rabbi, Dr. Isaac M. Wise, a national leader in the Jewish Reform Movement.

In 1859, Landa took the big plunge. He bought Merriweather's mill on the Comal River for $16,000. Just at the beginning of the Civil War, this was a risky time to do such a thing. Landa, like Lindheimer, sided with the Confederacy and he did own five slaves, but, after Lincoln's Emancipation Proclamation in 1863, he freed those slaves. From that moment on he was suspect. Harry Landa writes that his father's freeing of his slaves was "taken as a gesture of abolitionism." Landa then stood trial and was told to leave the country. He fled to Mexico with a load of cotton.

Meanwhile, Helena, with "seven small children tugging at her skirts," minded the store, directed operations at the flour mill, the saw mill, and the cotton gin. Later in the war, when the country was rife with rascals of all kinds - "bushwhackers, scalawags, and outlaws" - she locked the horse in the barn and kept a six-shooter handy.

On Landa's return, he paid special attention to his children's education. He built a small school in the back yard and hired teachers from Vermont. He attended services in San Antonio, but he also presided over religious services at home. Isadore, the oldest son, read the prayers. Helena baked unleavened bread and brewed a sweet raisin wine, while the job of Harry, the youngest, was to "open the door and let in the Angel," meaning to welcome Elijah.

The children must have changed to the public schools after a few years, because Harry speaks of his experiences there. "I did pretty well as a school boy until one of my teachers decided that I should learn German religious history and this I refused to do. I was given a lesson to learn by memory. I was to have it ready to recite at the next German religious hour. When the time arrived, I saw the teacher coming in with a big switch, so I grabbed my school bag and shot out of the window. Thus it was that I graduated from school through an open window at the age of twelve."

It was this same Harry who revived the family fortunes later. After tending store as a youth - his mother brought her knitting to keep him company - he moved on to other jobs in other locations. But back he came in 1890 when the family businesses were faltering.

Harry rebuilt the mills with new machinery, and persuaded the International and Great Northern Railroad, which had been here ten years, to build a spur to his property. He sent his parents on a trip and built a new house for them at their old location on the north end of the main plaza. After that he provided the town electricity by attaching a generator to his mill. His father died in 1896, but his mother became his chief business partner and constant companion. Together, they bought up all the property along the Comal River up to the head springs. They added more factories as the first modern industrialists in New Braunfels.

It was during this phase of expansion, that Helen Gould, daughter of Jay Gould the railroad financier and herself the principal stockholder of the International and Great Northern Railroad, came for a visit. She was interested in a "recreation grounds" on the line and she thought this the exact place for it. She proposed that she build a spur into the property and that Landa "improve" it. This he agreed to do. In 1898 Landa Park opened with great fanfare. Harry ordered barbecue for a gigantic picnic that involved a barrel of pickles and plenty of beer and baked beans and several hundred loaves of bread. Soon excursion trains trundled up every weekend from San Antonio. .

But these good times were not to last. Landa was obliged to sell the entire family estate in 1922. His mother's will had stated that all the property was to be liquidated and the proceeds divided among her heirs ten years after her death. Landa's empire was very prosperous at the time, capitalized at half a million dollars. He wrote that selling it "tore his heart strings."

The new owners faltered and then failed. Landa Park was closed to the public in 1927. Barbed wire surrounded it by 1933. But an effort by the Junior Chamber of Commerce spurred a bond election to buy the park. Grateful citizens of New Braunfels flocked once more to their beautiful picnic grounds in 1936. Since that time the park has been cherished as one of the most magnificent, most unique, of all the city parks in Texas. It was Harry Landa's gift to the city in 1898, but its final confirmation had to wait forty years.

COURTHOUSE AND MAIN PLAZA

When Harry Landa came back to revitalize his family fortunes in 1890, he found New Braunfels in the midst of changing from an old-fashioned town into an up-to-date Victorian city. It had been ten years since the International and Great Northern had charged into town, spilled out its goods, carried away the cotton crops, spurred commerce and manufacturing, and brought in all manner of building materials.

But Landa soon encountered the old ways after he was elected to the position of City Alderman and then discovered that the proceedings were held entirely in German. F. Stuvo, the City Secretary, "probably could not write one word of English," he said. Since Harry's comprehension of German was very limited, he suggested that "as we were a corporate body under the laws of Texas, the proceedings be held in English." His motion was accepted. F. Stuvo moved on to another job.

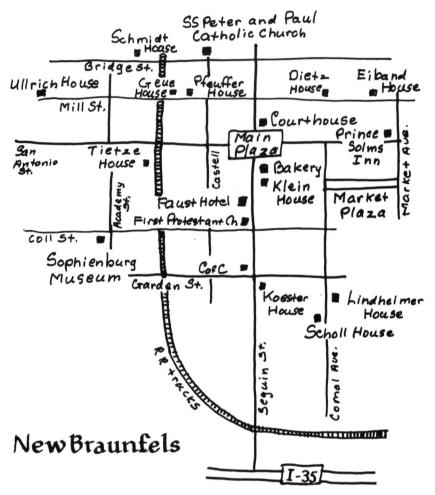

New Braunfels

New Braunfels was still very German at the core. But the new ways were coming. In 1892 a newspaper was finally printed in English. During the following year Landa's plant provided the town's first electricity.

Another step was taken after the big celebration of the town's first fifty years in 1895. People had noticed the neglected state of the main plaza. Set aside as a public space since the beginning, there had never been a plan for it. So a fountain was put in, and curbing, and then some trees and bushes.

This was followed by a new courthouse in 1898, one of J. Reily Gordon's last before he moved to New York. It was small, compared to his palaces in San Antonio, Waxahachie, or Decatur, but it had many of the same Romanesque characteristics. It was built mostly of limestone, but there is some granite at the doorways. The structure was placed at the side of the plaza. To put it in the center of the public plaza was not the idea here.

DOWNTOWN TODAY: SAN ANTONIO AND SEGUIN STREETS

Two streets branching off from Main Plaza form what's called "downtown." On West San Antonio there is a cluster of stores from the early part of the century. Two early ones are Henne Hardware (1893) and the old First National Bank (1894).

South Seguin Street stretches from Main Plaza out to I-35. Naegelin Bakery, at 129 South Seguin, was founded by Edouard Naegelin, who came in 1868 with a sack of flour and less than a dollar in his pocket. This bakery is known for its bear claws and elephant ears, cream puffs and chocolate eclairs, lemon snails and bags of German cookies such as iced molasses squares, springerle, and pfefferneuse. As a boy, Harry Landa loved to come here for slabs of gingerbread. I, too, am partial to these gingerbread planks - long and low, spicy and chewy.

Next door at 131 S. Seguin, is the Klein House (1846), one of the original homes. Stephan and Margaretha Klein built it of *fachwerk* construction with the help of the cabinetmaker Johann Jahn, their shipmate on the Herschel. In 1850, Jahn married their daughter, Anna Marie.

The Faust Hotel (1929) is at 240 S. Seguin. (See under Lodgings.)

The First Protestant Church (1875) at S. Seguin and Coll Street, is the continuation of the first community church and school. Additions to the handsome stone building of 1875 were made in 1889 and again in the twentieth century.

CHAMBER OF COMMERCE *390 S. Seguin. Mon-Fri 8-5,*
Sat 9-4, Sun 10-2 Ph: 210/625-2385 or 800/572-2626

SOPHIENBURG MUSEUM (1933) *401 W. Coll, Mon-Sat 10-
5, Sun 1-5. Admission. Ph: 210/629-1572*

In the 1930s, during the same years that Landa's
park was once again restored to the people of New
Braunfels, there was another community effort. In 1926 a
portrait of Prince Solms was sent over from Germany. It
was meant to hang "in the city museum." But there was
no museum.

With WPA funds and donations from local individuals
the building rose at last on the site of Prince Solm's
headquarters, on a hill southwest of the plaza. It was
named Sophienburg - as his headquarters had been - for
the prince's fiancee, the Princess Sophia of Salm-Salm.

Rock donated for this building was put up in a rough
state. This might seem bizarre unless you consider that
this was a common practice at the time. Other buildings
of a comparable nature are scattered throughout West
Texas, where building stone was available.

As well as the portrait of Prince Solms, his powder
horn, his hunting knife, his writing desk, and his folding
chair, we see the surveying tools Nicolaus Zink used to lay
out the town, a huge trunk that came with the Giesecke
family in 1846, and some of cabinetmaker Jahn's tools.
The charming rocker Jahn made for his daughter is here.
Also Joseph Landa's black carriage that he drove to
religious services in San Antonio, and Jean Jacques von
Coll's walnut doors with carved panels and hand-wrought
iron hinges that stood at the front door of his tavern on
the plaza.

There is an amazing assortment of implements from
the early days of the Naegelin Bakery: huge wooden
mixing bowls, the proofing cabinet in which the bread
rose, bread and tart tins made locally by the Henne
Tinning Company, long wooden paddles with which to put

the bread into the oven (like the ones you see today at Pizza Hut).

CONSERVATION PLAZA *1300 Church Hill Drive. From I-35, exit at #189, go N. 1 block, go through US 81 Business intersection, 200 yards to Church Hill Dr. Open during Wurstfest. Call for other hours. Ph: 210/629-2943. Admission.*

After World War II there was an alarming rush to discard the old and adopt the new. This was true all over the country. In New Braunfels, first the big department store that anchored Main Plaza (just north of Naegelin Bakery) burned in 1947. Then other structures were gone. In 1962 the big Landa mansion that had stood at the north end of Main Plaza was razed.

After that, watch dogs here banded together to form the Conservation Society. They were able to save some of the buildings that were slated for demolition, restoring some in place and moving others to this property slightly away from the center of town

You see an old store, a music studio, and cabinetmaker Jahn's home and workshop. But the best exhibit is the Baetge House built in 1852 of *fackwerk* and adobe brick up near Canyon Lake. It was dismantled and brought down here and stacked up. Finally high school students and their teacher took the lead in reassembling the house. Be sure to go up to the attic where you can study its construction.

MUSEUM OF TEXAS HANDMADE FURNITURE *1370 Church Hill Drive. (See instructions under Conservation Plaza) June through August: Tues-Sat 10-4, Sun 1-4. Call for other months. Daily during Wurstfest. Ph: 210/629-6504. Admission.*

Among the leaders in the Conservation Society were Nan and Bill Dillen, antiques dealers, who had moved here from San Antonio in 1945. They became intrigued with the furniture of the area after they discovered that a walnut draw leaf table they had bought was made by the master craftsman, Johann Jahn. This triggered their interest in all the area cabinetmakers, and they started an extensive collection.

In 1964 they bought the Andreas Bruested House (1858) when it was threatened by the path of 1-35 as it plowed through east of town. The house, of *fachwerk* construction, could not be taken over a bridge, nor could it be slid beneath an overpass, so the Dillens moved it here, not far from its original location and ultimately next door to the museum village of the Conservation Society.

Their collection looked well here. They found more and more items, and they enjoyed living here, but in 1983 they donated the house and its contents as a museum of antique furniture.

Now visitors can wander through the rooms and see pieces of the furniture as they were meant to be used. The collection is truly fabulous. Not only noteworthy pieces by Johann Jahn, but a sleigh bed by Heinrich Scholl, and a magnificent wardrobe by Franz Stautzenberger, who was trained in the household of the Duke of Nassau before he came to Texas.

Narrow, steep stairs lead to an attic crammed with more beds, chests-of-drawers, trunks. Outside in the barn there is even more.

WALKING TOUR OF OLD HOUSES

When we drive into town, we see an area that hasn't changed much since 1900. We see a Victorian bandstand and fountain in Main Plaza, and, over to the side, one of J. Reily Gordon's 1898 courthouses. We find mansions of the period pressing in closely on all sides of the plaza. We spy a small business district of several blocks that includes a hardware store that has been in business since 1893. And all over town we see houses covered with gingerbread trim.

With the coming of the railroad in 1880, jigsaws were employed to "decorate" the old cottages. By 1900, almost every home was embellished.

But the heritage here is deeper, older than this turn-of-the-century embellishment. With a bit of a search, you will find many old dwellings, some even dating back to the earliest years of the colony.

The first homes - crude wooden huts - were moved to backyards as the German settlers built more substantially with heavy oak timbers and stone. Their building methods included *fachwerk*, or half-timbering, an ancient medieval technique in which a heavy wooden frame was laid out on the ground, pegged together, raised up and then filled in with homemade bricks or rocks. Several examples of *fachwerk* houses remain. One of the most interesting, and one that is not on this tour, is the Tietze House (1854), at 196 Hill Street. (It faces the railroad tracks just south of San Antonio Street.)

For about ten years, from 1846 to the mid-1850s, the settlers built in this manner. Then they realized that hewn blocks of limestone could stand alone and they dispensed with the wooden framework.

Although German settlers here used the basic plan of the Anglo-American cottage, of one and one-half stories, subtle variations became their identifying marks. Sometimes they used casement windows that opened out instead of sash windows. Look for these casement windows at the Pfeuffer House on Mill Street. They frequently built small chimneys because they planned to use stoves for heating and cooking instead of large fireplaces. The two enormous fireplaces that are touted in Fredericksburg are thus very unusual. Thirdly, the Germans often built outside staircases that rose to doors in the gable ends of their homes. Children and guests climbed these stairs to extra sleeping quarters in the loft. You see these stairs in the famous Sunday Houses in Fredericksburg. Here, an example is found at the Schmidt House on Bridge Street.

As additions were made to these homes, the settlers tended to add the new in front of the old, or sometimes the new alongside the old. But rarely did they throw anything away. The first cottages remained in the yard as kitchens or workshops or smokehouses. The newer sections grew towards the street (as at the Scholl House) or towards the side (the Ullrich House). You find a house that grew remarkably towards the rear at the Pioneer Museum in Fredericksburg. At the Sauer-Beckman farmhouse at the LBJ State Park, you find at least four sections moving to the side, the last a facade of 1910 with the characteristic glass oval in the front door.

By the time of the Civil War new houses were larger, grander, and less distinctively German. Think of the magnificent Rode House out in the hills north of Fredericksburg. Here, an example is the Koerster House of 1859-60. The front elevation rises several floors with wide galleries stretching across each level.

Use of hewn limestone persisted farther west into the twentieth century, but in New Braunfels the arrival of the railroad in 1880 facilitated the use of lumber and, indeed, a wide variety of other building materials. The new courthouse in 1898 sported granite columns from Burnet. Granite was too heavy to cart long distances, but the rails brought the colorful stone here and to other spots such as Waxahachie, Fort Worth, Dallas, and San Antonio.

KOESTER HOUSE (1860) *421 S. Seguin.*

This was the home of the original town physician, Dr. Theodor Koester. After marrying a young woman from one of the early settler groups, Koester set up his medical practice and ran a pharmacy. This substantial brick home, completed just before the Civil War, shows how some of the German immigrants lived in family groups after they arrived in America. While the doctor had his office and his apothecary on the first floor, a full basement below accommodated a kitchen large enough for the his brother-in-law, August Tolle, to turn out a delicious "wheaten bread" for the community every morning.

LINDHEIMER HOUSE (1852) *489 Comal Street. Daily during Wurstfest; May -August, daily except Wed; Sept to April on Sat,Sun. Hours: 2-5. Admission.*

A visit to the Lindheimer House will be a good opportunity to inspect one of the early homes. Ferdinand Lindheimer built the structure of *fachwerk*, pegging the framework on the ground and then erecting it. He covered it entirely with plaster so the only place you see the half-timbering is in the cellar. He no doubt made small window

openings; the ones you see today are replacements. He omitted fireplaces, planning to use stoves instead. No outside staircase exists today, but Lindheimer included the characteristic door under the gable. He probably added the front porch that is seen in a photograph of the house on display just inside the door, but the porch was removed during restoration.

When Lindheimer finished this house in 1852, he left his first hut out in the yard as a kitchen. It still stands there today. Since his family stayed here until the house became a museum, and no additional rooms were added to the original five, this dwelling remains an unusually good example of the early ideas.

On stepping inside, you discover a trove of Lindheimer's possessions, all kinds of things that reflect every aspect of his life. A drawing of Mozart on the wall, an inscribed sketch of Pestalozzi, the Swiss educator, and his family Bible were obviously treasures he brought when he came. Guides point out a sword given Lindheimer by Prince Solms, plant specimens hanging on the walls, cases of his newspaper type. A beautiful walnut desk by Eugen Benno Ebensberger dates from 1870, two years before Lindheimer retired as editor of the *Neu-Braunfelser Zeitung*.

In addition to Lindheimer's walnut desk and cedar wardrobe, samplings of the work of òther early cabinetmakers in New Braunfels await the visitor. The most extraordinary piece is the rocking chair by Johann Jahn that stands in the front bedroom. Made for his family around 1855, this rocker descended to a grandson and is on loan here. It may be the most unusual of all the pieces of furniture you will see in New Braunfels. Of mesquite, a difficult wood to carve, with caned back and seat, its arm supports are carved like dolphins and its legs are exceptionally finely carved. A smaller version of this chair, in cherry, made for Jahn's children, is on loan to the Sophienburg Museum.

The other pieces of furniture here include some "assembled by Jahn" and a sleigh bed thought to have been made by Heinrich Scholl, Lindheimer's neighbor down the street.

SCHOLL HOUSE (1847, 1855) *550 Comal Street*

This house is an example of one that kept creeping closer to the street - first the early cottage in the rear, then a Greek Revival house of 1855, finally out front a white picket fence with three handsome gates made by the grandson of the original owner.

Heinrich Scholl came to Texas with his family in 1846, when he was about 18 years old. His father drowned at the port of Indianola, but he pressed on with his mother, brother and sister to New Braunfels. Trained as carpenters, the two brothers worked on many of the first houses, and later opened a sash and door company. As Union sympathizers, they resisted the Confederate draft by hiding out.

But Heinrich also became a skilled cabinetmaker. He made tables with beautiful inlaid trim. He made sofas, beds, and sets of scroll-back chairs. Many of these pieces still remain in this house. Even more astonishing, perhaps, is his workshop in back where his tools remain in perfect order and are still used by his descendants. Lonn Taylor, author of the definitive book on Texas furniture, *Texas Furniture, The Cabinetmakers and Their Work: 1840-1880,* writes of his amazement at finding these tools, especially "his nine-foot long horse-powered lathe, still installed in a shop behind the house he lived in a century ago."

COMAL, MILL, AND BRIDGE STREETS

Walking north on Comal Street, you pass the foundations of a woolen mill at the corner of Comal and Garden. Dr. Koester owned this property and had a distillery here until after the Civil War. He then he sold it to a group of citizens who bought and set up spinning frames and looms. They turned out yards of gray woolen broadcloth for the uniforms of the students at Texas A & M, as well as produced blankets, cashmere cloth, and eight kinds of knitting yarn.

At Napoleon Street, stop a minute to look at the Market Plaza, the second of the town's public spaces, an area that contained butchers and grocers throughout the nineteen century. It is now strictly residential. Two charming Victorian cottages - twins - stand side by side on the south side.

Linger a moment at the corner of San Antonio and Market Streets. The dwelling behind the Voight House, 308 E. San Antonio, is the oldest structure in New Braunfels. It was home to the first schoolteacher, Hermann Seele. With a friend he built it of cypress and cedar in July, 1845.

Across the street, the Prince Solms Inn, at 295 E. San Antonio, the former Comal Hotel (1898), is open as a bed-and-breakfast accommodation. Behind it, at 135 Market, is the Joseph Klein House (1852), moved to the backyard when the hotel was built. Klein, the brother-in-law of the cabinetmaker Jahn, owned one of his masterpieces, the mahagony corner cupboard, which now is shown at the Museum of Texas Handmade Furniture.

A block away, at 195 E. Mill, the Eiband House was the small home of Anselm Eiband who assumed the job of editor of the *Neu-Braunfelser Zeitung* after Lindheimer retired in 1872. Nearby are the Hohmann House (1853) at 273 E. Mill, and the Dietz House (1866) at 197 E. Mill.

The venerable Pfeuffer House (1846), 230 W. Mill, has the casement windows that were the mark of the early settlers. The builder, George Pfeuffer, a tanner from Bavaria, used black walnut for his doors and fitted out a kitchen in the cellar.

The tiny Geue House (1860s), 250 W. Mill, is only one room wide and two rooms deep. Johann Friedrich Geue was a master stonemason.

The Ullrich House (1855, 1870), 554 W. Mill, was the home of George and Margaretha Ullrich, who led the first wagon across the swollen Guadalupe River to the site of the future New Braunfels in 1845. Their home of sand brick was begun in 1855 and finished with an addition at the side in 1870.

At 394 W. Bridge, we encounter another Geue House, this one with walls of handmade brick. An older building in the rear has walls of *fachwerk* .

Next door, the Schmidt House (1850s), 354 W. Bridge, seems a composite of the early patterns. Here we even find an outside staircase rising to a door in the attic. The usual plaster and siding cover the *fachwerk* construction.

SAINTS PETER AND PAUL CATHOLIC CHURCH (1849, 1871, 1963) *Bridge Street and Castell.*

This was the original tract deeded to the Catholic bishop by Meusebach in 1846. At first the congregation met under a tree. Within a few years, the parishioners built a small chapel of black walnut. This was referred to as the "black walnut church." Later, when they expanded, they kept the core of this early building intact. The handsome stone church of 1871 was literally built around it. For twentieth-century changes, the parishioners saved the rock from the old county jail. They said it was a good match to the old stone of their church.

Of particular interest is the grotto at the side of the church. In 1918, after forty-five parishioners had died in the flu epidemic, the survivors promised to build a shrine for the Virgin, like the one at Lourdes, if the deaths stopped. No more died. So Father Wack, the priest since 1889, set out for Lourdes, France, to make measurements. On his return, he hired a stonemason from Nebraska and supervised the men of the church in their search for "honeycomb rock." They found this on three nearby ranches. At the old hospital grounds, they discovered hard flint for the back of the dome. Everybody in the parish helped in some way, if nothing other than washing the stones - no dirty rocks were permitted. On June 29, 1921, at the annual feast day of Saints Peter and Paul, the whole parish stood for a wide-angle photograph in front of the completed grotto. Pictured are women in big hats, young girls and boys dressed in white, and swags of greenery, draped from tree to tree and finally to a corner of the church.

LANDA PARK AND PRINCE SOLMS PARK

One of my favorite memories of New Braunfels is of a time in the spring of 1976 when our family drove down to the coast and then stopped here on the way back. On our return, we had passed through Panna Maria, the center of Polish settlements in Texas, and then through scrubby post oaks and unremarkable landscapes until we approached New Braunfels. Here we paused for the night. And here we came out to play in the evening. That night Landa Park seemed magical: green grass everywhere, water all around, paddle boats pushing off, the miniature train rolling along, ancient oaks standing guard. Our children crawled up into one of these ancient oaks, somewhat infirm and cumbersome, one of its long branches supported by two concrete piers and two posts. They delighted in this grandaddy tree. I thought it should be nominated for "oldest tree in Texas."

The park encompasses not only the picnic grounds, the giant swimming pools, the golf course, and other amusements, but also the former industrial complex of the Landa family. An old grain warehouse has become the Wursthalle for the annual Wurstfest, and here the famous accordianist, Myron Floren, arrives each year in a water-borne float from the river.

In the northeast corner, past the springs, is the entrance to Panther Canyon hiking trail. This trek back into a fold of the Balcones Escarpment is to one of those special places where you see the plants of the east and the west, and, also, of the north and the south.

What a gift to the City of New Braunfels. What a splendid park. This surely is the most remarkable of the city parks in Texas.

PRINCE SOLMS PARK, TUBING ON THE COMAL *Enter on E. Mill Street or from Liberty Street. Tubes available at entrance on Mill Street, or from private concessions near the river. Admission.*

Since our spring visit to Landa Park in 1976, city leaders have striven to link it with other natural sites downstream. With the proceeds from the Wurstfest, the city fathers bought Hinman's Island and Prince Solms Park. They also transformed the ruins of the old Torrey mill into a remarkable Tube Chute, a water slide that captures the flow of the Comal River and gives the tuber a twisting, dashing ride.

Never will I forget tubing down the river with Esther Kibbey, an artist who went down with me in late June, close to that proverbial turning point, the 4th of July, when Texas turns into an oven. Esther and I were tromping around New Braunfels and Gruene, getting a bit hot and sweaty, even irritable, when we headed out for the river and found our "tube ladies" on Liberty Street, sitting out under their umbrella. They fitted us with tubes, then sent us to change in their dressing room. They told us how to enter the park on the north side of the Chute. Since we didn't pay entering this way, we were allowed to go through the Chute only once, but we didn't care. We drifted on down the river, idly paddling our feet, shaded in the sunny patches by big, floppy hats.

We glided past old Camp Warnecke, through the small rapids there, past the Garden Street Bridge with its "Tuber's Exit," and on around the bend past The Other Place until we came to the Union Street Exit. Here we had to look sharp, to paddle ourselves carefully over to the landing, and to get ourselves and our tubes out of the water. The Union Street is the last - the very *last* - exit from the Comal before it joins with the swift Guadalupe at the edge of town.

At the landing we climbed up the steep bank on iron stairs, and, there at the top, we found ourselves in another world: a world of streets and cars and pedestrians, instead of a world of green ripples and overhanging trees and turtles basking on logs. We were glad we had worn shirts, hats, and shoes because now it would be a short walk back to the "tube ladies."

SCHLITTERBAHN *400 N. Liberty. Summer: 10-8. Call for spring and fall hours. Ph: 210/625-2351*

In 1966 Bob and Billye Henry bought the Landa Resort on a branch of the Comal River and began what would turn out to be a hugely successful water park. They built the first of several water slides, but, after a visit to Florida's Disney World in 1979, they expanded much farther. A dozen years later they had a network of waterways and tube chutes in their Schlitterbaln (or "slippery road"). The Henrys expanded again by purchasing the old Camp Warnecke a few blocks away. At Warnecke, the rapids on the main stretch of the Comal were natural - have always been an attraction - so the Henrys added this as Surfenberg, another asset in their already extraordinary park. Their operation now included both the cabins at the former Landa Resort and those at old Camp Warnecke.

The Henry children became involved as they grew up, Gary as general manager, Jeff as the chief designer, and Jana the head of marketing. As these children had babies of their own, the family saw the need for play areas for toddlers. Soon these were duly installed.

Schlitterbahn may be most thrilling for a ten-year-old, but there are attractions for every age. Because of family ownership, the place feels less commercial than a typical Water World. Guests are even encouraged to bring their own picnics.

MILL STORE PLAZA *I-35 (exit 188) Mon-Sat 9-9. Sun 9-6.*

The Mill Store in New Braunfels has always been a wonderful place to buy discounted sheets and towels. Now that the store has been enlarged to include fabrics and other linens, and a mall surrounding the original store includes around fifty other national outlets. You can easily spend a morning here, as we did, picking up cotton sheets and "rub down" towels at the Mill Store, summer shorts at Van Heusen, baby dishes at Corning Glassware Company, and shoes at Bass. The Smokehouse maintains a small shop. Naegelin Bakery offers cookies and sweet rolls and a cup of coffee.

GRUENE *N. on Union, east on Torrey St., which becomes Gruene St. Or N. on Loop 337 or FM 306*

Gruene is an old nineteenth-century cotton town with all the fittings. It was ignored in modern times, but suddenly was appreciated for what it was around 1975. Then the whole village was placed on the National Register of Historic Places. Nothing was to be disturbed. Shops and restaurant and modern amenities were to be fitted into existing structures.

What an extraordinary setting! Not stuck out on the

prairie nor lost in the woods, Gruene sits on a ledge of the Guadalupe River, indeed peers over the edge of it. The surviving structures are ranged gracefully around a broad meadow.

The Gruene family arrived at this location in 1872 after having lived many years in New Braunfels. Ernst Gruene sailed across from Germany in 1845 after reading an advertisement for the Verein, the immigration society. He saw that he would receive more acres if he came as a married man, so through his pastor he announced his intention to marry. He interviewed the applicants at their homes. He chose 19-year-old Maria Antoinette Kloepper because she continued at her laundry tasks in the yard throughout the interview. He decided, "any young woman so diligent is bound to make a good wife."

They sailed on the *Margaretha* and, at first, settled near New Braunfels. Their sons, Ernst, Jr. and Heinrich were born in the early 1850s.

By 1872, the younger son, Heinrich (by now Henry) had finished a stint of driving cattle to Kansas. Ready to marry and settle down, Henry, his parents and brother moved out here to a village (then known as Goodwin) and advertised for sharecroppers. Twenty to thirty families answered their call. Eventually the family bought more land, hired more tenants, and the place became known as Gruene.

An old frame store served the community at first. Then, in 1878, the Gruenes built Gruene Hall, probably the oldest dance hall in Texas. They added a water-powered cotton gin by the river. Much later, in 1904, they built the large brick general store across the road. This housed a bank, a post office, and a lumberyard. This red brick store parallels development in downtown New Braunfels of the same era.

By 1920 the Gruene empire began to fall apart. Henry D. died that year. The cotton gin burned in 1922. Boll weevils claimed the cotton crop in 1925. The red brick store managed to stay open until 1938, but Gruene

continued to decline. Major roads passed it by. Finally the population shrank to seven or eight people.

Gruene was a ghost town for thirty-five years. Nobody was quite sure what was here and finding it again in the 1970s had many elements of discovery and surprise. Early in the decade, a San Antonio developer had bought the property with the idea of razing the buildings and erecting condominiums at the edge of the river. But other people began to see the potential in the old structures here. The San Antonio developer was persuaded to give up his plan. He sold the property to others who would preserve the town

Saving Gruene Hall was relatively easy. It alone had never closed. The new owners decided to save it much as it was - a big dance floor with a stage at one one, screened sides that folded up, and rustic wooden benches and tables. They were soon ready to invite country and western singers and to stage dances on the weekends. It was not long before this was a very popular place again.

The ruins of the cotton gin became the setting for the equally popular Gristmill Restaurant. Here again, new owners left much intact. The brick hulk above the river had been the boiler house of the gin, oil having replaced water wheels. The new owners fitted a restaurant in and around these ruins and planned for guests to walk out to the other side where extensive decks overhung the Guadalupe.

And then there was Gruene Mansion itself, the fabulous old house that started as a stucco-over-brick, one-story affair in 1872, but was raised to two full floors with lacy Victorian porches all around and even a cupola at an upstairs corner in 1886. This house, of course, was ripe for a bed-and-breakfast. So were the mule barns down by the river, even the corn crib. Then other Gruene houses scattered around the village followed in their stead and became guest accommodations.

So, much to the surprise of many, this old ghost town sprang to life, becoming a major drawing card. A potter set up shop behind the red brick store. A T-shirt company moved in across the street. A winery settled into the electric gin that replaced the old gin down by the river. BBQ came along with the Rodriguez Family General Store, which had been moved in from Martindale.

RIVER ROAD *Turn north on River Road from W. Torrey or Loop 337. 11 miles to Sattler.*

At Gruene you admire the Guadalupe River surging along, churning downstream, and you may choose to rent a tube and float down.

Closeby is the old River Road leading north and passing many outfitters who will rent canoes or kayaks for this stretch of the river, one of the best white-water areas in Texas.

Driving along this River Road presents another sort of experience. Follow the signs north and soon you are crossing and recrossing the winding stream. The scenery is magnificent. Ancient cypresses bend over the water. Bluffs rear in some places. Dripping seeps and springs and mainenhair fern dot the banks.

This a narrow road with private property on both sides. You can't park or get out. Passing through is somewhat like driving along the Willow City Loop where private property presses closely to a narrow public road.

ANNUAL EVENT - WURSTFEST *10 days at the beginning of November. Wursthalle at Landa Park. Ph:210/625-9167. Admission.*

The Wurstfest was started in 1961 as a sausage festival sponsored by the Chamber of Commerce. By 1967 the backers were using half of the huge Wursthalle, a former warehouse in the Landa complex, but within a year or two, they needed all of it for an attendance of 56,000 people. About that time, the famous accordianist, Myron Floren arrived, and then continued to come every year. A few years later, the sponsors built the Marktplatz, outside the Wursthalle, and then, in 1983, they started the flotilla of floats on the river that inaugurates the festival every year - the Wurst Navy.

A Dallas man once said that what he liked about the Wurstfest was that the whole town participates in it. Civic groups run the concessions. No outside promoters, carnivals, or rides are permitted. This is not like the State Fair.

On our visit, we went down early on the first night, but not early enough to see the boat parade. If you want to see that, plan on getting there about five for the spectacle of the Wurst Navy steaming down the river and discharging it dignitaries at the pier. By the time we arrived crowds were already milling around the Marktplatz and people were finding places at the picnic tables under an enormous tent.

We discovered that the first night is the best time to come. This is when the residents of New Braunfels come as participants. They are dressed in German finery - lederhozen and dirndls - and they sit at the picnic tables and eat and drink beer and talk. Many speak both English and German, and some converse with visitors from Germany. We happened to sit next to the mayor of Braunfels, Germany, but he spoke only in German to his companions and we could not understand what he was saying.

At the food booths inside we had a hard time choosing between apple strudel or potato pancakes with apple sauce, a local favorite. Very popular were sausages on a stick, German potatoes, and sauerkraut.

Later we visited the Little Tent where we heard local bands and saw fantastic polka dancing by an older couple in a very fast tempo. Everyone here polkas, young and old.

At last, when we thought we had seen everything, we ventured into the huge Wursthalle and there was Myron Floren, holding forth in knee socks and black leather lederhosen, his accordian straps slung over his shoulders and his fingers flying over the keys. What an amazing personality. What energy in his whole body. What a twinkle in his eye. He played polkas and waltzes, but also old favorites like "Daisy" and "Roll out the Barrel." Everyone sang along with him. When he played "The Eyes of Texas" and the Aggie fight song, the place rocked.

LODGINGS: GRUENE MANSION INN   *1275 Gruene Rd. Ph: 830/629-2641.*

Old Gruene family homes, barns, and even a former corn crib form attractive units of housing all over this charming village. These units have private baths, kitchens, living areas. Each offers easy proximity to walking, canoeing and tubing on the Guadalupe, shopping, eating, and even dancing at the historic Gruene Hall.

LODGINGS: THE OTHER PLACE   *385 Other Place Drive,*
Ph: 210/625-5114.

The Other Place is a series of wooden cabins overlooking
a broad stretch of St. Augustine grass that slopes down to
the beautiful Comal River. The cabins have porches,
kitchens, everything you need for a lazy weekend. The
water is so clear you can see the rocky bottom and turtles
swimming in early morning, even from your porch. Since
the management rents intertubes, you can catch a shuttle
up to the public Tube Chute and float all the way back
down the river to the concrete steps here. You can walk to
dinner - or just about anywhere from this location. We
usually walk along the river all the way up to Landa Park.

LODGINGS: THE FAUST HOTEL   *240 S. Seguin   Ph:
210/5625-7791.*

The Faust offers a rare opportunity to stay in an
attractive, small hotel from the 1920s. It is one of three
built in the Hill Country on main thoroughfares, but the
only one that has survived in its original form. The hotel
in Mason is now a bank building, remodeled beyond
recognition. The one in Llano, which lasted longer since
Llano carried on a prosperous granite trade into the
1930s, is now an annex for county government.
    The Faust, originally The Travelers Hotel, faltered
during the Depression, but the bankers here, the Fausts,
stood behind it, Walter Faust even moving in and staying
until his death in 1933. Three years later the hotel was
named for him. During World War II, servicemen from
San Antonio came up with their brides for three-day
passes, and this became known as the "Honeymoon Hotel."
    Hard times followed the war, but in the 1970s the hotel
received a face lift. Fortunately, the new owners kept the
old touches, left intact the tile floor in the lobby, the small
but cozy rooms with old furniture, and the hexagonal tiles

in the bathrooms. The place was - and is - a rendezvous for local folks.

RESTAURANT: NEW BRAUNFELS SMOKEHOUSE *Hwy 46 and Hwy 81 (one block W. of I-35). Daily, all meals.*

This is the only restaurant we remember from our early visits. It was a landmark on I-35 and was always a favorite.

While it started in 1951 as a one-room store, a retail outlet for smoked meats, it has grown into a large establishment that serves regular meals in five dining rooms. The Country Store has been retained at the front door. Here you can buy smoked hams, turkeys, bacon, sausages, jellies, and jams.

A friend said, "Let's eat breakfast at the Smokehouse," and what a wonderful suggestion that was! We ate delicious Canadian bacon along with our eggs and grits and fluffy biscuits. The next time I went back the restaurant was serving breakfast in the "Yard" - a shaded brick terrace with an adjoining grape arbor and a tiny cafeteria. I could chose from among pigs-in-blankets, patty or link sausages, scrambled eggs, grits, biscuits and gravy. This was a great way to start the day. A lunch buffet offers homemade soup, sandwiches, barbecue, apple strudel, their special chocolate cake, apple dumplings, and beer on tap.

As is so often the case in New Braunfels, a quaint cottage is located next door to a newer attraction. Here we see a detached stone kitchen - the main house gone - a charming cottage with inviting rooms within, terraces and a bench and sheltering trees and vines without. A "summer kitchen" I thought, but of course this is what the settlers used all year.

RESTAURANT: PAT'S PLACE *202 S. Union. Open daily,*
11-10.

You won't hear about Pat's unless someone tells you.
The restaurant is so popular, with large crowds at every
meal, that Pat's Place does not advertise. All the locals
come here - this Austin-styled, informal place is their
hang-out - but you may not happen to meet one who will
tell you.
    Some swear by the grilled chicken breasts, others love
the spagetti and garlic toast. My favorite is a platter of
cheese enchiladas with chili on top and a large sprinkling
of chopped tomatoes and lettuce.

RESTAURANT: THE GRISTMILL *Summer, 11-10 daily,*
winter, Sun-Thurs 11-9. Next to the river in Gruene.

    Certainly the most colorful restaurant in New
Braunfels is this perch high above the Guadalupe where
you sit out on decks surrounding the ruin of H. D.
Gruene's cotton gin. The gin still shows great gaping holes
in the walls from an explosion in the 1920s, but the
designers of the restaurant made no effort to tidy these up.
Half the fun is seeing the ruins and walking through to the
decks on the other side. The other half is sitting almost
directly over the Guadalupe River - the decks have a
marvelous view - and ordering something like a
hamburger or grilled chicken.
    Once when I was down in New Braunfels with a group
of women, we ate supper at the Gristmill, sitting out on the
deck over the river, then we wandered over to the T-shirt
shop, and finally sat at the picnic tables by the side of
Gruene Hall. We remarked how pleasant it was to sit out,
how it reminded us of our childhoods. There was a full
moon overhead, as well as colored lights strung above in
the trees.
    We began to notice the music coming from inside the
hall - not a band, but two guitars and a harmonica in the

front room, the bar area. We just sat and listened for awhile. Then "Amazing Grace" drew us in and we sang along with everyone else. No one bothered us or asked us for anything. Those who wanted drinks went up to the bar. The music changed and an older couple began to dance - a fast polka. They were dressed in shorts and tennis shoes like the rest of us.

What a special moment. What a summing up of all the pleasures in New Braunfels.

Blanco

INTRODUCTION TO BLANCO

Where Highway 281 crosses the Blanco River is one of the great swimming holes in the Hill Country. The spring-fed river comes tumbling and dashing from limestone bluffs farther up in the hills, but here it is dammed in three places. Blanco State Park encompasses two green strips either side of the river: a canopy of towering oaks, pecans and St. Augustine lawns down to the water's edge.

We arrived late on the Sunday of a Memorial Day weekend - my husband and I - for a picnic lunch. The park was crowded, yet we were able to find a table in the shade on the far side of the river. We settled down with our picnic hamper, and then we began to notice the families around us. Three generations were enjoying themselves. The grandpas were sitting in aluminum folding chairs and reading the papers. The grandmas were barbecuing something for supper. Lunch was over, and members of the younger groups drifted in and out.

At 3:30 it was "nap time." We looked out to see some folks asleep in their chairs, some on pallets, and one old man stretched crosswise on a picnic table. Later we took

a walk and found families in every pool of shade, with a table or without. Our favorite spot was a stone table with benches on all sides, a matching crescent-shaped, high-backed bench behind it. All was encompassed by the dense shade of a motte of ancient, spreading liveoaks. This was the kind of picnic spot built by the CCC in the 1930s.

We went swimming and found the water marvelous. We crawled up on the dam, walked along up there, watched the teenagers push each other in, and then we descended down a slippery iron ladder to the other side. The younger children were playing there in a shallow place and scampering on a natural beach.

Later, with the shadows lengthening, boating was in order. Canoes and paddle boats formed bright spots of color down river, between one dam and the next.

Soon we were gone, but Blanco State Park had found a way into our hearts.

HISTORY

Blanco is an old county seat, dating back to 1858. Anglo-American settlers had arrived five years earlier and had settled south of the river. With the founding of the county, the emphasis shifted north of the river and the village took the name of Blanco.

In 1859 German settlers in the west voted to break off. They wanted to band with more of their own and form another county. Four years later, during the turmoil of the Civil War, they were able to sway the county vote to enable them to do this. Areas around Sisterdale and Boerne joined with parts of Kerr County to form the new county of Kendall. It was the only new county formed in Texas during the Civil War.

Trouble reared up in the northern portion of the county after the war. Lyndon Johnson's forebears had set up a large cattle operation near the present Johnson City. His grandfather, Sam Johnson and his great uncle, Tom, had made a great deal of money driving cattle to Kansas, but had lost it all and sold out to their nephew, James Polk Johnson. It was he who laid out Johnson

66

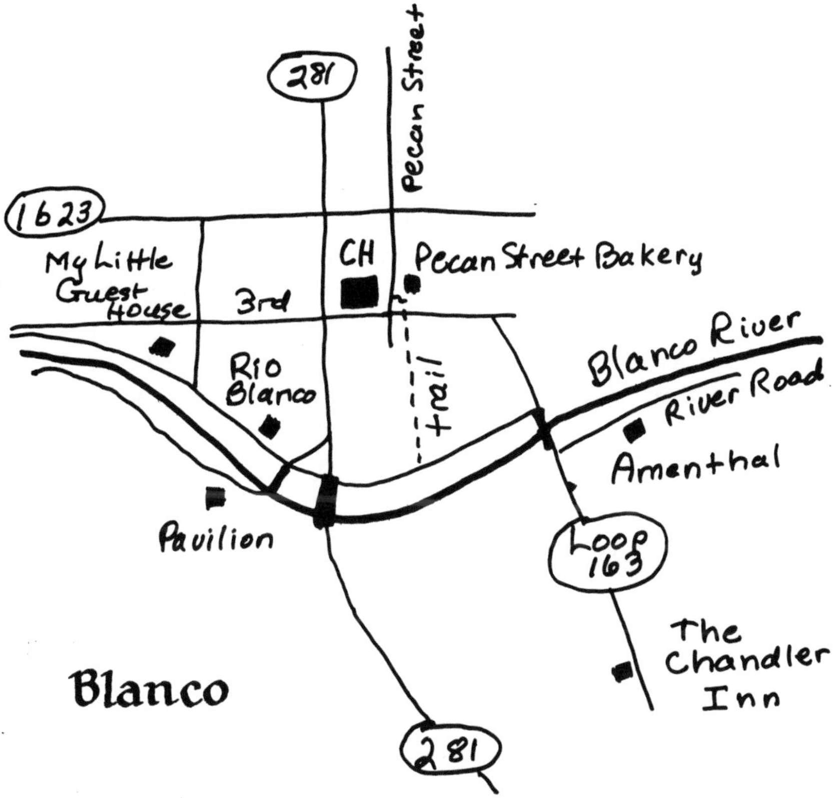
281
Pecan Street
1623
My Little Guest House
3rd
CH
Pecan Street Bakery
Blanco River
Rio Blanco
trail
River Road
Amenthal
Pavilion
Loop 163
The Chandler Inn
Blanco
281

City in 1878, gave it the family name, and then had his eye on the county seat. In an election the following year, Johnson City lost by only seven votes. In 1884, she lost by only fifteen votes. But in 1890, Johnson City won.

So, here was Blanco, no longer the seat but with a handsome limestone courthouse in the middle of the public square - a courthouse only four years old. What could be done now?

At first doctors and lawyers rented office space for fifty cents a month. A school moved in, then a bank around 1906. During the 1930s a bakery here made the bread for the CCC workers at the Blanco State Park. A hospital followed.

At length, in 1986, the courthouse, by then abandoned, fell into the hands of a San Antonio businessman. He planned to move it, stone by stone, to his ranch near Round Mountain.

This was too much. Local citizens rose up in protest, rallied their forces, schemed to get control. They learned how to raise money, and they raised enough to pay off the man from San Antonio. The group plans to use the old structure as a community center and regional museum.

Such has been the scene in Blanco County. Early, part was broken off to form Kendall County. Later, there was a bitter fight over the location of the county seat. And, since 1890, there have been two county courthouses, the "old county courthouse" here and a newer version in Johnson City, fourteen miles north. Both towns remain very small. Railroads never reached any point in this county.

COURTHOUSE SQUARE

The stately limestone courthouse of 1885 was designed by F.E. Ruffini of Austin, a young man who had come down from Cleveland ten years before. He had designed the Millet Opera House there, and, in the early 1880s, he was working on the plans for the Main Building at the fledgling University of Texas.

You can best see Ruffini's ideas if you stand on the north side of the building. He liked the style of the Second Empire, with its projecting central pavilions and receding planes on either side. This was a basic scheme he used again and again. His stone jail at Burnet (1884) has much the same look as the courthouse here, only it is a much smaller version.

You can determine the outlines of the original mansard roofs, but the wrought iron cresting is gone. A handsome double door with a lunette survives, but the corresponding door on the south side has been filled in.

The square is still the center of town activity. Shops and cafes line it on all sides. You find the Pecan Street Bakery here. Close by is a nature trail of one-fourth mile that leads down to the river. Blanco is the kind of place where you tend to walk from one spot to another.

AMENTHAL *(1883) 819 River Drive. S. of the river, east of the Loop 163 bridge.*

Once you get down to the river, you may want to find Amenthal, the childhood home of Lyndon Johnson's mother.

Before Blanco lost the county seat, before the records were carted off to Johnson City, Lyndon Johnson's family on his mother's side moved here. Joseph Wilson Baines brought his family to a spacious, two-story limestone house on the river bank, on the opposite side from town. He was a lawyer, trained in McKinney under ex-Governor Throckmorton. He served as Secretary of State in Governor John Ireland's administration in Austin from 1883 to 1887. Baines, whose father was George W. Baines, president of Baylor University during the Civil War, had helped establish a Baptist church in McKinney and became a leading layman in the Baptist congregation here.

Rebekah, Baines's daughter and Lyndon Johnson's mother, was born in McKinney in 1881 but arrived here at the age of six. She always recalled this house and its setting with pleasure. In 1954, writing in *A Family Album*, she mentions the orchards, the flower beds, the honeysuckle climbing up to the windows.

But this idyll was not to last. No doubt the removal of the county courthouse hurt Baines's law practice, but he also invested in farms that had suffered during a long drought. In 1904, near bankruptcy, he sold the house here and moved the family to Fredericksburg. He hoped to continue his law practice there, but within two years he was dead. His funeral was held in the German Methodist Church. Fredericksburg had no Baptist church, but the Baptist pastor in Kerrville came up to conduct the service.

At the time of the move to Fredericksburg, Rebekah was in her senior year at Baylor Female College in Belton. She then joined the family, gave lessons in elocution and wrote for the local newspaper. She made many friends; among them, Sam Johnson, the young state legislator, whom she subsequently married in

August, 1907. They wed at the Fredericksburg
courthouse - again, in lieu of a Baptist church - and
Rebekah then moved with Sam out to the Johnson Ranch
at Stonewall. Lyndon was born there August 27, 1908.

Rebekah's mother, Ruth Ament Huffman Baines, was,
by then, living in San Marcos, where she had gone after
her husband's death. She rented out rooms to college
students to supplement her resources. Thus began a
long family connection to the Southwest Texas State
Teachers College (established in 1903) where Lyndon
and all of his siblings matriculated. Rebekah and Sam
even moved there in 1930 to help the younger children
get through.

Amenthal, the Baines home here, still stands south
of the river, only a short walk from the state park. It is
still an attractive place, still suggests the enchantment
that Rebekah experienced as a young girl. For Rebekah,
Blanco was a place of happy memories.

BLANCO STATE PARK *Entrance off Hw. 281 just N. of the
Blanco River. Screened shelters. Admission. For camping:
Ph: 512/389-8900. For pavilion: Ph: 210/833-4333.*

In the early 1930s a group of Blanco citizens donated
105 acres on either side of the Blanco River to the
struggling state parks board. In June of 1933 the CCC
came to develop it. This was an early project for the
national program, the Civilian Conservation Corps,

which had only been in existence for a few months. Blanco State Park was in the first group of parks to be developed in Texas, along with Caddo Lake State Park, Davis Mountains State Park, and Meridian State Park. These formed the nucleus of the Texas state park system.

Until June of the following year, Unit 854 of the CCC built two dams across the river, roads, picnic tables and benches. They also built a limestone pavilion that is a classic of the era: low to the ground with huge chimney, arched openings, and handcrafted roof braces. It is very similar to the CCC pavilion at the Meridian State Park.

After finishing the work here, Unit 854 moved on to Longhorn Cavern (1934-1940) and then to Inks Lake State Park (1940-1941). The latter does not have a pavilion, probably because World War II cut short the projects of the CCC. (Congress officially ended the program in 1942.) These three parks - Blanco, Longhorn, and Inks - are the only ones developed by the CCC within the confines of this book. Others have come since then, of course, but they lack the distinctive stonework of the 1930s.

But all did not go well for this park. In the early 1960s Governor John Connally announced that it would close. Attendance had lagged. The property would revert to its original owners.

It was then that a local rancher stepped forward. Ira Caswell was a member of the Blanco Chamber of Commerce and a leader in town. He sponsored a write-in campaign to the governor to persuade him to change his mind. Then Caswell took the job of managing the park himself. With a helper (ostensibly hired to work on his ranch) he made repairs, planted trees, spruced things up. At night he and his wife sent out flyers to groups in Austin and San Antonio to come out and enjoy the park. Before long, there were crowds. By 1965 Ira Caswell could step back. He was replaced by a full-time manager.

Of course, all this is hard to believe now with the park as popular as it is. Visitors stream in from afar. But local folks come, too. They like to fish, to swim, to bird watch, to picnic, to walk. They enjoy the river scenery just as do their counterparts in New Braunfels or Lampasas. Indeed, these river parks in the hearts of Central Texas cities and towns are part of the special appeal of this part of the state.

ANNUAL EVENT: LIGHTING OF THE OLD COURTHOUSE *Friday after Thanksgiving. 6:30 P.M.*

Blanco welcomes visitors to the annual lighting of the old Blanco County Courthouse on the night after Thanksgiving. Shops around the square stay open late. Santa comes. Carolers serenade.

LODGING: MY LITTLE GUEST HOUSE *West of the entrance to state park. Stay on the public road. Write to Doris Cox, Box 67, Blanco, 78606. Ph: 210/833-5264 or 800/577-5264.*

Other than camping at the state park, there is one place where you can stay down by the river. It is a charming guest cottage with a porch overlooking the water, spaces to sleep five, and a full kitchen. The house nestles in a liveoak motte, and the porch has a big swing and tables and chairs for breakfast. This all seems too good to be true. But there it is, and Doris Cox operates this, her only guest cottage, as a special project. She arranges breakfast items and everything else you might need, and then slips away. You may want to move in - as I did.

In the early mornings, you spy those who have come out to fish, you see birds undisturbed. In the evenings, shadows lengthen across the park, people pack up to go home, the quiet river beckons a swimmer to venture far upstream.

RESTAURANT: PECAN STREET BAKERY AND CAFE *On the square, 306 Pecan Street. Open 8-4. Ph: 210/833-5737.*

The Pecan Street Bakery is the sort of place where you settle down to a meal of squash quiche with green chilies, tortilla soup, a salad, and corn muffins. Something special is cooking every day. And you can watch what is going on because the kitchen is set off in one corner of the large room. Breakfasts sound great: omelets, quesadillas, migas. And always look for goodies to take along with you - big cookies, brownies, carrot cake.

RESTAURANT: RIO BLANCO *On public road north of the river, just west of entrance to state park. Ph: 210/833-4982.*

Rio Blanco's broad, tree-shaded deck overlooks the river, close to the entrance to the state park. The offerings here include all kinds of Mexican dishes, hamburgers, stuffed bell peppers. Take-out is available, but some find the deck overlooking the water irresistible.

RESTAURANT: THE CHANDLER INN *Loop 163, S. of Blanco River. Fri, Sat 5:30-9:30. Sun ll:30-2:30. Ph: 210/833-4117.*

The Chandler Inn is in an old house in the country. Big rooms in the front have tables laid out with unmatched tablecloths edged with white lace. There is a pleasant view from the windows. The menu offers a weekly change of choices, but usually includes rack of lamb. There may be trout, red snapper, or scampi.

THE LUCKENBACH ROAD *RR 1623 from square in Blanco, RR 1888, RR 1376 to Hwy. 290, just E. of Fredericksburg. Luckenbach information: 830/997-3224.*

The road out from town parallels the Blanco River into the hills. This is an exceptionally beautiful drive. White cliffs border the water in many places. Eventually the river peters out and the road turns north. It climbs up to the divide between the watersheds of the Blanco and the Pedernales Rivers. Here there is a broad panorama west towards Fredericksburg.

Soon you pass the old community of Luckenbach. Started by the Luckenbach family, who later moved to

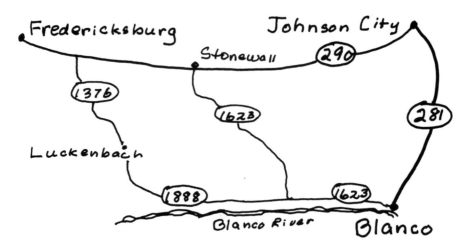

Doss, the village was continued by the Engels who had married into the family. There was a post office, a general store, a dance hall.

In January, 1971, Benno Engel sold the property to Hondo and Shatzie Crouch, a couple who were both natives of the region. They lived nearby in an old stone house on a ranch and were both interested in preservation. Shatzie, the former Helen Stieler and the daughter of a prominent goat rancher, was a leader in the historical association in Fredericksburg and also a refinisher of old furniture. She wanted to Luckenbach to continue as it was, with a genuine country store.

But not long after the purchase, the Crouches found out that the post office here would be closing. This dashed cold water on Shatzie's plans. Neighborhood business lagged, and soon Hondo began organizing events such as chili cook-offs and picnics on the 4th of July. Hondo was a natural entertainer and people gathered around. As his daughter, Becky Crouch Patterson, wrote later in *Hondo, My Father*, Luckenbach became his stage.

Shatzie drifted away, lost interest in the project, and she and Hondo separated in 1973. Hondo continued, even achieved national acclaim, but he died three years later.

In the next year, 1977, a song came out called "Let's Go to Luckenbach, Texas" by Waylon Jennings and

Willie Nelson. That put Luckenbach on the map. Four thousand people crowded in for the 4th of July picnic that year.

After that Kathy Morgan, an early partner, together with the Crouch children, kept the place going. Neighbors supported them. No one wanted it to change, or to close.

So, there it is still - a small place by the side of a creek, the patio for beer drinking out back, the store unpainted, the same stuff on the shelves, the pot-bellied stove warming the "saloon" on cold days, the rest rooms in a separate building at the rear. The dance hall is still open on a regular basis. The Fourth of July picnic - sometimes with Willie Nelson - still happens.

Fredericksburg

INTRODUCTION TO FREDERICKSBURG

I remember Fredericksburg years ago when in early December we went down to see the Kristkindl Markt, the Hill Country version of the famous Advent markets in Germany. We looked over the goods in the huge tent set up in the central plaza, but we were also excited by Main Street itself, decked out as it was in Christmas finery, every store fairly bursting with goods.

It was a bitterly cold day and we soon found ourselves at Altdorf's, in a cozy spot in the front room next to a tall tree decorated with tinsel and red bows. We ate juicy Reuben sandwiches and drank mulled wine. Our spirits revived, we went out and around the corner to the Christmas Bazaar at St. Joseph's Hall next to the Catholic Church. Later we heard a concert in the old Methodist Church, now a community center. In the evening, when it was very dark, we visited the tiny Schandua House, its kerosene lamps and candles aglow. This old cottage, shown as part of the annual Open House, has neither electricity nor plumbing.

The grays and browns of Fredericksburg take to the reds and greens of Christmas. It is a good time to be there.

HISTORY

Fredericksburg is an attractive small town, a German outpost from the 1840s, a distinctive place that has kept its

customs and traditions intact. It has a long Main Street with shops and bakeries and museums. The street is very wide - originally wide.enough to turn an ox team without backing up. Very popular today, Fredericksburg is one of the places you think of when you say "Hill Country."

The town began as a second "way station" set up by the German Emigration Company on the way towards its land claim north of the Llano River. The framework of the town was exactly that of early New Braunfels, its sister city. Both had communal governments. Both were laid out as grids and divided into half-acre plots that were distributed to the colonists. Both had warehouses for food distribution, a community church and school, and doctors hired by the society. In both cases, outlying lots of 10 acres surrounded the towns on all sides. At first these were intended as ancilliary farms, but around 1900 these outlots were subdivided as housing additions.

Meusebach, the Society director, had bought on credit 10,000 acres at this site, five or six miles north of the Pedernales River. He named the place Friedrichsburg for Prince Friedrich of Prussia, one of the principal supporters of the German Emigration Society. The first settlers arrived May 8, 1846 to a beautiful valley of post oak trees divided by two strongly flowing streams. They lost little time in cutting down the oaks for their first homes.

But this was the heart of Comanche hunting grounds and soon Meusebach was off, up towards Mason and points beyond, to make a celebrated treaty with the Indians. He promised them certain goods in exchange for their leaving this German colony unmolested. He arranged for some of the settlers to live north of the Llano River, in the Fisher-Miller Grant, thus fulfilling his obligation. He promised the Indians they would be treated like "brothers" in Fredericksburg.

This treaty, not withstanding, the colonists breathed easier when a federal fort was erected at the edge of town in 1848. As part of the federal responsibility to protect the western border after the war with Mexico, Fort Martin Scott was part of a chain that ran from the Rio Grande to the Upper Trinity River. This cordon included Fort Croghan at the present Burnet and Fort Worth.

With the fort came a military road that led from San Antonio out to various point in West Texas. The road brought the forty-niners during the following year, folks in a hurry to get to the Gold Rush in California.

Also with the fort came a demand for goods and services. The first private store opened in town. It was followed by others. The soldiers needed produce, meat, grains, hay for their horses. The fort also employed construction workers and teamsters.

Other installations followed the first line. Fort Martin Scott was abandoned after two years, but Fort Mason, forty miles north, superceded it. Fort Mason and others remained active until the Civil War, and Robert E. Lee was stationed there when the war began. He had been a frequent visitor in Fredericksburg during the 1850s.

The populace of Fredericksburg was loathe to confront the conflict of the Civil War. They voted against secession, as did most of the other counties in this region. Most refused to serve far afield; they preferred to join the Gillespie Rifles, the home guard for the frontier. Charles Henry Nimitz, grandfather of the famous admiral, was the leader in this section of the Texas Frontier Regiment, but after a short interval, he was designated the conscription officer for the Confederate Army. In this post he was unpopular.

Fredericksburg was bitterly divided during the war. Admiral Nimitz's other grandfather, Heinrich Henke, was a teamster for the Confederates. But his wife's brother was killed at the Battle of the Nueces, where a group of Union sympathizers were intercepted on their flight to Mexico. J.J. Klingelhoefer, an early chief justice or county judge, was opposed to the war on philosophical grounds, but one of his sons joined the Confederate Army and later was missing in action at Vicksburg.

Fortunes improved at the end of the war. The federal forts in the West were reactivated: Mason in 1866, McKavett in 1869. Further business came from cattle drovers moving their herds up to Kansas. Main Street was humming again.

By the 1880s, when the cattle drives were finished and the forts in Central Texas were finally shut down at the close of the Indian wars, Fredericksburg was well established as a market town for a broad region. Up and down the street, artisans lived next to their shops, behind them or above. The doctor lived here, the druggist behind his shop there, the wheelwright in his dwelling behind his workshop.

In the 1890s, though still very German, Fredericksburg "Americanized" to some degree. The name Friedrichsburg was Anglicized to Fredericksburg. After a jolly fiftieth anniversary of the town in 1896, Main Street was straightened and the old relic of the first church and community center was removed from the center of the street. A huge steam boiler for generating electricity was carted up from the rail terminal at Comfort. Yet, modernized to a degree, the old ways persisted. Everybody here was bilingual, the children more proficient in English than their parents. As Chester Nimitz would explain about his mother, she grew up speaking, reading, and writing German and, thus, she was not comfortable writing a letter in English. His grandmother Henke spoke English hardly at all.

Besides that wood-burning boiler, many other things came up to Fredericksburg from the rails at Comfort. Thus, getting a railroad here was a burning issue. When the San Antonio and Aransas Pass Railroad built west from San Antonio in 1887, it turned west from Comfort to Kerrville, and thus missed Fredericksburg altogether. Finally, in 1913 a tap road was completed up from Comfort. This line lasted until 1942, when trucking was well established.

The 1930s proved a great turning point here, as in other sections of the Hill Country. A paved road, Highway 87, was finally completed from San Antonio in 1936. During that era, the town was incorporated. Its streets were finally given formal designations (mostly English names now) and signs were put up. As in New Braunfels, some of the local families began to appreciate their local heritage. They formed the Gillespie County Historical Society and began to raise funds for the reconstruction of their old pioneer symbol, the Vereins Kirsche, the octagonal church and community center that had stood in the center of town until 1897.

Admiral Nimitz caused more hometown pride to swell during World War II. Many volunteered for the service this time. Any conflict over loyalty to Germany dissipated during this war. At the end, a huge parade and dinner at the Nimitz Hotel honored the returning admiral.

Now people wanted to be more up-to-date. They modernized their old houses, filled in breezeways with hollow tile, stripped off porches and laid concrete terraces, discarded old doors and windows, lowered ceilings and closed off fireplaces. They exchanged old gardens for "carpet grass," tore down tank houses and other extraneous outbuildings.

Yet there were some old families - and these included doctors, lawyers, and bankers - who were pushing for recognition and preservation of the old. They had banded together in the Gillespie County Historical Society and now they succeeded in purchasing the old Kammlah House for a Pioneer Museum. One of their members, the lawyer Arthur Stehling, bought the old Dietz hotel as a home and office in 1957. And, three years later, the group published *Pioneers in God's Hills*, historical sketches of the early settlers.

Meanwhile, the Lyndon Johnsons bought his aunt's ranch in 1951, and Lady Bird led the family over to a church in Fredericksburg after the newly formed Episcopal Church was located in the renovated, half-timbered Walter House.

In 1961, Vice-President Johnson brought the West German Chancellor, Konrad Adenauer to visit. Adenauer spoke to a large crowd in German and was widely understood. Admiral Nimitz also took part in the occasion. After the ceremonies Nimitz went out to visit two of his aunts but lost the secret service. He had to motor back to the LBJ Ranch instead of flying in the helicopter.

Nimitz was a great favorite here, and three years later, when the Nimitz Hotel was closing, plans were laid to establish a museum honoring the admiral. He agreed, provided the exhibits were dedicated to all the men and women who served in the Pacific War.

In 1967, another old landmark, the 1882 limestone courthouse, was renovated and converted into a handsome library.

After that, preservation efforts picked up momentum. First one and then another of the old structures were renovated. Soon no one was tearing down anything, and people began to regret selling the old doors with the carving or etched panes or taking the windows with the bubble glass out to use in the chicken house.

In the 1980s the city stepped forward with zoning rules, taxes on occupancy rates at overnight accommodations, and active promotion of Fredericksburg as a tourist destination. The city also bought the northern half of the central plaza to protect it from commerical encroachment.

So, now, at the end of the twentieth century, hordes of tourists are coming, a bed-and-breakfast trade is thriving,

and innumerable stores and boutiques abound.
Fredericksburg has experienced a radical change from its
days as an ethnic enclave, isolated and remote.
Sometimes, this development seems to have gone too far -
there is some tackiness now evident on Main Street and in
the replicas of early homes that are springing up here and
there - but the hardy spirit of the old town has held up so
far against this onslaught of growth.

ARCHITECTURE

How did architectural trends parallel history here?
After the initial log cabins, early houses were quite
small, one-and-one-half stories, built of *fachwerk*, or half-
timbering, and covered with plaster. Windows were small,
often casements, and chimneys were also usually small.
Additions poked out at either side, or the rear.

Almost everything here was built of limestone, quarried
locally. Both early and later structures rose in clean, neat
layers of the white stone. By 1850 a few houses grew to
two full stories, and most builders dispensed with the half-
timbering, now realizing that large blocks of limestone
could stand alone.

After the Civil War builders in Fredericksburg
continued with one-and-one-half story cottages, usually
side-gabled, but some experimented with front-gabled
stores that accommodated living space in the rear. Two of
these are the Lungkwitz House at 254 E. Main and the
Alberthal House at 414 E. Main.

Other styles seeped in. For example, a little of the Greek
Revival influence in the Felix Van Der Stucken House at
114 W. Austin Street. The Catholic Church, built around
1863, with its central, forward tower, was Old World
Gothic. The elegant courthouse of 1882, designed by a San
Antonio architect, was Italianate.

By the late 1880s several stores with French doors and
wrought iron trim went up on Main Street. The best
known, with its doors and iron trim still intact, is the
White Elephant Saloon, 242 E. Main. Soon larger
mercantile buildings were springing up. These had plate
glass show windows below and upstairs apartments with
large, airy rooms that enticed the owners to move from
cramped cottages in the streets nearby. The Hoerster
Building (1890), 242 W. Main, was followed by the Bank of

Fredericksburg at 120 E. Main, the Schandua Building at 205 E. Main, and the Patton Building at 232 W. Main.

Milled lumber became available by the end of the century. Small houses were then built of wood. Victorian details and gingerbread trim were also added to older homes, as was done in New Braunfels.

After 1900, people with a little money in their pockets could order from the Sears-Roebuck catalogs. One of the things they could obtain was an apparatus to make concrete blocks. These were used all over the country, especially in places where wood was scarce. The Baron's Creek Inn (1911) is a good example in town of a structure made entirely of concrete blocks, or "Basse Blocks," named for the brothers who ran the cement yard.

After World War I, yet another building method was tried. Houses were "rocked." Wooden frames were covered with concrete and then layered with irregular pieces of native stone in a masonry veneer. This was a common practice throughout West Texas.

A little red granite from Bear Mountain, four miles north, came into use at this time. Discovered in 1888, but heavy to cart and difficult to cut, the granite did not make its first appearance here until 1905 when it was used in the Central Drug Store built for a Swiss jeweler. Alphonse Walter contracted Stein Lumber Company to erect a building of molded concrete with a trim of limestone blocks and polished red granite panels. The red granite is also prominently displayed next door in another of Walter's buildings and across the street in numerous cornerstones. (100 block of E. Main)

The red granite was not used in large quanities until the First National Bank was built in 1936 and the new WPA courthouse in 1939. By then Fredericksburg had a smattering of other modern structures: bungalows and Tudor-style houses in residential sections, a 1929 Pueblo Deco theater.

The age of the automobile brought cars and trucks on highways running through town, and gas stations, including one at the old White Elephant Saloon. Motels soon followed. One of the first of these still thrives just south of Main Street on the San Antonio highway as the Peach Tree Inn.

Soon after World War II, a Buick agency cropped up, right there on Main Street, in a glass and metal building.

But that Buick dealership was the end of the line. Nothing that modern showed up again. Fredericksburg, like another Santa Fe, was ready to turn back the clock.

Suddenly the trove of sturdy limestone buildings became cherished for what they were. First one and then another of the old structures were restored. Original facades emerged from behind layers of paint or cement plaster. Masonry was repointed, fireplaces opened up, porches rebuilt.

By the end of the 1970s, Fredericksburg had Altdorf's Restaurant in the old Hanisch home, the Peach Tree Gift Shop (and soon to be tea room) in the old Bonn home, the Schandua Building restored with its owner living upstairs, the original Methodist Church acquired by the Historical Society, and the old Nimitz Hotel stripped down to its rock walls, its Alamo gable from the 1920s discarded, and a ship's prow rising once again over Main Street.

A new bank built in 1984 was not a particularly handsome building or attractive addition to Main Street, but it demonstrated the trend towards fitting in, blending with its neighbors, respecting the past.

Then came a different twist - a move away from congested Main Street. In the 1990s there was a sense of reaching out for the woods, the creek bottoms, the natural sites on the outskirts. Bill and Sylvia Varney took the Lehne-Itz House south of town and made it the hub of an expansive herb garden. The house itself, an 1882 stone cottage like many in this region, is now surrounded by a bower of greenery. The owners of the Peach Tree Tea Room doubled its size, extending it down towards the creek, making this very attractive place more accessible to weekend crowds. The Fredericksburg Inn and Suites preserved an old half-timbered house for its breakfast spot and faced the rest of the complex towards a meadow overlooking Baron's Creek. All of these changes added a new dimension, a balance to the tightly packed grid in the center of town.

What a marvelous architectural collection! Fredericksburg has retained an enormous amount. Most of it lines Main Street and the adjacent thoroughfares, but many other old structures survive out on the edges. Everywhere you look there's more. You won't be able to see everything on your first visit.

COURTHOUSES AND CIVIC CENTER *Main Street between Crockett and Adams Streets.*

Here you find the courthouses – the old one and the newer one – the post office, jails of various eras, a monument to John O. Meusebach, a park, and the reconstructed community church of 1847.

VEREINS KIRCHE AND ARCHIVES MUSEUM *112 W. Main. Mon-Sat 10-4, Sun 1-4*

A year after Fredericksburg was founded, the colonists began construction of an octagonal community building - a church, a school, a meeting place. It was quite small, eighteen feet by eighteen feet, made of wood and topped by an octagonal cupola. It was placed in the center of Main Street and also in the middle of the large central plaza that had been marked off cross-wise to the main thoroughfare. And there the Vereins Kirche - "Society Church" - stood for fifty years. It served as a community church, but then as various denominations broke off, it fell to the lot of the Lutherans. At length, they, too, abandoned it, and the little building was used as a testing hall for school examinations.

Then, in 1896, there it still stood in the center of things when old-timers were planning the fiftieth anniversary of the town. It was then stripped down to its bare bones and used as a pavilion during the festival. After that, it was torn down, consigned to the dump heap.

However, that old community church, with the distinctive shape that reminded some of a coffee mill, an octagonal building like you will still find in parts of Germany, had captured the imaginations of the folks here. In a sense, it was their hallmark. So, in 1934, they reconstructed the little building, and you see it now, not in the middle of the street this time, but alongside Main Street, just to the north of its former position. It serves as a repository for county relics and is open on a regular basis. Both the cornerstones, from the original building (which had been used as a chicken watering trough) and the later red granite marker, are mounted by the front door.

Step inside for a look at wonderful photographs showing Main Street in the old days, the original Vereins

85

Fredericksburg

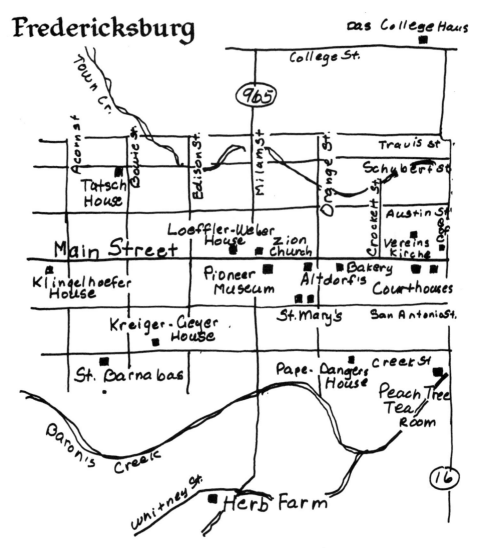

Das College Haus

College St.

965

Town Cr.

Acorn St.
Bowie St.
Edison St.
Milam St.
Orange St.
Crockett St.

Travis St.
Schubert St.

Tatsch House

Austin St.

Loeffler-Weber House

Main Street

Zion Church

Vereins Kirche

Klingelhoefer House

Pioneer Museum

Altdorf's

Bakery

Courthouses

Kreiger-Geyer House

St. Mary's

San Antonio St.

St. Barnabas

Pape-Dangers House

Creek St.

Peach Tree Tea Room

Baron's Creek

Whitney St.

Herb Farm

16

Kirche in various states of disrepair, and the White Elephant Saloon when it was used as a gas station.

1882 COURTHOUSE - PIONEER MEMORIAL LIBRARY
115 W. Main Street. Mon, Tues, Thurs 9-6, Wed 9-7, Friday, Sat 9-12.

Across Main Street from the Vereins Kirche is the old courthouse from 1882. It reigned here for many years, until it was replaced by the 1939 courthouse erected next door. It was scheduled for demolition in 1965 when the

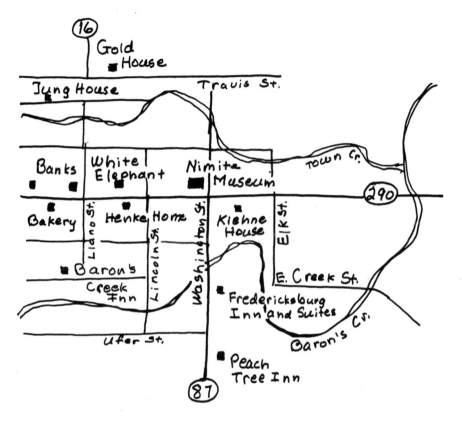

Eugene McDermotts of Dallas offered to pay for its
restoration. This was completed several years later, and
the building became an attractive public library. Lady Bird
Johnson came for the dedication. Her parents-in-law,
Sam and Rebekah Johnson, had been married in this
courthouse in 1907.

An English architect named Alfred Giles, who was
working in San Antonio at the time, won the contract in
the early 1880s to design the building. He was drawing
plans for the residences at the Fort Sam Houston, and the
courthouse here bears a certain resemblance to those. He
favored the Italianate style with its rough and smooth
stonework, corner quoins, segmentally arched windows,
one-story porches, and unpretentious doorways. He
specified two kinds of limestone, one that was softer for the

walls and a harder and paler kind for the trim. The wrought iron cresting, standing-seam metal roof, and galvanized iron cornices were brought up from San Antonio.

But this courthouse is more like his houses of the time - like two of them back to back, with a connecting wing - and less our idea of what we would think a Victorian courthouse was supposed to be. We look for four-square buildings with side doorways that face out to public squares. And, especially, we look for towers, or at least cupolas. Giles' courthouse in Fredericksburg shows none of that. But, curiously, a couple of years later he designed another courthouse of about the same size and style that builds up to a central tower. The wooden tower on his courthouse at Floresville is small, but effective.

GILLESPIE COUNTY COURTHOUSE OF 1939   *Corner of Main and S. Adams St.*

Next door is the WPA Courthouse that replaced the older one during the Depression years when federal funds were available. It is a classic of its kind: flat roof, yellow brick walls, vertically banked aluminum windows and spandrels, heavy wooden doors with beveled glass panes, terrazzo floors and marble wainscoting. The facade is divided into attic, mid-section, and basement, and, at the bottom, it shows the red granite from Bear Mountain a few miles north. This base is beautifully cut and polished. Designers of the WPA projects were encouraged to use the materials at hand. Trucks were then available to haul this heavy granite into town.

OLD JAIL (1885)   *117 San Antonio.*

Very plain and no nonsense in the style of West Texas, this old calaboose is solidly built of limestone, offers only a narrow, unpretentious front door, and a stark visage. One feels there were no extra comforts here.

This building served until the 1939 courthouse provided a lock-up on the third floor. After that, other uses were found for this building.

This is the place to obtain maps, brochures, and advice about Fredericksburg. Also find information about lodgings, festivals, the peach season, and hunting. Public restrooms are located in the rear.

MAIN STREET

The following are some of the principal points of interest on Main Street.

The KLINGELHOEFER HOUSE (1847), 701 W. Main Street, dates back to the beginnings here. Johann Jost Klingelhoefer arrived with his family in 1847. He received this lot and immediately set to work building the family home. Some of the *fachwerk*, or half-timbering, is still visible on the front section under the porch. Narrow, steep stairs inside led to the children's sleeping loft. The stairs outside now are not original.

Klingelhoefer prized his freedom in America, became a citizen soon after arriving, and served as the third Chief Justice. He stayed loyal to the Union during the Civil War. He grieved for his oldest son, August, who volunteered for the Confederate Army and then was missing in action near Vicksburg.

The BETZ-KAMMLAH HOUSE, 602 W. Main Street, was built a few years later, in the mid-1850s. The family omitted the half-timbering here, focusing instead on big sections of limestone used as building blocks.

The LOEFFLER-WEBER HOUSE (1846-7), 506 W. Main, built during the first winter, is the oldest house on Main Street. The original section is log. A later owner added more room. He was Johann Martin Loeffler, a cabinetmaker. Look for one of his chairs in the "first kitchen" in the Pioneer Museum.

ZION LUTHERAN CHURCH, corner of Main Street and N. Edison, is the oldest church building in Fredericksburg. It dates back to 1854, when the first structure arose, though there have many changes and additions through the years. Several families broke away from the community church in the Vereins Kirche and eventually bought this lot for $45.

The PIONEER MUSEUM COMPLEX at 309 W. Main, is a remarkable group of early buildings. Plan to spend time here. (See below.)

The WISSEMANN-HANISCH HOUSE (or ALTDORF'S RESTAURANT), late 1840s, 301 W. Main, was started by Conrad Wissemann, son of a Lutheran minister. He came at the age of 30, worked as a carpenter and also as a teamster on trips between here and San Antonio. He built the first four rooms, the ones that face the the street.

Wissemann sold this house to another son of a Lutheran minister, Paul Hanisch, a pharmacist who had trained in Germany and arrived on the scene in 1872. The front room on the west became his shop. The family parlor was on the east. Other rooms began to appear in the back. In 1976, when the last of the Hanisches died - 95-year-old Elizabeth, Paul's daughter - the property was willed to Zion Lutheran Church. A year later it was sold and became Altdorf's, a popular restaurant and beer garden. Half the fun of eating here is exploring the premises.

The ITZ HOUSE (late 1860s), 320 W. Main, was used as a saloon until Prohibition, and later as a meat market. The latter was run by Ernest and Elgin Itz in the 1930s.

Altdorf's

Ernest lived with his wife, the former Sophie Lehne, out at the site of the present Herb Farm. The family ran a cannery out there.

The KRAUSKOPF BUILDING, next door at 312 W. Main, was built in 1900 by Oscar Krauskopf for farm implement sales. His father, Engelbert, a cabinetmaker and gunsmith, had worked at this location. His sons and grandsons have continued the business, but they now have headquarters in the south part of town.

Engelbert, an early arrival, made guns for everyone who came to town. Famous Indians came to see him, as well as the officers at the frontier forts. He even made a gun for Robert E. Lee.

Now, as we move closer to the Market Square, we encounter a mercantile block, most of which was owned originally by the Schmidts. The German Emigration Company granted this family four lots beginning at the corner. The corner space is now occupied by the HOERSTER BUILDING (1890), 242 W. Main. Anton Hoerster bought the space from a Schmidt descendant in 1878. His building was one of the first two-story mercantile buildings with an apartment above. Like the others, it was constructed of local limestone, and like the

others, it had plenty of plate glass on the lower floor. A single bathroom held forth upstairs. In a line of bedrooms, each was fitted out with a wood stove. It was a lot of work to get the wood upstairs.

Next is the PATTON BUILDING (1897), at 232 W. Main. A. L. Patton, a young man from Missouri, came to Fredericksburg in 1871 when he was twenty. He married into one of the prominent families, the Wahrmunds, set up shop as a merchant, bought this land, and eventually built this structure as a store and home. He and his family had been living around the corner at 107 N. Orange. That house still stands. The Pattons had left it to their eldest son when they moved here.

SCHMIDT'S HOTEL (1860s), 218 W. Main Street, represents the interests of the Schmidt family, who provided the competition to the Nimitz inn at this end of Main Street. In the old days, there were stables and a big barn in back. Now the building serves as a law office. Through the years there have never been any significant changes to the exterior.

Last in this row is the SCHWARZ BUILDING (1907), 216 W. Main. This property, owned by the Schmidts, fell to the lot of Charles Schwarz after he married into the family. He and his wife, Maria, received it at the division of the family estate in 1899. A one-story building here had served as dining room and kitchen to the hotel next door. Schwarz, a merchant who had worked at other stores on the block, built this imposing edifice in 1907. He hired stone masons who had just finished the new Catholic Church. They did a fine job for him, fashioning stone finials at the corners, a broken pediment in the center, tall arched windows. Just as at the new St. Mary's there is a little red granite here. Cornerstones give the date, "1907," and the name, "Chas. Schwarz."

GEORG'S OLD WORLD BAKERY, 225 W. Main, is a marvelous place to stop for a cup of coffee and a pastry. The huge selection includes gingerbread bars and lebkucken. At Easter time they make pastry bunnies holding real eggs. Another specialty is an Osterlamm - an Easter lamb - a sponge cake baked in a special mold and then dusted with powered sugar. This was once my birthday cake.

Now we pass the civic center, the post office and the two courthouses. The numbers of the streets change here.

They switch from the west 100 block to the east 100 block at the courthouses.

The BANK OF FREDERICKSBURG, (1897), 120 E. Main, is a striking Romanesque limestone building, a landmark. It sports a horseshoe window in front, beautiful carving in the limestone beneath the window, and a jaunty tower at the top.

The architect was Alfred Giles of San Antonio, the same man who designed the courthouse of 1882, while the owner was Temple D. Smith, a banker from Virginia who came to open the first bank in Fredericksburg in 1887. He lived with his family upstairs - behind the horseshoe window. He tried to learn some German, he was an avid hunter, and he was a ceaseless promoter of the railroad to Fredericksburg, finally driving in the last spike when it arrived.

His funeral service in 1926 was held here at the bank. His wife, originally from Indiana, continued to live here after his death. She served as as vice-president of the bank. But the end was in sight. On February 19, 1932, both this bank and the second one (in rented space in the Patton Building) closed simultaneously. When they were reorganized, joined as one, the new bank stayed here until a new building was ready across the street. That building - the former home of the First National Bank - is currently the location of Showcase Antiques.

Continue a tour of this block next door at the former CITY DRUG STORE (1905) built by a watchmaker from Switzerland, Alphonse Walter. You see his initials in a red granite panel on the front. (He was also a pioneer in the use of molded concrete blocks. See these on the sides of the building.) Then, in the next building you find Walter's clock and watch shop that he built in 1908. The most remarkable feature here is a clock face in polished red granite right at the center top of the facade.

A few doors down is the PALACE THEATER (1929), another landmark with its brightly tiled accents. A movie palace that has never closed. A Pueblo Art Deco accent for Main Street.

Then at the end of the block is Bank One, a modern limestone bank that the San Antonio architect O'Neil Ford designed for Main Street in 1984. It is not wholly successful in its attempts to blend with the older buildings, yet it is not an anomaly either.

Cross Llano Street at the corner, circle back to the west, and find a table near the front window of the FREDERICKSBURG BAKERY, 141 E. Main. Here you can rest a moment with tea and cookies and look back across the street at the granite top knot above the jeweler's store, the theater, and the new bank. Sometimes you have to cross the street for a clear view of these buildings.

The bakery holds forth in an old structure Louis Priess built in 1889. It is limestone with French doors above and plate glass windows below. Originally, the entire facade was done with French doors, but later renovations changed this.

Outside, find the cornerstones in matching limestone: on the left, "Luis Priess," and on the right, "1889." DOOLEY'S FIVE AND DIME, next door to the west, was built by the same man in 1914. Here you find yellow brick instead of limestone, and large red granite cornerstones that say "1914" and "Louis Priess." (Priess had now Anglicized his name.)

Then, at 121 E. Main, you will find "R. C. Bonn" in a granite panel above the door, "1913" at the left corner, and, on the right: "R. C. Bonn, a convincing fact that Nagel Brothers have the best granite for buildings and monumental work." This is accompanied by drawings of a man and a woman etched into the granite.

At 119 E. Main is the old FIRST NATIONAL BANK. Here a base of red granite extends across the front, and the date "1936" is prominent as well as the cypher of the FNB.

The BURRIER-MAIER COMPANY (1916) put up more granite cornerstones. "The Famous Bear Mt. Red Granite owned and operated by Nagel Bros. Monumental Works, Fredericksburg, Texas."

Finally, on the corner, an old building was embellished with a granite cornerstone fifty years after it was put up. Limestone construction in 1874. Red granite cornerstone in 1924.

In the next block east, we find the SCHANDUA BUILDING (1897, 1901) at 207 E. Main. It is large and impressive, built in two sections, the first in 1897 and the second a few years later. John Schandua had inherited the land. It had passed down through his family from the original allotments. He lacked the money to build, however, so he went to the Masons for help. They agreed to loan him $700 for five years provided they could use the upstairs room as their meeting place. Schandua agreed, built the building, repaid the loan within two years, but promptly died. His brother then married his widow and put up the other half of the building. The Masons continued to meet in their room on the west, but the Schandua family moved into new quarters on the east. They left the Schandua House, 111 E. Austin Street, that is now featured on tours of old homes. The contrast between the tiny cottage and the quarters here is striking.

The FELIX REINBACH BUILDING (1904), 229 E. Main, represents a further development of the downtown stores. Here we have cast iron framing plate glass windows below, but an upper facade of galvanized metal. Ornate pilasters border the windows and door. A frieze shows an elaborate pattern of swags and stars.

Felix Reinbach married Admiral Nimitz's aunt, Elise Henke, in 1905, the year the admiral was graduated from the Naval Academy. The Reinbachs lived here until 1910, when they moved to a house down on S. Creek Street. No doubt a house and yard at the edge of town were more convenient for a family with small children.

Close by is the HENKE HOME (1866), 247 E. Main, where Elise Henke and her sisters and brothers grew up, and where Admiral Nimitz was born. His mother, Anna, was the eldest daughter in the family. His father, Chester Nimitz, was the son of Charles Henry Nimitz, the innkeeper across the street. Chester Nimitz died not long after he and Anna were married and before the birth of their baby, young Chester, in 1885.

Anna and young Chester lived here or across the street in the Nimitz Hotel until 1890. Then she married a younger Nimitz son, William, and went with him to Kerrville to manage another hotel.

The Henkes had bought this house in 1866. Heinrich, born in Germany, had arrived here in 1856, married 15-year-old Dorothea Weirich, served as a freighter for the Confederates, and then established a meat market here. Butchering was done in the backyard, while sales were made from the porch. After a few years, Heinrich spread his operation into a shop on the corner. All but one of his seven sons followed him into the meat business; Richard and Hugo continuing here, William establishing another shop on West Main Street, August and Henry, Jr. running still a third in Kerrville, and Otto raising cattle on his ranch halfway between Fredericksburg and Kerrville.

On my last visit to Fredericksburg I found the Henke home open as a gift shop. It is now possible to see the small room where Admiral Nimitz was born.

The HENKE MEAT MARKET, corner of Main St. and Lincoln, is also open as a modern gift shop. You can still see a marble-topped counter, a huge butcher block, and a walk-in refrigerator unit. A friend, who is an old-timer in the Hill Country, remembers, of course, when this was a meat market. It passed down through Richard to his son, Udo, who kept the shop open for many years, well past the time when Admiral Nimitz passed it in his Victory Parade in 1945.

The DIETZ BAKERY, 218 E. Main, is open Tuesday through Saturday, 8:00 A.M. until everything is sold out. Then you will see a sign on the door that reads, "Closed, Sold Out." This is a bakery of long standing in the Dietz family. Bread is their specialty.

The WHITE ELEPHANT SALOON (1886), 242 E. Main, was built by John Kleck in 1888. He had a long bar running along the west wall. Men played billiards, dominoes, and skat here.

Large blocks of tooled limestone form the front walls. The original French doors are still in place. Kleck finished off the facade with an extravagant wrought iron cresting and a statue of a white elephant. He hired A. W. Petmecky to make this elephant of cement. Petmecky borrowed a wooden elephant from an itinerant merry-go-round operator and used it to make the mold. The wonderful white elephant, symbol of hospitality, has always served as one of the landmarks in Fredericksburg.

The KEIDEL BUILDINGS, 248-258 E. Main. All the buildings from the White Elephant Saloon to the corner are part of the Keidel compound. A family of doctors who came early, they spread out from one building to the next. They bought the White Elephant Saloon in 1905, built the Keidel Medical Building next door in 1909, bought the Lungkwitz House (1868, 254 E. Main) in 1920, and remodeled the Priess Building (1883) on the corner into the first modern hospital in 1939. The large two-story house, from which this activity spread, stands in the midst of the compound, at 252 E. Main.

The first of the Keidel doctors, William, came with the original settlers and served as physician for the German Emigration Society. Trained in Germany, and himself the son and grandson of doctors, he sent his son Albert to school back in Germany as soon as the Civil War drew to a close. Albert returned in 1878, magnificently trained in pharmacy, surgery, obstetrics, and other areas of internal

White Elephant Saloon

medicine. There were many in Galveston and San Antonio who wished he would tarry in their cities, but Albert came back home.

It was this son, Albert, who bought the house on Main Street in 1881, doubled its size in 1888, and set up offices in the east wing. It was Albert who bought the White Elephant Saloon so he could place recovering surgery patients in the wooden addition at the rear. (He leased the saloon.) And it was Albert who sandwiched in the Keidel Medical Building on the west side of his lot in 1909. His four sons had followed him in the medical profession, and he arranged spaces for all of them in the new building. Werner and Felix, dentists, would practice upstairs. Also Victor, who followed his father as a surgeon and family practitioner, and Kurt, a pharmacist, would practice downstairs.

But still this was not enough room. After Albert's death in 1914, more changes followed. Felix bought the Lungkwitz House in 1920. Victor bought the Priess Building, a large former store with upstairs quarters, on the corner. Eventually Victor converted this into a modern hospital and also added a large wing at the rear. The Keidel Memorial Hospital - honoring William and Albert - served the community from 1939 to 1971, when the Hill Country Memorial Hospital was completed.

The STRIEGLER HOUSE (1908), 310 E. Main, was an impressive home built for a young businessman just after the turn-of-the-century. It is curious to see what was included, and what was not, at that time. There was electricity, yes, and indoor plumbing. There was one bathroom, and it was upstairs. The large L-shaped house was built of enormous limestone blocks - not concrete blocks. There was some red granite in the two cornerstones in front. Tall windows and transoms above the doors aided ventilation, and all the rooms connected with porches on either the upper or lower level. But there were no fireplaces. The family used only stoves.

The NAUWALD BUILDING (1847) at 328 E. Main now houses the gift shop for the Nimitz Museum next door. This was the home of Bertha, the oldest daughter in the Nimitz family, who helped her father run the hotel after her mother died. Bertha and Charles Nauwald had a large brood of their own. Charles ran a general store in the front of the building, while the family lived in the rear. Later owners changed the facade.

98

The NIMITZ MUSEUM is next at 340 W. Main. This is the fabled stagecoach inn established by Admiral Nimitz's grandfather, Charles Henry Nimitz, in the mid-1850s. (See below for details of the museum.)

Nimitz had left Germany after a teenage stint in the merchant marines and arrived here with the first colonists in 1846. He married Sophie Mueller and served in the Texas Rangers. Before long he and Sophie started this inn, which grew to include forty rooms, stables and a campground in the rear, a ballroom with a small stage, a brewery, and a bathhouse with four hand-soldered tin tubs. This bathhouse was quite a luxury at the time. Grandpa Nimitz liked to say this was "the last bath before El Paso."

Grandpa Nimitz was a jovial host. He loved to tell tall tales - especially if his grandchildren were within hearing. He immensely enjoyed practical jokes and would even play them on his guests. One of his favorites was to stash some of the hotel's silver in departing guests' luggage, wave them off, and then rush them back for a mock trial. Perhaps it is not surprising that this man added a steamboat section to his hotel in the 1880s. This four-story unit included a hurricane deck, a pilot house, and a crow's nest. The rooms at the top were said to be cooler than others in the hotel.

Sophie Nimitz died in 1877, only six years after the birth of the last of her twelve babies. But Bertha, the eldest daughter, was settled next door, and she helped with the various arrangements.

Grandpa Nimitz loved the changes in the seasons and the opportunities offered for entertainments. He held a children's Christmas Eve party around a huge cedar tree in the middle of his parlor. His dance on New Year's Eve was the talk of the town. At Easter he sponsored a community egg hunt in his backyard. All through the year he sponsored dances in the ballroom and theatrical performances on the small stage. Apparently, there was never a dull moment.

Young Chester loved all the activity, and he adored his grandfather. After he graduated from Annapolis, he and the white-bearded old gentleman posed for a memorable photograph. Slender, handsome, young Chester is resplendent in his uniform. A large copy of this picture hangs as a backdrop to the main desk in the museum. You can catch a glimpse of it through the front door.

Chester Nimitz was then gone for long spells, and the life at the hotel began to change. Grandpa Nimitz deeded the inn to his eldest son, Charles Henry, Jr., in 1906, and five years later the old man died. Charles Jr. in 1926, sold the hotel to a consortium of local owners who tore down most of the old structure and built a modern hotel. They sheared off the steamboat section, straightened the lines, covered the remaining rock walls with concrete plaster, added one-story porches, and finished it off with an Alamo gable at the top.

The modern hotel stayed in business until 1964. It was here that Admiral Nimitz came for a victory dinner in October 1945. The old ballroom, behind the lobby, had remained intact, and it was there that the admiral sat with family and friends. It was a moment of glory for the town, his family, and the hotel.

In 1964, when the hotel closed, there were plans to convert it into a museum to honor the admiral. He agreed with the idea, but requested that the museum honor all those who served with him in the Pacific War.

Funds came from various sources, but slowly. It was not until 1983 that the final dedication took place. By then the Japanese had built a garden at the rear, relics of the war were set up a block away, and, amazingly, the steamboat facade was back.

When the KIEHNE HOUSE (1850), 405 E. Main, was restored in the early 1970s, there was a stir of excitement. Old doors were found in the attic, and these doors had their original hardware. Friedrich Kiehne was a blacksmith who had made most of his own hardware. He had worked in the backyard, shoeing horses, making the horse shoes and the nails,too. The details in his house were outstanding. Solidly built of limestone, it is thought to be the first two-story stone house in town.

So, there is it - Main Street. Old houses and businesses, a church, bakeries, banks, beer gardens, museums, the original hospital. Almost everything of limestone, but some with a little granite trim. Magnificent. There is not another street like it in Texas.

PIONEER MUSEUM COMPLEX *309 W. Main, Mon-Sat 10-5, Sun 1-5. Admission. Ph: 830/997-2835.*

This museum embraces three historic Fredericksburg houses as well as a collection of other structures such as a barn, firehouse, log cabin, and a blacksmith shop. Each of the three main dwellings passed down through the original families until it came into the possession of the Historical Society. Some of the family's possessions came with each house, making this museum considerably more special than many. Further, fine examples of the furniture made by local cabinetmakers are found here.

KAMMLAH HOUSE (1848).

Outside the Kammlah House, the principal structure, a guide once said to me, "Stand here and look at the side view. There was no concern at all at how one roof line meets another. There were five or six additions, and it is easy to see them here."

The front part, on Main Street, is the typical early German cottage of one-and-one-half stories with front porch, plaster over *fachwerk*, casement windows, and an outside door in the attic. A small chimney pokes up at the lower end of the roof line on the east side. Then there was one addition after another, and these are what you experience as you visit this house. Elise Kowert in her *Old Homes and Buildings of Fredericksburg* describes it as "a house that grew and grew."

Begin your tour inside the front door with one of the guides, all natives of the Fredericksburg area, who will begin by telling you about the large room across the front of the dwelling. This - two rooms at first - was the original house, built around 1848, on the town lot that Heinrich Kammlah received from the German Emigration Company. He soon added the two rooms behind it, a kitchen and a bedroom. Later the family added a "second kitchen" behind these two rooms. It is one of the finest rooms in the house - with its enormous fireplace, its work table, dry sink and cupboard, all originally used by the Kammlahs.

On my last visit there I was escorted by my favorite guide. She grew up in the country and came into Fredericksburg as a teenager. She led me about and, in her distinctly German accent, pointed out many things I had not noticed before. In the front room she pointed to the *fachwerk* (half-timbering), showed me the holes for the wooden pegs, the places where it was spliced, the short pieces used in it. She said this *fachwerk* was originally covered with plaster and that to clean it now was troublesome.

She said the floor was the third one laid in this room. Around 1870 the Kammlahs opened a store in this part. Just when they took down the partition between the two rooms is not known. She said the front door was original. and the hardware as well. The casement windows also have their hardware intact, but she indicated that glass was not used at first.

She said the long table against the back wall was used in the store - "too long for a home." She explained that when customers were waited on family members took them to this table, but they did not stand behind it as we would today.

We passed through the "second kitchen", a marvelous place at Christmas with swags of greenery and red bows and peppermint sticks in glass jars in the cupboard. Even the shelf liners here fit in with the theme - white cloth with bright red embroidery. My guide said the liners were found in a trunk and the words spell out several lines from one of Schiller's poems.

On this particular day she went with me to the back part of the house, to a large section built over a cellar. Here there's yet another kitchen, the third, and a large space for dining, a parlor, and bedrooms. The cellar itself was used for the store as well as the family. Cured meats, whiskey and wine were kept down there.

At the top of some very worn stone steps is a small parlor with several pieces of early Fredericksburg furniture that are worth special attention. A walnut rocking chair was made by Peter Tatsch, the cabinetmaker who lived on Bowie Street in another house with an extraordinary hearth and chimney. A fine safe, with hand-blown glass in the doors, stands in the corner. In the center of the room is a round table with a pedestal base that was owned and used by Meusebach in his home at Loyal Valley.

All of these pieces are shown in Lonn Taylor's definitive *Texas Furniture: The Cabinetmakers and Their Work, 1840-1890*, as well as a wardrobe in the adjoining bedroom. This one was signed by the owner: "C. Welgehausen, Crab Apple, Gillespie County." My guide opened the door to the wardrobe to show me the writing.

Behind the parlor and the bedroom is a large area, the "attic," where more treasures await. Here is Admiral Nimitz's cradle, also featured in Taylor's book, and wash bowls and pitchers, some from the Nimitz Hotel. I also spotted the announcement of Chester Nimitz's parents' wedding.

After the death of Heinrich Kammlah (Henry I) in 1875, his son took over. It was Henry II who presided over the glory days of the store and who added the back part of the house. After his death in 1923, the store was closed. With the death of his son, Henry III, in 1942, the family scattered and lived here only sporadically. By 1955 they were ready to sell.

So it was that the Gillespie County Historical Society bought the Kammlah House from the heirs in 1955. The Society then began the process of restoring it to its present state. You won't find a better introduction to Fredericksburg, its architecture and its furnishings, than here.

FASSEL HOUSE

The Fassel House next door began as a small rock cottage on an adjoining town lot that the Kammlahs purchased in 1852. They sold the property in 1871, and by 1876 Mathias Fassel had bought it and started to enlarge the original cottage, the rock room that is now the back bedroom. He added what is now the large kitchen, and later he built the two rooms at the front and the porch. He also erected a shop for his business between the porch and Main Street. He was a wheelwright who specialized in wagons and buggies.

Many would pass through the shop and the home to the Catholic Church immediately behind. This was a short cut from Main Street. Apparently, women would shake off wood chips from their long skirts and petticoats before entering the house.

Elise Kowert, interviewing a surviving daughter for her newspaper series, was delighted to hear of social events in this house, which was a gathering place for family and friends. The daughter remembered the gatherings after the midnight services on Christmas Eve at St. Mary's. She said the coffee pots covered the top of the woodburning stove.

The Fassel house was also used as a kind of funeral home for relatives and friends in the country. They brought the deceased here and held the service and procession from this house.

Ownership passed down to a daughter and her family. After her death, other members used it as a Sunday House. In 1967 the remaining heirs sold it to the Historical Society.

WEBER HOUSE (1904)

The last of these, the Weber House, truly was a Sunday House, and one of the most authentic in Fredericksburg.

Alwine Weber, daughter of Conrad and Louise Klingelhoefer Wehmeyer, was born and reared on Main Street. Her father was a baker. Her mother, Louise, was one of the daughters of J. J. Klingelhoefer, who amassed quite a bit of property. At her mother's death, in 1903, Alwine inherited a town lot at San Antonio and South Cherry. Since she and her husband, August Weber, were living seven miles out on the Kerrville Road, they decided to build a Sunday House on this lot during the following year.

The frame house was a simple one-room structure with no modern conveniences. The family brought in what they needed for their short stays. Devout Lutherans, faithful members of Zion Lutheran Church, they came in on the weekends for services, choir practice, a little shopping, and visiting with friends and family.

Alwine and August Weber both died in 1929. Their daughter and then their son owned the house. After their deaths, the son's wife gave the cottage to the Historical Society in 1972, and it was moved here. She also donated some of its furnishings: a small bed, the kitchen cupboard, a long table and benches.

Sunday Houses ran their course by the Second World War. The tradition had started back in the era of wagons and buggies. But with advent of the automobile, families could easily come into town for the day. After cars came into general use, many of the former Sunday Houses were enlarged and used as permanent dwellings.

CHURCHES AND SUNDAY HOUSES

Directly behind the Pioneer Museum, in the 300 block of San Antonio Street, stand the magnificent Catholic Churches - a pair of them, one old, one not so old, a wonderful example of how everything here has been

preserved. The old St. Mary's, the Marienkirche, was completed in 1863 after a grueling three years during which the entire congregation helped with its construction. The massive limestone church is dominated by a large tower in front. Tall, pointed Gothic windows complemented vaulted ceilings inside. At first the aisles were paved with stones, and under the pews was sand.

This church served the congregation until the new St. Mary's next door was completed in 1906. Then the older sanctuary became a school. The windows were squared off. A second floor was incorporated within the structure. After a number of years, new schools were built across the street, and this building was used for other purposes. Finally, in 1988, efforts began to redo the windows and restore the church to its original appearance.

Once we stood outside the churches on a summer evening about seven o'clock. The Saturday evening mass was just over and people were coming out from the services. We asked one of the parishioners about the painted designs inside. He said they were mostly covered over in the 1970s, "when they also moved out most of the statues." Then we stood there and looked at the many buildings of the church complex, commented on the rustic stonework in the old St. Mary's and the enormous stones used in the new one and the Austin stone (or cast stone) in the church structures to the west. He said the latter were put up after World War II. He also told us that one of his ancestors had helped shingle the first church. His family had been there from the beginning.

In the same block, west from St. Marys, is the original Methodist Church. Built in 1855, it is now the property of the Historical Society. The Methodists, like the other denominations, had broken away from worship at the Verein Kirche, the community church. Their early church, however, has suffered so many renovations that it is hard to determine its original shape.

Near these churches are more Sunday Houses, similar to the Weber House at the Pioneer Museum, but none as authentic or true to character as that one. Three houses at 404, 408, and 410 W. San Antonio have long been identified as Sunday Houses. Whether these were truly used in that way, as the Weber House was, is open to question. But at any rate they are exceedingly small structures that look the part.

On the other hand, the Gentemann Sunday House, 108 S. Milam was truly used as such, having been built by the Gentemanns in 1882 as a retreat from their farm northwest of Fredericksburg. Their stone house is one room wide on a very narrow lot, only twenty-two feet wide. Eventually they added to the back. This dollhouse is still occupied today, though larger now than it was a hundred years ago. Remarkably, it stands almost exactly across the street from the Weber Sunday House in the Pioneer Museum.

ADMIRAL NIMITZ STATE HISTORICAL PARK *340 E. Main Street, daily 8-5, (except Dec 25). Admission. Ph: 210/997-4379.*

Admiral Nimitz wanted the exhibits at the old hotel to honor all the men and women who served with him in the Pacific. Thus it was set up to chronicle the war there, becoming a museum of the Pacific War. The old hotel would hold the main exhibits. A park a block away, the History Walk, would show airplanes and tanks and amphibious boats. Later, a garden was built in the area of the former corral of the hotel. This is the Garden of Peace, a gift from the Japanese people.

Finally, the steamboat facade of the hotel was rebuilt, with the dedication in 1983. But this facade could be misleading. Inside, the spaces are organized as a museum, not as the old hotel. Only a few vestiges remain. Just past the lobby is a large room where a movie about Nimitz is shown. This is Grandfather Nimitz's ballroom. It was not changed during the renovations of 1926, nor was it disturbed during the reconstructions of 1978 and the years following.

Upstairs, on the second floor, a few bedrooms symbolize the old hotel. Here you see "Robert E. Lee's bed," the spool bed from the room he occupied when he came to visit in the 1850s.

For more about the history of the hotel, the Nimitz family, and the Henkes, turn to sections about them under "Main Street."

ADMIRAL NIMITZ'S CAREER

Chester Nimitz was living in Kerrville with his mother and his stepfather, William Nimitz, when he applied to the

Naval Academy at Annapolis. He was working at his
parents hotel when he met two young lieutenants in the
army who·had come out to the Hill Country for gunnery
practice. He was fascinated to learn that they had gone to
West Point without paying tuition.

He contacted his congressman about an appointment,
but Congressman James Slaydon told him that would be
impossible in his district. He explained that there were
multitudes of army families who had designs on West
Point for their sons. "But what about Annapolis? I have
an opening." Chester had never heard of it. But he
decided to give it a try. His stepfather, a graduate of the
Worcester Polytechnic Institute in Massachusetts, tutored
him in math. A favorite teacher helped with grammar,
geography, and history. Even the principal of the high
school helped tutor Chester Nimitz. And then he was off!

Away from the Hill Country. Gone for good, really.
Though, of course, he came back to visit his family. Just
after he graduated from the academy in 1905 (7th in a
class of 114) he posed in his uniform for photographs with
his white-bearded grandfather, and also with his mother
and stepfather, as well as Dora and Otto, his half-sister
and half-brother.

A new life opened up for Chester Nimitz at Annapolis.
He went out to sea almost immediately. His sailing
instructor was the father of Admiral Bill Halsey, his buddy

in the Pacific during World War II. In fact, all the principals of the Pacific War were there at that time: Admiral Halsey was class of 1904, Admiral Spruance the class of 1905, and Admiral Fletcher the class of 1907. There were only 700 men in the academy then and everyone knew everyone else. The navy in those days was like a club, and Nimitz continued to see his friends wherever he went. Later, he met his future wife through a Navy buddy. He and Catherine Freeman, of Wollaston, Massachusets, were married in 1913.

Nimitz had been sent out to the Pacific on his first tour of duty after graduation. After that he became deeply involved with submarines. At the age of twenty-seven he was asked to address the Naval War College on this subject. He capped this part of his career by supervising the construction of the submarine base at Pearl Harbor in 1920.

In 1922, he attended the Naval War College for eleven months. He pointed out later how this was instrumental in his preparation for his role in World War II. He said the "enemy was Japan" in all the war games. The challenge was to plan logistic support for a march across the Pacific Ocean. The studies in geography, strategy, and logistic problems prepared him "more than any other experience."

In 1925, Nimitz was selected as one of six to organize units of the NROTC at leading universities. Nimitz was assigned the University of California at Berkeley. Chester and Catherine Nimitz liked Berkeley so well that they lived there after his years of active duty. (Nimitz is buried nearby at the Golden Gate National Cemetery. Like all the others, his is a regulation headstone, though his is marked with five stars instead of a religious symbol. He and Catherine had arranged to be buried with Admirals Spruance, Lockwood, and Turner, as well as their wives.)

Throughout the rest of the 1920s and the 1930s, Nimitz alternated sea and shore duty. While out to sea, he insisted on blending the new aircraft carriers with the rest of the fleet. He also insisted on doing night maneuvers - not popular in the U. S., but a specialty of the Japanese. He took an intense interest in underway refueling, a procedure he had coinvented in 1917 and which he continued to develop. Amphibious landings were another emphasis. All of these were crucial to his success in World War II.

Beginning in 1939, Nimitz was in Washington as the Chief of the Bureau of Navigation. Here he knew President Roosevelt, who personally selected his top naval officers. Here Nimitz himself became acquainted with all the top naval officers, learning the special qualifications of each.

Nine days after the Japanese attack at Pearl Harbor, President Roosevelt tapped Nimitz to head the Pacific Fleet. "Tell Nimitz to get the hell out to Pearl and stay there till the war is won." Nimitz, with only three stars at that time - ranked below twenty-eight others - did as he was told. He did not question the orders, but he did take a few days rest by riding the train out to California. Once in San Diego, he boarded a plane for Hawaii, arriving in Honolulu on Christmas Day - a dreary, rainy day, when charred remains were all around, the air was still acrid from burning oil, and bloated bodies were still rising to the surface.

His first job was to raise morale. He said that the principal officers would keep their jobs. What they needed to do now was roll up their sleeves and get to work. He was given command of the fleet on board the *Grayling*, a submarine, on December 31, 1941. His four-star flag was raised for the first time.

Nimitz realized that the damage could have been much worse. The Japanese had not struck our oil tanks. They had not hit our carriers, which had been out to sea. They had not damaged the submarine base that Nimitz had built in 1920. And they had not hit the repair facilities.

Nevertheless, everyone was scared and nervous during those first six months. Nimitz had trouble sleeping. His doctor told him to set up a shooting range for relaxation - when aiming a pistol you can think of nothing else. Nimitz wrote his wife that his job might not last long.

The turning point was the Battle of Midway in the early days of June, 1942, exactly six months after Pearl Harbor. The Japanese fleet greatly exceeded ours. We were the underdog in every way. But this engagement was truly amazing, "a miracle," some said. Our movement was a surprise attack against the flank of the Japanese armada, in which dive bombers knocked out four of their six aircraft carriers and 332 airplanes. The death toll of 2,155 skilled and experienced men included most of their best-trained naval pilots.

Nimitz's role was this. He listened carefully to what his intelligence officers were telling him, paid attention to the code breakers, and, finally, was willing to act on what he heard. The messages in Japanese code indicated a maneuver at Midway. To take them by surprise would be the key to success. This would be a flanking operation, in which our vastly inferior flotilla would attack the flank of their fleet and knock out their carriers.

Though not an airman, Nimitz knew the day for the battleship was past. He understood the role of the carriers, that modern warfare was an air battle. When the USS *Yorktown* came in damaged, he moved with lightning speed to have it minimally repaired so it could proceed to the battle of Midway.

When Admiral Halsey came in ailing, Nimitz moved at once to appoint Admiral Spruance to take his place. Admiral Spruance had keen intelligence and judgment, and he knew when to quit. He was willing to strike hard with all he had, but he knew when enough was enough. Nimitz said later that Admiral Spruance's judgment and wisdom spelled the difference between victory and defeat.

Nimitz himself could not follow the fleet. He realized immediately upon reaching Hawaii that he had to stay at the communications center. On the other hand, Admiral Yamamoto, his Japanese counterpart, made a big mistake in tagging along. His presence on his enormous flagship meant "radio silence" for all, muzzled communications, and kept the Japanese two steps behind the action.

In the end, Nimitz outfoxed the Japanese naval command, and in time, even the Japanese talked about it. After the war, when events were analyzed, they gave Nimitz due credit. In their view, three admirals stand out in military history: Lord Nelson, their own Admiral Togo, and Nimitz.

Nimitz said of Midway that it was "the most crucial battle of the Pacific War." Over three years of fighting remained, but the Japanese were on the defensive after Midway. With the loss of so many of their carriers, planes, and pilots, they were forced to stay closer to the Empire. The war continued, but the balance of naval power had shifted.

THE MUSEUM OF THE PACIFIC WAR

When entering the museum, the first items you encounter are mementos of the Nimitz family, a few things from the hotel, Chester's high chair, and a baptismal gown. There is a photograph of Chester and Catherine at the time they were married. Other exhibits in this area outline his story up to the time of Second World War.

Then you move into a separate gallery, a small room devoted to Pearl Harbor and the start of the war. A huge photograph on the wall shows President Roosevelt addressing the joint session of Congress. Punch a button on an old-fashioned radio and hear his voice in his eloquent "Day of Infamy" speech. Look around at pictures of the destruction, the line of battleships hit from the air, the devastating fires, and bodies washed ashore. Don't miss the photograph here of Mitsuo Fuchida, the air ace who led the Japanese attack. Then turn around to the center of the room to see the rusty hatch of the USS Arizona, a relic, which, like everything else in this room, is very moving.

Upstairs on the second floor is an enormous electronic wall map which shows the islands in the Pacific Ocean. With the flick of a switch, the story begins and in just a few minutes you follow the entire course of the war. Lights flash at Pearl Harbor, arrows show air missions, destroyers dart across the screen, fireworks explode at Midway.

In this room hangs an immense Japanese flag. Its huge sun with red rays on a white field was flown on Admiral Yamamota's flagship.

Against another wall is Nimitz's pistol. There are photographs here of the admiral on the shooting range. His doctor had recommended the target range for his nerves.

From this room it is an easy transition to the rest of the exhibits: displays on the various battles, graphic photographs of the destruction in Japan, films showing authentic battle footage. Punch another button and hear Paul Tibbets, the pilot of the Enola Gay, the plane that dropped the atom bomb on Hiroshima.

Finally, with the war over, one sees photographs of signing the treaty on the battleship, the USS Missouri. On the next floor, one can follow the rest of Nimitz's life.

First, the glorious parades in Washington and New York and down to Texas for a tumultuous homecoming. In Fredericksburg there were seven marching bands, speeches in front of the courthouse, a visit to the Henke House, and then a dinner downstairs in this building. It was held in the ballroom, the only room that has remained undisturbed since Grandfather Nimitz's days.

The exhibit then chronicles Nimitz's life in Washington where he served as Chief of Naval Operations and then out in Berkley, California, where he and Catherine lived after the era of active duty. (Five star admirals do not retire.) During this time, they had many visitors, and some of them were Japanese. Nimitz did what he could to help with restoring Japanese shrines and antiquities after the war, and he became known as a friendly presence in the United States.

Upstairs in the museum is a remarkable photograph showing Mitsuo Fuchida as a visitor in Nimitz's home. In the picture is the Nimitz guestbook. Then in the next case is the guestbook itself. You can see that Fuchida had signed his name, put in his address in Japan, and then, under "comments", had written "No more Pearl Harbor."

THE GARDEN OF PEACE

Next we move outside to the area behind the Nimitz barn, to the site of the former corral, to a walled area that encloses an authentic Japanese garden. Designed by professionals in Japan, it was built under the direction of six craftsmen who came to Texas.

Ideas for this garden began after Nimitz's death in 1966. He had done what he could to restore peace, harmony, and understanding between the United States and Japan, especially in regard to one of the Japanese heroes, Admiral Heihachiro Togo. After the great Japanese naval victory against the Russians in 1905, the Emperor gave a garden party in honor of Admiral Togo at his imperial palace. He sent invitations to American naval officers stationed in the Bay of Tokyo and young Chester Nimitz, just out of Annapolis, was one the seven who attended. His group was actually able to visit with Admiral Togo for a few minutes. The admiral had spent seven years in England, had studied naval history there, and was fluent in English.

When Admiral Togo died in 1934, Nimitz, as Captain of the USS *Augusta*, flagship of the Asiatic fleet, was asked to march with his crew in the funeral procession in Tokyo. He also attended private rites at Togo's home.

At the conclusion of World War II, Admiral Nimitz was flanked closely by Captain Layton, his intelligence officer, who spoke fluent Japanese. With this aide in tow, Nimitz took off immediately after the festivities of the signing ceremony to visit Admiral Togo's flagship, the *Mikasa*, which had been moored at the Yokosuka Naval Base. Encased in concrete, it was revered as a national monument. Nimitz was shocked that this ship had been looted. (Admiral Halsey had taken already the flag, which he thought would make a great trophy for the Russians.) But Nimitz's reaction was very different. Forthwith, he posted a marine guard. There would be no more looting.

As the years passed, Nimitz's attitude of clemency became known. In his retirement years in Berkeley, California, he was often visited by Japanese naval officers who kept him abreast of developments. On one such occasion he heard of the fate of the *Mikasa*. During the occupation, the Russians had insisted it was a "fortress," and as such should be destroyed. The United States and Britain prevented this. But after the occupation was over, the pacifist sentiment was such that the Japanese nation ignored this old battleship. It fell into use as a dance pavilion..

Admiral Nimitz wrote an article for a Japanese magazine reminding the nation of the importance of their great naval hero. He then donated the proceeds from the article to efforts to restore the ship. Word got out. The Japanese responded overwhelmingly. They not only restored his ship, but Admiral Togo's home as well.

When it came time to plan this garden - paid for largely by Japanese naval officers, but also by many others in Japan and also some in Fredericksburg - the designers had Admiral Togo's study copied, dismantled, and then shipped for reassembly in Texas. This is the little house that you see at the far end of the garden. Sliding screens open to the outside. Rush matting covers the floors. It is built without nails.

The rest of the garden takes certain elements from Admiral Togo's in Japan. The pond is shaped like his. As in all Japanese gardens, the running water represents the stream of life, the stones are the "backbone," and the plants are the building blocks, or the "flesh." Here we see Japanese black pines, magnolias, crepe mytles, and a liveoak, but no cherry trees. The latter would quickly have grown out of scale.

Closer to the Nimitz barn is a dry garden, a stone garden, with boulders surrounded by raked gravel. This represents the sea swirling around the islands in the Pacific. The designers were afraid they could not find the right kind of rocks in Texas, but when they went north of Fredericksburg up towards Enchanted Rock and saw the granite there, they were delighted. This was just what they wanted for the boulders. For the "sea" they used crushed granite because a coarser texture of gravel could not be raked into patterns.

At the dedication on May 8, 1976, visiting Japanese admirals consecrated the garden with sake (rice wine) and sand from the Togo shrine near Tokyo. They were joined by retired American admirals. Lady Bird Johnson came from Stonewall. President Johnson had originally started the ball rolling by asking his Chief of Naval Operations to speak to his contacts in Japan, but now Johnson was dead. The Japanese and American admirals later visited LBJ's grave.

Nimitz himself would have been pleased with this garden. He loved his own, and when Mitsuo Fuchida came to visit he found Nimitz in the driveway, beckoning him on a short tour. There, in the hills of California, Admiral Nimitz had built his own miniature Japanese garden with black pines and carefully placed stones around a small pond, the kind of garden Fuchida knew from home. "Lovely," he wrote later, "not big, but just like in Japan."

HISTORY WALK OF THE PACIFIC WAR

The final section takes you a block away to an outdoor exhibit where you find tanks, guns, planes, Admiral Nimitz's barge, amphibious landing craft, and a Quonset hut. The most arresting sight here is a Japanese Val dive bomber, of the type that dropped the bombs at Pearl Harbor. This one, damaged, is shown in nose-down position. It was sent by Australians from Gaspata, a Japanese air base on the island of New Britain. There are few of these left anywhere. Towards the end of the war those still flying were used as Kamikaze (suicide) aircraft. As such, these tiny planes were very dangerous and did a great deal of damage.

NEIGHBORHOODS

After a look at the center of Fredericksburg and the buildings on Main Street, drive along the other streets in the Historical District: San Antonio and Creek, Austin and Schubert. There are many, many old houses here, all with markers, and most within plain sight of the road.

A few of special note include the Jung House (1871), 108 E. Schubert, with its exquisite stonework and the

Tatsch House (1856), 210 N. Bowie, known for it enormous, outsized chimney. The Kreiger-Geyer House (1848), 512 E. Creek, has long been regarded as an excellent example of the early styles with its *fachwerk*, small chimney, casement windows, and original door. A trace of gingerbread alludes to later remodeling.

At the Pape-Dangers House at 213 E. Creek, you can see one of the original log cabins. The Pape family arrived with a sick mother and everyone in the community helped build a small shelter for her. It's amazing that this one is still standing.

Around 1900 the town spread out from its core. Developers took the original 10-acre outlots on the edges and made "additions." These were early subdivisions and paralleled developments in cities across the country. Among the first here was the Wehmeyer-Saenger Addition, near the west end of Main Street at South Cherry. This had been an outlot belonging to J. J. Klingelhoefer, but at his death in 1886, it went to two daughters, Louise Wehmeyer and Henrietta Saenger. In 1903 they subdivided it and sold the lots. By then, houses were primarily wooden.

Another of the early expansions was the Vander Stucken-Gold Addition north of Travis Street between N. Llano and N. Lincoln. Lot Number One was reserved for the handsome Gold House (1901), 212 E. Travis. Built of huge limestone blocks, it also had a porch with intricate gingerbread trim. Edward Stein later recalled making this as a youth in his father's lumber yard, Stein Lumber Company.

116

A third subdivision was southeast of town along East Creek Street in a bend of Baron's Creek. This area is very scenic - a beauty spot, a place where art teachers take their classes to draw the dip down to the creek, the bridge, the trees along the bank, and the fields on the other side. F. W. Langerhans, a bootmaker, developed this property. His house of large limestone blocks built between 1901 and 1904 still stands at 411 E. Creek. The others that followed were of wood. The whole pocket here still looks like the first years of the century.

Later, in 1930, the Lehnes developed the property at the present Herb Farm, on Whitney Street south of town. And in 1977 the Sunrise Village Addition was formed at the corner of S. Creek and Highway Street. One of the outlots here had belonged to Admiral Nimitz's aunt, Elise Henke Reinbach Kiehne. She had lived here since 1901 in a house bordered by a swept yard and flower beds in the shapes of circles and diamonds and stars. But, after her death in 1976, the property was sold and subdivided. So it has been with the outskirts of Fredericksburg.

SAINT BARNABAS EPISCOPAL CHURCH *601 W. Creek.*

Peter Walter bought town lots here, farmed, and also worked as a teamster, hauling goods to and from San Antonio and out to the forts. His half-timbered house built in 1848 was one of the early ones.

Though his family kept property up the street, they sold his old cottage to a fledgling congregation of Episcopalians in 1954. This was the first church of that denomination in Fredericksburg. And it was here that Lady Bird Johnson brought her family. Although reared as a Methodist in East Texas, she had joined the Episcopal Church while a student at the University of Texas in Austin.

This first tiny chapel received wide publicity as Vice-President and then President Johnson was shown stooping to enter. But, in 1964, the church built a new sanctuary next door, and this old cottage became a chapel.

Lady Bird Johnson continued to come to Saint Barnabas after her husband's death. Once she brought over a young reporter who was with her for an interview for the *New York Times*, and she motioned to the windows and said, "Probably the only place you will see a cactus blooming in a church window."

117

She was referring to the stained-glass windows by Becky Crouch Patterson installed in 1991. Becky, the daughter of Hondo and Shatzie Crouch and the author of his biography, *Hondo, My Father*, is very talented. Her windows are a blaze of color. They show geometric designs, as well as angels, stars, sheep, doves, and cactus.

Her family, too, had attended this church. In 1976, Hondo's funeral service was here, with "sunflowers at the door" and a reading of his special poem.

FREDERICKSBURG HERB FARM   *402 Whitney (S. on Milam from Main St.) Mon- Sat 9:30-5:30. Sun 1-4.*

On one of my favorite days in Fredericksburg I drove out to the Herb Farm with Laverne Lee of Mason. We sat out on the covered porch, drank herb tea, and gazed at the flowers and greenery in the surrounding gardens. We poked around the various small buildings and looked in at the Herb Haus Bed and Breakfast. All of it seemed enchanting.

Laverne was especially interested in the focal point, the Lehne-Itz House of 1882. This small stone cottage with two doors and a porch across the front is very much like her ancestral Hasse House from the same era. She was intrigued to see this house used as a store. Hers, of course, has been open to visitors as a guest house for a number of years. (See Hasse House under Mason and Art.)

The stone house was built by Henry Lehne after he bought the property in 1881. He eventually owned several outlots and, just before he died, in 1930, he had his property subdivided into the H. Lehne Addition. This house and a few acres passed to his daughter Sophie, the wife of Ernest Itz. With his brother Erwin, he ran a butcher shop in the old Itz house on Main Street. Sophie and Ernest added a wooden addition at the rear and operated a cannery during the 1930s. Ernest died in 1944, Sophie remarried and moved away, then Ernest's sister-in-law lived here.

In 1991, Bill and Sylvia Varney bought the property and increased it to fourteen acres. They had come from Houston a few years before and had run a number of operations on Main Street. But here, they "made the prairie bloom." Bill, a nurseryman, planted eight gardens, one in the shape of an enormous star. Sylvia, an artist with a different touch, made vinegars and all sorts of things with herbs and flowers. Together they have made a paradise - and just a few blocks from Main Street. (See the Tea Room and Herb Haus B and B below.)

LADY BIRD JOHNSON MUNICIPAL PARK   *Hwy. 16, 2 mi. S. of Fredericksburg. Ph: 210/997-4202.*

Oak Crest Park was renamed for Lady Bird Johnson and dedicated in 1969, the year the Johnsons came back to Texas. She and Lyndon Johnson were both here, as well as a huge crowd gathered around. This was an appropriate recognition of Mrs. Johnson's efforts as First Lady to raise the general awareness towards the environment. She had led the campaign to revitalize the parks and public spaces in Washington. She had then led many trips out to places of historical or scenic importance in the rest of the United States. Back in Texas, she would continue these efforts. She helped with the hike-and-bike trails along the Colorado River in Austin, sponsored annual awards for highway maintenance workers, and, finally, on her 70th birthday, founded the Wildlife Research Center.

Part of this property was formerly the outlot of the Tatsch family - and their old cottage is still there - but the park has continued to be expanded and developed. It now includes an 18-hole golf course, ball courts, and a swimming pool. There are spaces for 113 campers. Liveoak mottes, picnic tables and playgrounds dot the area. It is quite scenic and very popular for both locals and visitors to Fredericksburg. On a visit you see families picnicking everywhere.

A GERMAN CHRISTMAS IN THE HILL COUNTRY

Long ago in the cold of northern Europe, when the days grew short and the nights seemed interminable, people found ways to lighten the gloom, to cheer the heart. Fire was welcomed, light was a beacon of hope. Warmth and light eased the burden in a time of darkness. Norsemen burned a huge Yule log in honor of their god Thor. Druids hung mistletoe to ward off evil spirits and ate something that resembled plum pudding.

As pagans became Christians, and their customs changed to Christian customs, the holly, the mistletoe and the Yule logs assumed new meanings. No one remembered that the original meaning of "Yuletide" meant the "turning of the sun," the marking of the winter solstice. December 25 became established as the birthday of Jesus, though of course no one really knew when that was exactly. The day was celebrated as a religious holiday.

At first the feasting, dancing, shooting of guns, and making of bonfires continued uninterrupted - all the old revelry and cheer of the season - but eventually Puritans in Europe, and especially those in the United States, frowned on the merriment. They denounced Christmas trees and presents, eggnog and fireworks. Nothing was proper but a church service. The Puritans in Massachusetts even managed to pass a law making the celebration of Christmas illegal, punishable by fine.

Such was the scene - more or less - when the first German colonists arrived in Galveston in 1844. Christmas celebrations here were then relatively simple affairs: a nice meal somewhere, a little alcohol, some shooting. But the Germans came from a tradition of celebrating the season with zest: a month of outdoor markets, roasted sausages, mulled wine, the ancient honey cookies known as Lebkuchen, marzipan in countless shapes, massed choirs singing *Silent Night* - all culminating in a lighted tree and presents on Christmas Eve. Oh, it was glorious! Certainly not traditions they wanted to leave behind. Dour Puritans had not tampered with the Christmas spirit in Germany.

Indeed, the Christmas tree as we know it originated there. The medieval Roman Catholic Church had observed the saints day of Adam and Eve on December 24. Live trees, set up in churches, were decorated with apples to commemorate Adam and Eve and were accompanied by mystery plays that included their story. Later, when they lost religious import, the plays and the trees were banished from the churches, but the parishioners began setting up trees at home. Finally, Martin Luther blessed the Christmas tree, explaining his vision that the candles were the stars of heavens, the presents from the Christ Child.

Unabashedly, the German colonists sang around their tree - an oak - on that first Christmas in Galveston. Before long many others joined them. In the early 1840s Queen Victoria's young German husband, Prince Albert, began setting up trees for the royal family. Slowly at first, but gathering speed by 1900, Christmas trees then became popular. Favored, too, were German ornaments - papier-mache figures, richly decorated, or glass Santas or bunches of purple grapes. Many of us remember these molded or blown-glass ornaments from our childhoods. They were widely available before the Second World War.

In the Hill Country, families treasured these ornaments, carefully wrapped and stored from year to year. All the accounts of Christmas here are the same. A tree was selected early, but not set up before the afternoon of the 24th. Then a special place was reserved for the tree, a separate room or a hallway. Children were shunted aside. The house was kept dark. Then, after an early supper, the family gathered around a tree blazing with lighted candles and sang carols before they opened the gifts.

The whole week between Christmas and New Year's was a time of visiting and feasting. Boxes of Christmas cookies had been laid aside, and these were brought out along with cake and wine and coffee. The week ended with a big dance at the Nimitz Hotel on New Year's Eve. There was a midnight supper and dancing until dawn. In contrast, in Methodist Mason County, the year ended with a party and a religious service at church, followed by fireworks at midnight.

ANNUAL EVENT: CHRISTMAS IN FREDERICKSBURG

The high point of the Christmas season in Fredericksburg is the second weekend. Since 1980 shopkeepers have sponsored a Kristkindl Markt on Market Square, across from the courthouse. The idea for this is taken from the Christmas markets held all over Germany during Advent. The market is open all day Saturday and Sunday.

On Saturday evening, from 3 to 9, the Gillespie County Historical Society holds open house. Visitors see a varying selection of houses and churches decked out for the season. Always included is the Schandua House, a cottage donated to the Society in 1963. This one is lit by lanterns and decorated with greens. It is a place where you can see how it was to live without plumbing, gas, or electricity.

On Sunday, the Lions Club sponsors a community choir, made up of singers of all faiths. Altogether, this second weekend offers many treats. Be sure to find the special breads and cookies at the bakeries and ornaments at the Christmas market.

ANNUAL EVENT: EASTER FIRES PAGEANT *Easter Eve. Gillespie County Fairgrounds. 3 mi. S. on Hwy. 16. 8:15 P.M. Admission.*

Easter here has its traditions, too. In Germany there were fires on the hillsides in the spring. Promoting new growth, they were ancient fertility rites.

In the early days in Fredericksburg fires on the hills around town indicated Indians were sending signals. This was, of course, frightening to the children, but they were told that Easter Rabbits were up there, stoking their fires to dye Easter eggs.

What a story! And what a tradition! Since the spring of 1847 when Meusebach was negotiating with the Comanches, Fredericksburg youths have gone up into the hills to build fires on Easter Eve. Easter Rabbits at work.

And since 1947, the 100th anniversary of the first spring, there has been a pageant at the stadium on the fairgrounds on Easter Eve. Hundreds of "bunnies" abound. It seems almost every native of Fredericksburg has worn a bunny costume at one time or another. More than bunnies, the pageant tells the entire story of Fredericksburg's founding.

Afterwards the pilgrimage begins to the hills to see the fires - about eight in the surrounding area, some sponsored by families, some by Boy Scouts. Drive out FM 965 towards Enchanted Rock and you are sure to see several, beginning with one on Cross Mountain at the edge of town.

ANNUAL EVENT: FOUNDERS DAY *Saturday nearest May 8. Grounds of the Pioneer Museum, 11-5.*

Since the beginning, folks in Fredericksburg have marked the passing of the years. Every twenty-five years they have commemorated their founding with a special festival. In 1896, the 50th anniversary was accentuated with the first appearance of electricity. For that event the old community church, the Vereins Kirche in the middle of Main Street, was dismantled and the shell of it was used as a pavilion around which traffic circled.

This shell was torn down the next year - an obstruction in the midst of a town turning modern - but the memory of it lingered. A one-dimensional framework of it, a symbol, was erected in 1921 for the 75th celebration, and beneath it passed the new automobiles, the transportation of that age.

There was a big event in 1946, a smaller one in 1971, and then a ten-day affair in 1996. But since 1971 there has been an annual celebration as well. On the Saturday closest to May 8, the actual day of the founding, many join together in an all-day gathering of craftspeople, food vendors and musicians.

LODGINGS: BARON'S CREEK INN *110 E. Creek, Ph: 830/997-9398 or 800/800-4042.*

Baron's Creek Inn is not far from Main Street, or the Nimitz Museum - only a two block walk - yet it is quiet here, much quieter than in any of the accommodations there. The inn is large, with three-room suites, microwave ovens and refrigerators. A modest breakfast is left in the suite, but you can easily augment this with items from the shops in town.

The big house was built as the family home of Max Eckert in 1911. He chose "Basse Blocks," the molded concrete blocks that resembled limestone, and this house is a prime example of that construction material. Later, in 1941, the family built a large addition at the rear. Bathrooms were included at that time, as well as a larger kitchen.

In 1983, two of the Eckert daughters sold out to some young developers who decided to leave the layout much as it was by forming four suites, two on each floor, with bathrooms in the rear. The cottage in the yard, the "Sunday House" makes a fifth unit.

LODGINGS: DAS COLLEGE HAUS *106 W. College, Ph: 210/997-9047.*

Das College Haus is a traditional bed-and-breakfast where your hostess will serve a full breakfast in the dining room, give touring ideas and directions, and send you along for your day in Fredericksburg. Bebe Curry, a German teacher at a nearby college, has developed the property over several years. The two-story house from around 1910 has three suites with private baths opening out to a porch upstairs, and another room and bath below.

College Street is a few blocks north of Main Street. The inn is due north of the center of town. It is a pleasant walk back to the activities there.

LODGINGS: THE HERB HAUS *Fredericksburg Herb Farm, 402 Whitney (S. on Milam from Main St.) Ph: 830-997-8615 or 800/259-HERB.*

A stay at the Herb Farm means a respite in a small cottage at the edge of the gardens. With two bedrooms, a fully equipped kitchen, and a bathroom with herbal soaps and lotions, this could be a home-away-from-home for several days. A breakfast of teas, coffees, juices, herb breads and jams is delivered out from the kitchen of the Herb Farm.

This small house from the 1940s was originally the home of a midwife who offered a brief stay to those recovering mothers who would be going back out to ranch life. Even then, this cottage was a place of rest.

LODGINGS: THE PEACH TREE INN *401 S. Washington (Hwy. 87, S.) Ph: 830/997-2117 or 800/843-4666.*

The Peach Tree Inn is a convenient and attractive old "motor court" a few blocks south of Main Street on the San Antonio highway. Erected in the 1940s, it is built in a U-shape projecting back from the highway, with a courtyard and large trees in the middle. Most of the units are one-story cottages. Rates are moderate and rooms are usually available during the week, but you must call ahead for the weekends.

While some rooms have refrigerators and microwave ovens, free coffee is provided for all in the office, and, on the weekends, juice and muffins as well. I have often found guests taking their morning coffee out to the benches under the trees in the courtyard.

One evening in May I came back to find several groups sitting out and a small girl chasing a firefly. I was so taken by the low hum of voices that I pulled out a chair and sat on an upstairs porch until nine o'clock, the time when most people seemed to go in. The owner told me that the communal aspect of the grassy area was what was special about his place. He said this ambiance predated television and air-conditioning and harked back "to the days when people sat out."

LODGINGS: FREDERICKSBURG INN AND *SUITES* *210 S. Washington (Hwy. 87, S.) Ph: 830/007-0202 or 800/446-0202. Fax: `210.997-5740.*

If you want something up-to-date, but with the same convenient location, try the Fredericksburg motor hotel just north of the Peach Tree Inn. Here you find a completely modern complex of rooms and suites, microwave ovens and refrigerators, a swimming pool on a lawn that dips down to Baron's Creek, and fax and copy service in the lobby.

Even though this might sound like the standard new facility, in truth the compound faces to the side and is tucked behind one of the original half-timbered houses in Fredericksburg. The property is large enough that the planners could face the big entry porte cochere to the side and run the parking towards the back. The lobby is joined to the old Mueller-Petmecky House, which has stood on Washington Street since the 1840s. Breakfast is served there - juice, cereal, toast, donuts, and muffins - but another attraction is a history of the house on a table in the corner. It seems the Muellers were related to Charles Nimitz, the innkeeper. Admiral Nimitz's family here is so large that you find the connections all over town.

RESERVATION SERVICES
Gastehaus Schmidt, 231 W. Main St. Ph: 830/997-5612.
Bed and Breakfast of Fredericksburg. 240 W. Main St. Ph: 830/997-4712
Be My Guest. 110 N. Milam. Ph: 830/997-7227

Bed and Breakfast services are available by special arrangement in Fredericksburg. Especially noteworthy are cottages out in the country near Luchenbach, Doss, or Enchanted Rock.

RESTAURANT: ALTDORF GERMAN BIERGARTEN AND
RESTAURANT *301 W. Main Street, Mon-Sat 11-9, Sun 11-4.
(Closed Tuesdays) Ph: 830/997-7865.*

A favorite place for us is the front rooms or the beer
garden at Altdorf's, the former Wissemann-Hanisch House
(1840s) that was converted into a restaurant in 1978. We
like the feeling of a family home here, the rooms added at
the rear, screen doors out to the back porches. We like to
sit outside in warm weather, order sausages and
sauerkraut, enchiladas or Reuben sandwiches. Altdorf's is
like an old friend. We are willing to wait when the crowds
line up.

RESTAURANT: THE PEACH TREE TEA ROOM *210 S.
Adams, Tues-Sat 7-10 A.M., Mon-Sat 11:30-2:30.
Reservations recommended. Ph: 830/997-9527 or 800/225-
3355.*

Come for breakfast here of homemade granola or
pancakes with butter pressed into a heart shape.
Everything at the Peach Tree is delicious, some of the very
best food in Fredericksburg is served here. People talk
about the chicken salad, but what we will never forget was
a peach ice cream pie with a chocolate crust and peach
sauce on top. The chocolate chip cookies - with Ghirardelli
chocolate chips - are so good, so wicked, that you better
buy several if you want to arrive home with any.

Cynthia Collins Pedregon and her husband, Hector,
bought the property in 1972. Her mother was Enid
Collins, designer of the famous handbags, and her
brother, Jeep Collins, is the jewelry maker. The family
migrated to Fredericksburg from a ranch near Medina.
Enid had gone to college with one of the Stieler women and
the large Stieler clan was very friendly to them when they
came. Cynthia's friendship with Becky Crouch Patterson
(her mother was Shatzie Stieler Crouch) has led to a
collaboration on two charming cookbooks. Becky did the
illustrations. (She is the same artist who designed the
windows at St. Barnabas.) Cynthia was signing piles of a
new edition of the second one when we were there for our
breakfast visit.

The core of the restaurant was part of the Peter Bonn
complex. The older Bonn home is next door at 206 S.

Adams and is used for storage or occasional yard sales. It was already here when Peter Bonn bought the property in 1869. Later, in 1895, a son, Adolph Bonn built the stone house that is now the restaurant. It passed down through the family until 1949 when it was sold to be used as a store.

Cynthia and Hector bought it in 1972. At first it was was a gift shop, but gradually they added desserts, and finally a full-scale menu. In 1994, they doubled the space with a wooden addition. This is similar to how the Stagecoach Inn in Salado has expanded through the years. And, for the same reason. The food here is wonderful, and everyone wants to experience it.

RESTAURANT: DER LINDENBAUM *312 E. Main. Daily 11:30 - 10 P.M., Ph: 830/997-9126.*

Authentic German food is offered at another venerable structure. This one is the old George Wahrmund House on Main Street. The chef, Ingrid Hofmann, trained in Germany, prepares such delicacies as peppered steaks and schnitzels, homemade noodles and porkchops in mustard sauce. She also serves up pan fried trout with warm German potato salad and delectable steamed squash. Some of the desserts are brought in, but others she makes. We ate a memorable peach cobbler with a struesel topping.

The restaurant is small and attractive, a delightful place to linger, to perhaps celebrate an anniversary. Adjacent is a beer garden with lots of flowers, tables, and chairs. Musicians play on the weekends.

TEA ROOM AT THE HERB FARM *402 Whitney (S. on Milam from Main Street) Desserts daily: 11:30 - 5. Lunch: Tues-Sat, 11:00-3. Ph: 830/997-8615.*

At the Herb Farm tables are arranged in the 1882 cottage, in its appendages, and out under a covered porch where the can visitor look into a bower of greenery. Every setting is delightful, a refreshing change from the bustle of Main Street. Once we were there for lunch in a pouring rain, so we sat inside.

Everything is made with herbs. Soups, salads, even desserts. We were served beautiful plates of salads, bowls of tomato basil soup, fresh foccacio bread with olive oil for dipping, and a tomato quiche. We were too full to add dessert, but behind us there were exclamations about a raspberry rum cake. Other selections were on display by the door. They included carrot cake, and peppermint fudge brownies.

FRIEDHELM'S BAVARIAN RESTAURANT *905 W. Main St. Ph: 830/997-6300.*

Several people recommended Friedhelm's. It is very popular for its "real German food." So off we went for a supper of schnitzels and sauerkraut, excellent steamed vegetables, and dark pumpernickel bread. Yes, the food is good. And, yes, this place is very popular. We arrived early, as suggested, we sat in the front room and we saw the crowds lining up, but it wasn't until the waitress told me to peek around the corner that I understood the dimensions of this place. She said: "Walk around there and look." I could hardly believe what I saw. There was a huge room with an enormous bar, tables everywhere, an immense crowd.

Enchanted Rock

INTRODUCTION TO ENCHANTED ROCK

Here we come to a special area of low mountains, green meadows, billows of bluebonnets and red paintbrush, low-water bridges over scenic creeks, rock fences half-hidden in shrubbery, stone ranch houses and barns and small rural churches: the heart of the Hill Country.

I have a friend who likes to drive slowly on the back roads in this area. She is a naturalist, and her quick eye spots tree roots in granite, road runners, quail, horned owls. She especially likes to drive at dusk when the wildlife is stirring. She is certain she will spot something then - and she always does. Once it was a jack rabbit with the setting sun behind his tall ears. Another time it was a family of armadillos coming out for an evening snack. Many times there were deer bolting and then sailing over fences. One evening it was a view of the back side of Enchanted Rock, the great granite dome poking up above the surrounding hills in that magical hour of the day.

THE RANCHERS

The area north of Fredericksburg towards Mason and Llano was settled in the 1850s behind the line of the federal forts. This was ranching country, and very little of it was cultivated, only some fields in the stream valleys where soil had washed down. German settlers came up from Fredericksburg or New Braunfels. A few Anglo-Americans pushed west from East Texas. All met here, and all raised cattle, and later sheep or goats. It was the only way they could make a living. Even the Methodist pastors, circuit riders, had a "Missionary herd." Their cattle were branded with MV for Missionary Verein.

The ranching families - the Rodes, the Martins, the Rusches, the Mosses - settled on creeks with running water and probably near springs as well. They built log houses for the first years. They fended off Indian attacks - the Rusche boy once hid in the rushes of an island in Crabapple Creek when he was pursued. They endured the turmoil of the Civil War, some served with the frontier guard, some volunteered for the Confederate army, and at

least one Unionist sympathizer was killed by "Confederate bandits."

Many of the area settlers participated in the massive cattle drives that originated in Texas in the second half of the nineteenth-century. In 1868, Crockett Riley and Damon Slator (married to the eldest Moss daughter) drove one of the first herds up to the markets in Kansas. Many other cattle drives followed. John Oatman, in his Llano County history, writes of one herd that was gathered from individual ranchers at Crabapple Creek, Loyal Valley, Mason, and Llano.

Since there were many sons in most of these families, and since these sons tended to stay on as ranchers, the compounds spread out across many acres. The Mosses - the former owners of Enchanted Rock - acquired most of the southern half of Llano County. There were seven sons in this family, and all stayed in the cattle business. The Rusches, with five sons, built an empire southwest of Enchanted Rock. The four sons and the grandsons of Gottlieb Brandenberger remained at Hilda.

An exception was the Martin family where the hegemony passed to a woman, the wife of Louis Martin's nephew. Anna Martin was not only a woman but also an exceptional leader in the communtiy: storekeeper, country banker, speculator in land and cattle, and the first woman president of an established bank in Texas.

RELIGIOUS AFFILIATIONS

While there may have been similarities in other aspects of the ranching families, in matters of religion there were differences.

Close to Fredericksburg, within 10 to 25 miles, lived many Lutherans who maintained close contacts with their mother church, the Zion Lutheran Church in Fredericksburg. These pioneers lived in town at first, hauled sand and lifted rock to build Zion Church, and even served as elders. When they moved north, they banded with other members of the congregation to form "branches" of the mother church. Their pastor would visit occasionally, holding services in homes. They went back to Fredericksburg from time to time for services in the main church, and eventually some built cottages for the weekend activities: the Sunday Houses of Fredericksburg.

These ranchers sent their teenage children to town when it was time to prepare for confirmation. The youngsters would board with relatives or friends while they attended the course of instruction. Confirmation Day was Palm Sunday, but the young people, having lived there since the previous September, had had plenty of time to get to know their contemporaries in Fredericksburg. Many of the sons and daughters of these ranching families chose their spouses in town.

These "branches" in the country broke off and formed independent congregations late in the nineteenth century. These country congregations built the small chapels that you see today. Supporting a pastor was difficult, so the country congregations shared their preachers: Cave Creek with Crabapple, Cherry Spring with Doss.

Catholics who moved out to the country stayed affiliated with their church in Fredericksburg. They returned on a regular basis to their Sunday Houses built close to St. Mary's, but they did not form rural congregations in the same manner as the Lutherans.

The Methodists, however, followed a different course. Converted by German-speaking missionaries to a life of pious devotion - free of the evils of drinking and dancing, card playing and social clubs - the Methodists sought a Promised Land far to the north, well out of the orbit of the beer gardens and dance halls of Fredericksburg. Many left in 1855 and 1856, their pastor Rev. C. A. Grote, leading the exodus. Congregations were organized at Hilda, Lower Willow Creek, Upper Willow Creek (Art) and Castell. Rev. Grote settled in Castell, established the Llano Valley Circuit, and, as a circuit-riding pastor, was able to visit all of his communicants on a regular basis. He could offer the sacraments and oversee the preparation of the young people for confirmation. As early as 1858, a church was erected at Art. Thus there was no need to return to Fredericksburg for church services or for companionship of any sort. The young people found their marriage partners among the neighboring Methodist families. The Llano River Valley between Mason and Llano remains one of the most solidly Methodist areas in the state today.

ARCHITECTURE

While Fredericksburg is built of the limestone from the surrounding mesas, and Llano displays a few buildings of granite, there is another building material that figures prominently as you move north. This is Pre-Cambrian sandstone, an ancient material thrust up on the edges of the Llano Uplift. First you see it in a fine rock fence at the Marschall-Meusebach Cemetery at Cherry Spring, then in the Marschall House at Prairie Mountain, in the church at Hilda, and finally everywhere in Mason, Art, and Castell. It is a distinctive reddish stone, much darker than the creamy limestone. Finding houses made of it in Mason is like hunting for Easter eggs.

The Rode House (1880) and barns at Cherry Spring are built of unadorned, cut limestone blocks - magnificent structures - but only half a mile away is the fine fence of sandstone surrounding the Marschall-Meusebach graveyard.

A few miles north, at Prairie Mountain, the Marschall House (1875 - 1888) is hewn sandstone blocks with limestone lintels and sills, a combination of ruddy stone with creamy trim that we will see again in Mason.

The church at Hilda (1902) has walls of sandstone, corner quoins of white limestone, and window surrounds of pale yellow brick. Quite a combination! But effective,

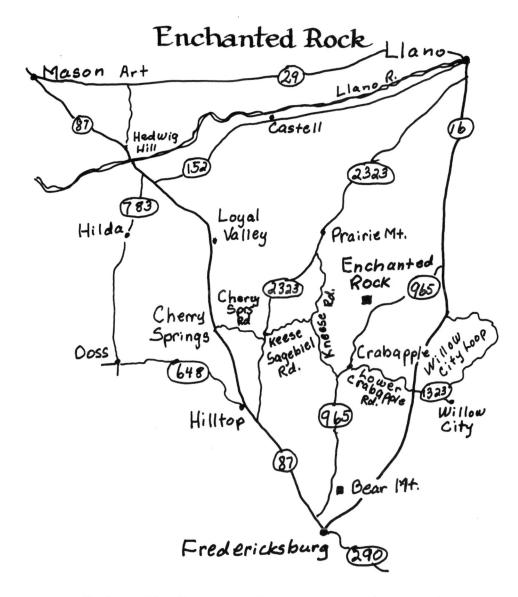

Enchanted Rock

Mason Art — 29 — Llano
Llano R.
87
Hedwig Hill
Castell
16
152
2323
783
Loyal Valley
Prairie Mt.
Hilda
Enchanted Rock
965
Cherry Sprs Rd.
2323
Keese Rd.
Cherry Springs
Keese Sagebiel Rd.
Crabapple
Willow City Loop
Doss
648
Lower Crabapple Rd.
1323
Willow City
Hilltop
965
87
Bear Mt.
Fredericksburg — 290

nonetheless. The German architect, Richard Grosse, also combined these materials masterfully in Mason's Seaquist House. For his Lutheran Church there, however, he omitted the limestone and just used sandstone and brick.

A few hundred yards above the Hilda Church stands the Brandenberger House (1916), evidence of the next phase: concrete and granite. The Brandenberger family tore down two previous rock houses here, reused the sandstones to put up a large two-story dwelling, and then embellished it with a concrete porch and columns across the front and a granite slab over that door the notes the owner, the date, and the brand of the ranch.

This was, of course, at the same time that concrete and a sparing use of granite were popular in Fredericksburg. This is one of the few places where I found even a small piece of granite incorporated into a building out here in the countryside.

BEAR MOUNTAIN GRANITE QUARRY *4.3 miles north of Fredericksburg on FM 965.*

A scenic drive north towards Enchanted Rock takes you past a local landmark, Cross Mountain - site of a lighted cross - and then heads up towards the source of the beautiful red granite that forms the base of the 1939 courthouse and various cornerstones and markers in Fredericksburg.

The granite here was first quarried for the columns of City Hall in San Antonio in 1888. It was hauled down by ox teams. Later the stone won prizes for its excellent quality at the World's Fair in St. Louis in 1904 and at an exhibition in Philadelphia in 1929. Prized - but hard to quarry, haul, and dress - it has been little used in this vicinity. Only at Llano (the center of the industry) and at Marble Falls (at the edge of Granite Mountain) will you find collections of buildings in granite.

RUSCHE CEMETERY *FM 965, 6.5 miles N. of Fredericksburg.*

All you will see of the Rusche Ranch is their charming graveyard by the side of the road. The family of Nichlaus Rusche came up from Fredericksburg to Crabapple Creek in 1856, built a log house and later a rock house, supported the local school and Lutheran church. The five sons stayed in the vicinity, and eventually together they owned 6,000 acres.

The earlier burials are marked by obelisks of limestone, but later - around 1910 - the family switched to the red granite from Bear Mountain. There is the customary German curbing and gravel paths, but here, with so few graves and in such a lovely setting, you think the formal

German style of graveyards is best when tucked into a patch of woods.

CRABAPPLE COMMUNITY *Lower Crabapple Road, 1 mile E. of FM 965.*

The community center for the ranchers of Crabapple Creek is set in another beautiful setting. The old limestone church, St. John's Lutheran (1897) served communicants here after they broke away from their mother church in Fredericksburg. They arranged to share a pastor with St. Paul's at Cave Creek.

Continue east of here for a tour of Willow City Loop. Lower Crabapple Road becomes Eckert Road, then FM 1232 at Highway 16.

WELGEHAUSEN RANCH *FM 965.*

On the way up to Enchanted Rock, we pass the Welgehausen Ranch with its picturesque cluster of old farm buildings gathered near its main house.

Friedrich Welgehausen had arrived from Germany in 1845 and moved up to this area, but it was not until ten years later that he bought this tract. It was the Crownover Survey, 640 acres deeded to Arter Crownover for his services during the Texas Revolutionary War. Crownover, who lived in Fayette County sold the tract in 1855 and Welgehausen bought it for $600 the next year. He and his descendants remained until 1976.

The Houstonians who bought the ranch in the 1970s restored the Welgehausen's original log house. They moved it and had to reconstruct parts of it, but you can still see the original log house, along with other structures that followed it.

ENCHANTED ROCK STATE NATURAL AREA *18 miles N. Fredericksburg, FM 965. Daily: 8-10. Ph: 915/247-3903. Camping reservations, Ph: 512/389-8900.*

Enchanted Rock is the magnificent, seemingly bald, granite mountain - or batholith - that rears majestically among the lower, verdant hills of the Sandy Creek area. My husband once compared the view of Enchanted Rock from the east to the pyramids outside Mexico City.

Both were considered sacred - the man-made pyramids an integral part of Pre-Columbian religions and Enchanted Rock a special place for many Indian nations. Indians who visited it revered the mountain as a holy place, a special site for revelations, healing, and renewal.

The mountain originated in ancient times, perhaps a billion years ago, when, in an era of upheaval and mountain-building, hot magma (or molten rock) thrust up through older rocks and pushed a large "bump" above the crust of the earth. The magma did not break through the crust, however, forming a volcano with lava flows, but instead remained below the surface and cooled slowly into large crystals. This is granite: magma cooled slowly, with large crystals resulting. Over time the area was covered by layers of sedimentary rock, but these layers have eroded now revealing a mountain of granite.

All ventures today start at the headquarters near the gate. Here you check in for primitive camping, rock climbing, a four-mile loop trail, or merely to prepare yourself for a climb up the face of the Rock. Pause for a moment at the exhibits. There is a diagram showing how granite is formed. There are also photographs and explanations of vernal pools.

As you start up the trail you will need to keep several things in mind. First, Enchanted Rock and its close neighbors are exfoliation domes; that is, they erode by spalling or sloughing off concentric layers, peeling off like the layers of an onion. If you look to the left at the neighboring hill, you can clearly see this process.

Second, be sure to notice the ferns on the lower levels. They hide just beneath the edges of large boulders, in this way conserving enough moisture to survive.

A little higher up you will encounter odd shapes, similar to enormous mushrooms. These so-called "pedestal rocks" have been formed by water and wind erosion.

Next, be on the lookout for dikes, cracks in the granite where magma of a different color and texture has pushed up. If the protruding magma eroded at a different rate, the dike will either protrude or recede. We have found dikes running up and down the Rock and also sideways across it.

By now you will have seen many depressions in the Rock, some just holes with small rocks in them and others quite large with grasses, shrubs, and even trees. These are vernal pools, one of the special aspects of a granite mountain. Even though at first glance there appears to be no vegetation on the mountain, there is really quite a bit.

A vernal pool begins with a few rocks in a small hole. A rain storm comes, causing the rocks to strike against the hole and enlarge it. Then lichens, an elemental plant life, break down the rock, ever so slightly, forming miniscule bits of soil. But those bits of soil are enough to support mosses, which then lay down matted matter that builds more soil. Grasses can then grow, and some of the vernal pools have developed into beautiful islands of waving green prairie grasses. Finally, the soil builds until shrubs and even trees can live on the face of the rock.

There's a liveoak on top of this mountain. Small and scrubby, to be sure, but a liveoak nonetheless. That's how you know you've reached the top. "How much farther?" you ask. "When you see the liveoak, you've reached the top," someone answers.

Also, at the top, there is a wonderful view in all directions. This place feels like the top of the world.

Coming down, you will observe all the same phenomena again. And perhaps you will notice, as I once did, another treasure - a completely natural Japanese garden in Sandy Creek: a few stones, some reeds, running water, small trees. I had Japanese gardens on my mind that day, having just visited the Nimitz Museum in Fredericksburg. How extraordinary I thought to find a perfect example of a stylized Japanese garden in nature itself.

WILLOW CITY LOOP *Go 13.5 miles N. of Fredericksburg on Hwy. 16. Turn on FM 1323. Proceed 12.7 miles to Willow City. Follow signs to Willow City Loop. The 13-mile loop ends at Hwy. 16.*

Willow City Loop is the ultimate place for bluebonnets. Nowhere else do they show off to such an advantage. The route takes you up on a granite ridge, somewhat barren, with thin vegetatation. You think maybe the bluebonnets haven't come out this year. But then it swoops down into a valley where the lustrous blue stretches in all directions, up hillsides and down, along an old stream bed, and then into the far reaches of the landscapes, like the distant blues in a Renaissance painting. The bluebonnets mingle here

with granite boulders, live oaks, cactus, and a few other
wild flowers. At the very end of the loop we once saw white
poppies making the same effect, forming another carpet as
far as the eye could see.

A friend once asked me where was the best place to see
bluebonnets and I told her of this place. When she
returned she commented that when they descended the
loop "it was like entering the gates of Heaven."

Just a word about the nature of this drive: the entire
route is public, but it is an exceedingly narrow county
road, and all the property on either side is private. You
will pass innumerable cattleguards separating one owner's
fields from the next, but there are not any fences to keep
livestock away from the road.

RODE HOUSE, CHERRY SPRING *1/2 mile E. of Hwy. 87
on Cherry Spring Road.*

One of the landmarks on a trip north to Mason is the
old Dietrich Rode House at Cherry Spring. It rises
spectacularly in the hills - all three floors of it, a huge
house, with none in Fredericksburg to compare. Dietrich
Rode was rancher who had done very well for himself. He
arrived up here in 1853, brought more land as he could,
raised sheep as well as cattle, and finally built this
enormous house in the winter of 1880.

The road to Mason ran in front of the southern
exposure of this house, so it is the southern facade that
displays the original front porch and main entry. Now as
we drive up we approach the back entry, and here we see
all the limestone barns and outbuildings that further
contribute to to make this such an outstanding
compound. A little way down the road is a small limestone
church from the turn-of-the-century, a reminder that
Rode was a devout Lutheran, a shepherd of the flock in this
region.

Dietrich Rode had arrived in Fredericksburg from
Germany in 1846. As an eighteen-year-old, he soon
received an outlot of ten acres on which he built a log
cabin. He married Katharina Klaener in 1851, and
together they helped organize Zion Lutheran Church the
following year. Dietrich served as one of the first elders.
When they moved north, they dismantled the log house
and took it along, but they also took along the zeal of the

Lutherans. Dietrich applied for a license to be a lay minister. They held services in their home, and Dietrich prepared the youth in the neighborhood for confirmation. The youngsters came for a six month's stay on his ranch. The "big house" completed in 1880 included a chapel on the second floor and also an ample central hall downstairs where Katharina served lunch after services.

The Rodes also road up to Castell once a month to bolster the faith there. Dietrich conducted services in homes or under trees until 1893 when the Castell congregation built their first church, a simple rock building north of the Llano River now used as a hay barn. Mrs. Rode was said to always arrive with a big honey cake. The Rodes then invited all the members of the Castell congregation to stay with them when they traveled down to Fredericksburg.

Dietrich Rode's health failed in 1902. Katherina died in 1904, and he succumbed the next year. By then the Lutheran neighbors knew they needed another place to meet. They built Christ Church in Rode's honor here on the ranch. It was completed in 1907. The church members arranged to share a pastor with St. Peter's in Doss, and that practice continues today. Services alternate, depending on when the minister is here: first and third Sundays at 10:45 and second and fourth Sundays at 9:00.

MARSCHALL-MEUSEBACH CEMETERY, CHERRY SPRING *1/4 mile E of Hwy. 87 on Cherry Spring Rd. Iron gates mark entry. Park on road and walk in.*

Just a short distance away from the Rode complex is the private graveyard of the Meusebach and Marschall families. It is not clear why this graveyard is here instead of near their homes at Loyal Valley (a few miles north on Highway 87) or Prairie Mountain (FM 2323).

John O. Meusebach, the representative of the German Emigration Company in the 1840s, and the founder of Fredericksburg, bought land up here and moved his family to what became known as Loyal Valley in 1875. His great friend, Wilhelm Marschall - another nobleman who had denounced his title - lived here as well. In 1884, he purchased the impressive sandstone house at Prairie Mountain after its owner was ambushed and killed. There

139

were seven children in each family and by 1884, a Marschall son had already married a Meusebach daughter. In 1889 and 1894, the same thing happened again. Thus, three marriages between the two families led to a strong coalition.

Meusebach died the day after his eighty-fifth birthday in 1897. He lived for one year after Fredericksburg celebrated its fiftieth anniversary. He had been too feeble to attend the festivities, but his old friend, Charles Nimitz, came up to tell him about it. These two also had children who had married each other, Lina Nimitz and Meusebach's eldest son, Ernst.

Meusebach's tombstone is marked with his motto: "Texas Forever." Marschall, who died at 80 in 1902, is buried under a stone of polished red granite with an incised bouquet of flowers that looks like old-fashioned crewel work.

The graveyard itself is striking: a white gate in an enclosed fence, several cedar trees, only the graves of the Marschalls and Meusebachs. The very fine rock fence - dry-stacked stonework with precisely squared-off corners and carefully arranged coping stones - is always noted by observers and admirers of rock fences in the Hill Country.

Meusebach's house and orchards at Loyal Valley have been gone for decades, and the village itself is a ghost town, but Marschall's home still stands. I was intrigued by the photographs of both the house and the big barn in D. B. Alexander's *Texas Homes of the Nineteenth Century*, but I despaired of seeing them, remote as they were and well off the beaten track. But once I did, at dusk, after a sunset ride north from Enchanted Rock. Deserted now, but still majestic, the Marschall House loomed in the evening shadows. It was hard to see the details, the limestone window sills and lintels played against sandstone walls and the broad segmental arch over the front door, but I was thrilled nonetheless. The big stone barn I could barely discern behind thick shrubbery.

LANGE MILL, DOSS *2 and 1/2 miles N. of Doss on FM 783. Turn right. Proceed 1/2 mile*

Another remote spot also featured in D. B. Alexander's *Texas Homes of the Nineteenth Century* is the large limestone mill house by the side of Threadgill Creek north of Doss. The location is as idyllic as his photograph. An abandoned limestone mill house overlooks a low-water bridge across a creek. A spring-fed stream rushes down the bank behind the mill. Large cypresses line the waterways.

Milling began in the area when the Doss brothers set up a grist mill and a distillery in 1849. A flood washed them out after a few years, but the Lange brothers bought the property and started again in 1859. Despite various mishaps, they succeeded with a burr mill for flour and corn until 1888 when the roller mills put them out of business.

Doss is only a crossroads community, like others in this region. St. Peter's Church, a branch of the Lutherans that shares a pastor with Christ Church in Cherry Springs, occupies one corner of the intersection. At the other side is a signboard that shows directions to sixty local ranchers. The names are the familiar ones from Fredericksburg: Itz, Crenwelge, Henke, Evers, Arhelger, Bierschwale. German ranchers have not sold, in line with the old saying, "The only way to acquire property out here is to inherit it or marry it."

HILDA UNITED METHODIST CHURCH, HILDA *16 miles S. of Mason, FM 783.*

The Methodist Church at Hilda (1902) of sturdy, reddish-brown sandstone with a white wooden steeple surmounted by a cross, stands as a sentinel just inside the border of Mason County. It proclaims: "This is the Land of the Methodists! Let there be no drinking, no dancing, no joining of social clubs, no cards, no carousing! This is the place of worship, hardwork, and clean living - the Promised Land."

Gilbert Jordan observes in *Yesterday in the Texas Hill Country*: "Entirely Methodist from the beginning, the Llano Valley of eastern Mason County and western Llano County has remained to the present day the most purely Methodist area in all of Texas. Mormon-like, my people came to the wilderness and created an isolated religious enclave. Brother Grote was their Brigham Young."

German Lutherans and reformed Evangelicals were converted to Methodism in Fredericksburg by German-speaking missionaries. Adhering to Puritanical standards,

141

they became restless in that town of beer gardens and dance halls. Why, even the Lutheran minister played cards! So, not long after helping to build a handsome church (which still stands on San Antonio Street), many plotted their escape. Jordan calls this "the Methodist move towards Mason." Methodist families came as pioneers to Hilda in 1855. Others followed to communities along the Llano River and Willow Creek. There were four charges (congregations) originally - Castell, Upper Willow Creek (Art), Lower Willow Creek, and Hilda - but later these grew to eight and included Mason.

The congregation here was organized in 1858, and Gottlieb Brandenberger and Fritz Kneese donated land four years later for the first church. This early church - also used as a school - was probably similar to the one still standing in a field south of Highway 29 at Art. Both were of the same era but far simpler than St. Mary's Catholic Church in Fredericksburg (1863).

At the turn-of-the-century the Methodists here built the stone parsonage nearby. With its hipped roof and small front gable, it looks like houses of the same era in Fredericksburg.

Then they set out to build this handsome church. They hired Richard Grosse, the German architect living in Mason. They hauled stone, and they freighted lumber from Llano, the nearest rail depot. The pastor built the pulpit, the altar railing, and the communion table. Others worked on the pews. Grosse did a masterful job of combining the local sandstone with limestone quoins and pale brick in a triple band above the lancet windows. His signature circular window is also banded with brick. The church is a little masterpiece in the hills. People come from near and far to see it - as is evident by the signatures in the guest book.

The church has been maintained, but little has been changed. One of the most attractive features is the unpainted beaded paneling that sheaths the lofty interior. It is wonderful that the folks here never painted it. It is also a marvel to think of the parishioners laboriously hauling all of this wood from Llano.

BRANDENBERGER HOUSE (1916), HILDA

Just up the hill from the church, sharing the same glorious view, is one of the homes of the Brandenbergers,

142

the family who gave the land for the church and cemetery. Five years after Gottlieb and Maria Brandenberger came in 1855 they replaced their log cabin with a home of ruddy sandstone, the rocks chiseled and hewn with wooden mallets.

Later their son James built a house next door, but in the early twentieth century he tore down his house and that of his father and built a much grander abode. He saved the hand-hewn rocks and used them again. He also used concrete this time - for grand galleries across the front on both floors. The final touch was a granite slab above the front door with his name, the date, the brand of his ranch, and the likeness of a longhorn steer with ear markings that showed it belonged to his herd.

Three years later when James's son, Walter, came back from the war in France to marry his childhood sweetheart, Gertrude Geistweidt, he built a rock house a half mile from his father's. The kitchen had a sink with cold running water. There was a privy (no indoor plumbing until 1926), a smokehouse, a washhouse, wood stoves and kerosene lamps. In 1929, Walter bought a Kohler light generating plant, which sufficed until the REA lines were built out here in 1938.

For a glimpse of that earlier lifestyle - the era before electricity - visit the Boyhood Home of LBJ in Johnson City or the Sauer-Beckmann Farm at the LBJ State Park. In Johnson City, you see Rebekah's faucet for cold water in the kitchen, the privy, the smokehouse, the porches that made life bearable in the summertime. At the farm, you see meals cooked on a wood stove, foods chilled in a make-shift refrigerator, cows milked by hand.

A final comment about this era in Hilda comes from Stella Polk, the Mason County historian. She was a 17-year-old teacher in Hilda at the end of World War I. She remembers the muddy roads that kept cars at home, the few "unreliable" telephones, the almost total lack of communication with the outside world. She relates that the war's end came, but nobody knew. Then the next morning she awoke to the pealing of bells. That sent the message. "It was the most joyous pealing I have ever heard."

MARTIN RANCH, HEDWIG HILL *8.8 miles S. of Mason on Hw. 87.*

The story begins with Louis Martin, a young man who went north after several years in Fredericksburg. He had arrived from Germany in 1846 and married Elisabeth Arheleger. Their child was the first in the colony. She was named Hedwig after Louis's mother.

He served as the first sheriff of Gillespie County, from 1848 to 1851, but after that he ventured north to Lower Willow Creek above the Llano River, where he farmed and raised cattle. In 1858 he bought a store at the Llano River where the Military Road crossed. He established a post office here and named the community for his daughter and his mother: Hedwig Hill.

At this point he hired his nephew, Karl Martin, to run the store for him, but Karl soon tired of it, and Louis hired others.

With the coming of the Civil War, he fell on hard times. After the federal soldiers pulled out of Fort Mason in 1861, Louis Martin, a Unionist, was not safe. And only a few years later, in 1864, he was killed by Confederate bandits as he was hauling cotton to Mexico.

His widow brought his body back to Fredericksburg and buried him there. In 1870, she sold the store at Hedwig Hill to the last person Louis had hired to run it, John Keller, Sr.

ANNA MARTIN

That might have been the end of the story had it not been for the nephew's wife. No one expected a woman to take charge in those days, but Anna Martin was a dynamic young woman who was determined not to take adversity lying down.

In the same year that Louis Martin was killed, his nephew Karl became an invalid. His wife, Anna, with two sons now, sat back and watched the family businesses unravel. Then, after Louis's widow sold the store, Anna borrowed $150 to stock a second store. Before long, she was dealing in livestock and land, and then she was banking. A bank in those days meant your word and the safe-keeping of the money. Anna sent the money off to Austin.

144

Karl died in 1879, but Anna was well established by then. In 1883 she built the family home that still stands above the north bank of the Llano River. It was rock, like the others in that day, and the lumber no doubt came from Austin. She hired a carpenter to build a wooden front porch, the central staircase, window frames and doors, and to install pine flooring. Today the house remains much as it was, and is still the headquarters of the Martin Ranch, but there is now a concrete porch across the front.

Anna Martin

By 1893 Anna Martin had her eye on Mason. At an auction of the assets of a prominent town leader she bought a building on the square. Eight years later she established her bank there, the Commercial Bank, which still occupies a prominent position in Mason, though sold out of the family in 1958.

By 1900 the Martins were closing down operations at Hedwig Hill. They closed the store and the post office. Anna built a small house in town on El Paso Street. Her son, Max, built a house of concrete blocks on the square in Mason around 1910.

Anna Martin remained the president and chief executive officer of the Commercial Bank until her death in 1925. Her sons, Charles and Max served originally as vice-president and cashier of the bank, but it was Anna herself who was a towering figure in the community. There were many who came for her counsel.

ANNUAL EVENT: WILDFLOWER SEASON *April to June*

The wildflower season is very special in this region between Fredericksburg, Mason and Llano. *Texas Highways Magazine* regularly sends out photographers to shoot scenes of bluebonnets and rock fences near Hilda. The Willow City Loop becomes more popular every year.

One of our favorite spots is the short stretch between Art and Hedwig Hill. White poppies, bluebonnets, fuscia phlox, daisies, paintbrush, and wine cups make a carpet there, with spreading liveoaks and blue hills in the distance.

LODGINGS

Though there are no towns as such out here, a few of the ranches open for lodgers. Not long ago there were guest rooms on the second floor of the Rode House. Now the Hasse Ranch house is available as a bed-and-breakfast. (See under Mason.) And there's the hunting camp of the Martin's, on their 5,000 acres along the Llano River. They provide eight air-conditioned cabins and a main lodge. This would probably be best for groups. Contact Homer and Tracy Martin, 915/347-6852

RESTAURANT: HILL TOP CAFE *10 miles N. of Fredericksburg on Hwy. 87. Wed-Sun, 11-10. Ph: 210/997-8922. Reserve for weekend nights.*

Hill Top Cafe is an old filling station on the Mason highway. It is white frame with green trim, an unlikely place for some of the best food around. But step inside, glance at the cakes and cobblers laid out for the day, look at the specialities on the menu, try the grilled shrimp or the sorrel and celery soup made with herbs from the garden, and you will be a believer like many others.

Johnny Nicholas is Greek. His wife, Brenda, hails from the Cajun country of Louisiana. What you find is a delightful mix of these two cuisines: Greek lamb or shrimp dishes, scallop bisque, pork boudin, gumbos. Johnny's Aunt Alice moved nearby and sometimes you can order her tiropetas. Delicious!

On Saturday nights you will need a reservation. Johnny sings and plays the piano then. But I like the unhurried pace of a visit at noon. Once Johnny himself waited on us, another time, his ten-year-old son.

This is my place for Italian cream cake. The first time I ever tasted it was here after a memorable meal on an Easter Sunday, after Greek lamb and vegetables. Their's is still my favorite version: four layers of light yellow cake with heavy, rich frosting. None other quite comes up to it.

Mason

What drew me to Mason was photographs of handsome stone houses and barns in Drury Blakeley Alexander's *Texas Homes of the Nineteenth Century*. I came, and I liked what I saw. Mason is a small West Texas town filled with sandstone houses and churches, a stone courthouse, a stone jail - everything of the reddish Pre-Cambrian sandstone that is abundant here on the edge of the Llano Uplift.

Two young women greeted me at the Chamber of Commerce on the square. Both were members of pioneer families here. Both were enthusiastic about sprucing up the square, especially relating to the Main Street Project of the 1980s that was going on then. One worked at the Chamber of Commerce, but the other one, not tied to the office, invited me to hop into her car for a quick tour of Mason.

And what a collection there was! An Italianate house of sandstone and limestone, a very fine Queen Anne mansion, and even a bungalow of solid masonry construction. The County Judge had found a pile of stone and built his house of it. Previously, the rock had been in a store, and before that in the pioneer fort at the edge of town.

149

One of the fascinating things here is how some building materials have been used again and again. Not only the rocks from Fort Mason and the rocks from a defunct Episcopal Church - the Episcopalians don't seem able to take root here - but also rock from fences around the county and some highly carved limestone blocks that an early builder, Thomas Broad, used in his houses. It was carved limestone trim from one of his early houses that went into the makings of the town mansion. Carved grapes and tulips and geometric patterns now form a border around the front door of the Seaquist House.

On that first visit to Mason I knew I would be coming back, and, standing there in the Chamber of Commerce, my eye fell on a brochure for the Hasse House, an 1883 sandstone cottage a few miles east of town. So back I came with my family to the Hasse House, to swing on its front porch, to walk around town, to tour the site of Fort Mason, and, finally, to drive fifty miles west to the remarkable ruins of Fort McKavett.

Later, I came with a friend who liked to drive around town and spot each of the many stone cottages of the pioneers. "Oh, there's another one!" she cried. It was like finding Easter eggs.

She liked the way everyone was living here, using the old as a matter of course. She liked the tricycles parked at the doors, the rockers on the porches. She instinctively understood that these sandstone houses - plain or fancy, early or late - are Mason's treasure.

MASON COUNTY HISTORY

Mason is a place where some of the ranchers in the wide open cattle country got together and made a town, a county seat, a market center, a place with a few amenities like doctors and schools. But developments here were very slow, especially in comparison to the rapid growth in places like Fredericksburg or New Baunfels.

Originally, the town grew in the shadow of Fort Mason, one of the old posts of the Indian frontier, which lingered here from 1851 until 1869. As long as the fort survived, progress in town was slow. After all, settlers nearby could use the post office at the fort, buy supplies there, even put up an offender of the frontier law in the post guard house.

It was not until 1869, when the last of the soldiers rode west, that local leaders made a serious attempt to develop a

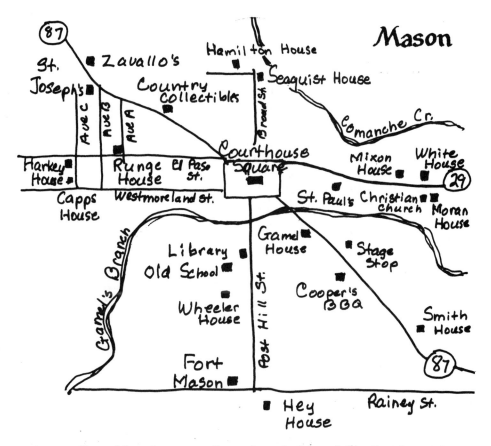

Mason

town. Local landowners then donated land for the square. Stores went up, a jail, a courthouse in 1872. Churches sprouted. Ranchers built small homes in town for their families. These were functional, not fancy, though larger than the Sunday Houses in Fredericksburg.

So who were these ranchers, these local leaders? They were not just the Germans who had spread up from Fredericksburg. Mason had attracted a wider variety. Some had stayed after duty at the post. Some were attracted from the Deep South, as part of the natural progression west. Others came as adventurers to the cattle kingdom of waving grasslands. They hailed from the midwest, the Eastern seaboard, even from Europe. One of the town's founders, James Ranck, came from Indiana in 1860, when Robert E. Lee was "still up on the hill." A colony of Irish settlers migrated a few miles west and developed a stop on the cattle trails north to Kansas. The Irish Crosbys joined with several ranchers from the South to build the first church, the Catholic Church, in 1876. A Swedish bootmaker, Oscar Seaquist, eventually had enough money to buy the town's mansion.

Mason County, then, was a mix, with roughly the southern half of the county German and the northern half "English." The town of Mason sat squarely in the middle. Various contingents found themselves at odds during the Civil War and later during the Wire Fence War in the early 1870s, when the introduction of barbed wire caused conflict over water holes that were blocked off. But underlying tensions erupted most explosively in a feud that broke out in 1875. This was the Mason County Hoodoo War - "hoodoo" for "who do it?" Originally this was a dispute between cattlemen, involving rustling, but soon the fight pitted "Americans" against "Germans."

Old antagonisms from the Civil War still smoldered. Anglo ranchers hailed mainly from the South, and most had fought in the Confederate Army, but their German neighbors had largely avoided the war. Most, though not all, were Unionists. Some had tried to leave the area. Some had served in the Frontier Guard. But all had a bad name, a reputation of not going along with the general effort. Now, with a cattleman's tiff to trigger it, old enmities surfaced.

Only the Texas Rangers could deal with a situation like this. They established order once again, but it took two years to do it and a dozen men were killed in the meantime. At the end, in 1875, the new courthouse went up in flames. C.L. Sonnichsen, in his classic study of Texas feuds, *I'll Die Before I Run*, says of this conflict, "it matched any Texas feud in bitterness and intensity."

With peace restored, the town continued in typical nineteenth-century fashion. Another court house went up. Stone from the fort went into the makings of the large school which still stands south of the square. Its designer, Richard Grosse, had recently arrived from Germany. His work added immeasurably to the architectural fabric of Mason.

By the time Grosse arrived, in the 1880s, relations between "Americans" and "Germans" were more peaceful. Bridges had been built from one community across to the other because young Anglo men had married German women. George Todd wed Bertha Mebus, Anna Martin's sister, after the Civil War. Wilson Hey, the British cowboy, rancher and county clerk for thirty years, married Hannah Korn. C. C. Smith, a rancher from Georgia, married Caroline Hoerster, daughter of one of the first German families in the county. And, in 1881, a widower, John Gamel, rancher and town founder, wed Alice Kettner, a Catholic like himself. Her family, like those of the other young women, was prominent in the county.

These marriages and other circumstances seemed to pave the way for the German-American National Bank founded in Mason in 1904. On its board sat both Anglo-Americans and German-Americans. Kettners and Lemburgs, Donops, Geistweidts, and Richard Grosse worked with the Bridges, the Hamiltons, the Gamels, and J. W. White. White was its president for 35 years. He had moved up here in a ranching deal with his renowned uncle, George Littlefield, the cattleman and banker in Austin. They had bought the 25,000 acre Mill Creek Ranch from John Gamel in 1889. White had then married and settled down here.

Not many years later, however, White arrived at the square to find a crowd staring at the word GERMAN painted in red on the side of the bank. White quietly told the group that the name was being changed. Henceforth, it would be known as the Mason National Bank.

This was during the last years of World War I, when everything German was in disrepute. School was not to be taught in the German language. Church services were to be conducted in English. Further, much controversy ensued over enlistment for the armed services. Many German families still maintained ties with relatives in the Old Country. Some individuals were not even citizens of the United States.

World War II aggravated this situation again. Though fewer families had connections with Germany, and though all condemned Hitler, it was another thing again to fight against the Fatherland, to "bear arms" against one's native country. (As you will see below, this was Robert E. Lee's dilemma in 1861. Though he favored the Union and opposed secession, he could not bring himself to "bear arms" against Virginia.)

Some of the young German-Americans in Mason County volunteered, as did most of the "English", or Anglo-Americans. But some German-speaking farmers and ranchers took agricultural deferrments to avoid service in that war.

Passions from all these conflicts have been slow to die. As late as 1966, the county historian, Stella Gipson Polk, was loathe to give a straightforward account of the feud of the 1870s. She says that her people were on both sides. " I am both German and American." Instead she gives three or four contemporary, but conflicting, accounts. The reader is left to wonder exactly what did happen.

Elderly people in town still won't talk about some of the ancient quarrels. Divisions have been too sharp. Perhaps the best comparison would be to places in the border states of Tennessee, Kentucky, or Missouri where people were divided during the Civil War, and bitterness continues to smolder.

You won't hear about any of this in town, of course. But you can grasp something of the situation if you walk around the public square. You won't see a memorial to the dead of any war there. And you won't find any acknowledgment of the German heritage, as you do on the central plaza in Fredericksburg.

But here on the square is a monument to the ranchers, to the trail drivers who rousted cattle north to the markets in Kansas. In 1985 a list was taken and posted here at the monument. Here were the heroes of this town. Here was glory all could share.

MASON COUNTY COURTHOUSE AND PUBLIC SQUARE

The square in Mason says a great deal about the town - spare, western, a bit austere. The space is a generous two blocks, and it is filled with shops of all sorts, an old movie theater, a venerable lumber yard. The buildings are mostly sandstone: some quite handsome, some no doubt built with rock from the old fort, some covered now with stucco.

People are friendly in the stores. It is fun to poke around. Yet there is a certain soberness here, a certain intangible something in the air. This is, after all, the place where the Puritanical Methodists escaped the frivolities of Fredericksburg. You still sense this somehow today.

The courthouse, built in 1910, is equally sober and plain. Designed by a Dallas architect in the prevailing mode of the times, Neoclassical, it has plain sandstone walls, classical porticos on four sides, and a dome. All of it sits quite low to the ground, as compared with others of this era that are built over basements. Sandstone, of course, was cheaper than imported materials, and Mason did not have a railroad.

A recent paint job has softened the former brilliance of the white concrete columns to a subtle beige, outlined the windows in dark green, and blackened the faces of the clock in the cupola. It looks handsome now, more up-to-date.

The lawns around the courthouse are deep and green and shady. St. Augustine grass stretches in every direction. Pecan trees, huge now, were planted in the 1930s. A low stone wall surrounds the grounds. It is not the same stonework as the courthouse. You will see chunks of granite and quartz in it. Indeed the wall is formed of unworked stones, all around, set in concrete. It was built in 1927 and 1928.

On the east side of the courthouse is a small building built as a public rest room about the same time. If you look closely, you will see fantastic rocks of all sorts, stuck into the concrete in any way pleasing to the builder. This small building is a marvelous introduction to others in this town where people built with their rock collections.

A new fire station in 1940 also showed the new styles. Native sandstone here is banded with yellow bricks, but at the sides are what I call "stone quilts" - two marvelous murals of varigated stone. The one on the east side has a center of "pudding stones," just the kind of thing I was looking for after I read *Dugout to Deco*, Elizabeth Sasser's delightful book about West Texas architecture.

A final stop on the courthouse lawn is at the Trail Driver's Monument, erected in 1985 on the eastern edge. This honors not a rebel soldier, nor a World War I doughboy - Mason was too divided for that - but a list of the outstanding ranchers. Anna Martin is the only woman included.

MASON HOUSE (1876) *100 Liveoak St. NE corner of the square*

This stage coach inn is truly old, dating back to the beginning of the town. James Ranck from Indiana, who donated land for the square and pushed development in the late 1860s, persuaded his half-brother and his British wife, the S. F. Bridges, to come to Mason and then to build an inn. The sight of the struggling community was a shock to Mrs. Bridges. In the year that they came, 1870, the Lehmann children were stolen by the Indians from Loyal Valley, a few miles south. She would not consider letting three-year-old Cora go out to play. (This is the same Cora who later married J. M. White, George Littlefield's nephew.)

The two-story inn is surprisingly large, but the small, irregular stones are painted white today. The spaces are divided into apartments. But a peek around back is rewarding. The rock wall of the corral remains. The small building to the east was the stage stop.

CHAMBER OF COMMERCE *108 Ft. McKavett. Ph: 915/347-5758 On the square.*

COMMERCIAL BANK *100 Moody. NW corner of square. Hours: Mon-Fri 9-3*

This was the bank Anna Martin established in Mason when she moved in from Hedwig Hill in 1901. (See Enchanted Rock Section.) She remained President until her death in 1925. Her sons and grandsons continued until they sold the bank outside the family. A few years after that, in the early 1960s, the new owners erected this building. They used a limestone fence hauled in from the southern part of the county. With little mortar used between the stones, the walls of this bank were meant to resemble the original limestone fence.

There are several remarkable pictures of Anna Martin and her family inside. There is also a display of the work of Gene Zesch, cowboy artist, whose carved wooden figures show all the aspects of ranching, but always with a bit of humor.

MASON NATIONAL BANK *103 Westmoreland*

The Mason National Bank (the former German-American National Bank) is housed on the southeast corner of the square in what was formerly a hotel. Erected in 1929 by the County Judge, Carl Runge, and E. O Kothmann, the Fort Mason Hotel was too grand for its place and time. It failed almost immediately. Runge and Kothmann were still paying back the debt to their subscribers years later. But the yellow brick hotel continued in operation under other owners, and some people can still remember going to dances there.

In 1966, the Mason National Bank bought the defunct hotel, knocked off the top two floors, and totally remodeled the shell into a modern facility. The facade of the old hotel was obliterated altogether with a coating of pebbled concrete.

GROSSE LUMBER COMPANY *109 S. Liveoak SE corner of the square*

You don't always spot a lumber yard on the town square, but the Grosse Lumber Company dates back over a hundred years and its inconspicuous office is very much part of the local scene. Richard Grosse trained as an architect in Germany before arriving here and beginning to put his mark on the town. He designed the new Grammar School in 1887, the Seaquist Mansion in 1891, the jail in 1894, the Methodist Church at Hilda in 1902, and the Lutheran Church here in 1905.

Since railroads never reached Mason, Grosse freighted lumber from Brady, the extension for which was completed in 1886, the same year he arrived here. He, no doubt, ordered machine-made trims and flourishes and had these carted into town. He died in 1944, but his sons and grandsons continued the lumber business.

MASON COUNTY JAIL (1894) *South of the courthouse, on the square.*

Richard Grosse's jail is a forbidding place - massive, straightforward, masculine, only the least nod to its Victorian heritage in an abbreviated tower over the door. It is still used. Traditionally, the sheriff lives below, and his charges stay above.

OLD GRAMMAR SCHOOL (1887) *Post Hill St., just S. of the square*

The Old Grammar School is like a decorated cake. If you walk around to the front of it you will see carved limestone blocks tucked in among the sandstone, some of the latter said to be from the fort. The carved limestone pieces show the names of the school board and also the date. Other carved pieces show stars and other designs in the corner quoins.

A darker stone forms string courses between the windows and also a geometric pattern like a cross at regular intervals. "Dimpled," or tooled, limestone stands out in the segmental arches over the windows. All was done with a light touch. Richard Grosse, the German architect, seems to have known instinctively how to combine these materials.

This was the first big school in Mason. It was in continuous use until the 1950s. Now it serves as a community center.

MASON COUNTY M. BEVEN ECKERT MEMORIAL LIBRARY (1990) *210 Post Hill Street. Open: Mon-Thur, 1-5:30, Fri 9-1:30, Sat 10-noon*

The architect of this 1990 library tried to relate this new building to the Grammar School of 1887, which stands close by. Sandstone was hauled in from a ruined fence in the country. He contrasted the sandstone of the walls with bands of dark brick over the openings.

From this you can see that Mason continues with the same Pre-Cambrian sandstone from its first days until now. This continuous use of the distinctive dark reddish stone makes a unique town. You will see early buildings of it at Art, in Llano, and Castell, but no other place can compare. This modern building continuing the old traditions is the icing on the cake.

Here, at the new library, you will find mementos of a well-known writer, Fred Gipson, the author of *Ole Yeller*. He lived here most of his life, from 1908 to 1973 - exactly the same span as LBJ, who was based sixty miles south. Gipson's calling, though, was far different from Johnson's. He captured in his stories the look and feel of the land, the folk tales of its peoples, the old-time expressions. "She talked a blue streak." "I'll set and be waited on." "Younguns."

Ole Yeller is his most popular book, always in print, and it is indeed a marvelous story about a young teenage boy and an ugly yellow dog, that, at various times, saves the life of each member of the family during the absence of the father on a cattle drive to Kansas in the 1860s. The ending is sad. But Papa returns from the cattle drive to assure his son that, yes, life is bad, but also good, "A man can't waste all the good parts worrying about the bad parts."

158

Even so, I found myself partial to another of Gipson's books, *Hound Dog Man*, written earlier and closer I think to the peoples and habits of thinking and living in Mason County. A teenage boy, a Huck Finn, goes out with an older companion and mingles with the settlers down by the Llano River. German women have married Anglo men by this time, the late nineteenth century, and some of the differences between them become apparent in the story. The lone representative of the Hispanic culture, Mexico Jesus, is considered a "greaser" who should know his place - away from the dinner table or the whiskey jug passed around a campfire. The teenager thinks Mexico Jesus is treated unfairly, but, like Mark Twain's Huck Finn, he concludes, "But that wasn't the way things went."

WHEELER HOUSE (1871) AND BARN *Post Hill St. and Bryan St.*

As you leave the museum and move up Post Hill Street you come to an early house, a "town house" for a big rancher, a house that is now stuccoed and painted white so that you can't see the stonework, can't recognize its antiquity.

This small dwelling was built by the stonemason, August Brockman, in 1871 when he moved up to Mason from Hilda. Six years later, however, he sold it to W. E. Wheeler, whose family then lived here for a long time. Wheeler was one of the important ranchers. Like John Gamel, he was married to one of the Crosby sisters, and, with the other Crosbys, helped sponsor the building for the Catholic Church in 1876.

Take a close look at the barn on this property as you move up the hill. It is thought to be the only structure remaining from Fort Mason. It was a tack house, part of the stables. Small slits for windows would have afforded protection from Indian attacks. The stonework here is exposed, not covered with stucco.

FORT MASON *At the top of Post Hill Road.*

With the close of the Mexican War, the federal government undertook the defense of its new southern border and also of the pioneer frontier of the state of Texas. Forts were established along the Rio Grande, and then, beginning in 1848, at Fredericksburg (the new settlement

of the Germans), at the present Burnet and so on up to
Fort Worth. Very soon another line was needed because
western expansion of white settlers pushed on beyond
these forts. Fort Mason in 1851 was followed by Fort
McKavett the next year and so on up to Fort Washita in
Oklahoma (Indian Territory).

At first the forts were garrisoned by mounted dragoons,
the only mounted troops of the day, as well as units of
infantry. But in 1855 the glorious Second Cavalry arrived,
one of the most spectacular fighting forces this nation had
seen. The First and Second Cavalries were specially
formed by Jefferson Davis, the Secretary of War and a
graduate of West Point, who personally chose all of the
officers. The fighting force marched down from Jefferson
Barracks in St. Louis with Albert Sidney Johnston at its
head. The second in command was Robert E. Lee. The
third was George Thomas, a Virginian, one of the few
Southern officers who subsequently did not quit the
Union. His loyalty Lincoln suspected at first, but he
turned out to be a great general who served with
distinction. Thomas was later known as the Rock of
Chickamunga.

Texas was the training ground in the 1850s, where a
career officer could gain experience and could advance his
position. Colonel Robert E. Lee was here, with
interruptions, from 1855 to 1861. He spent time in San
Antonio, some at court-martials down on the Rio Grande,
but in early 1861 he was the Commander of the Second
Cavalry and was headquartered here at Fort Mason.

The Second Cavalry maintained the post at Fort Mason
until the outbreak of the Civil War. It was abandoned by
federal troops then, but the Confederate forces maintained
nominal control. It was owned by absentee owners, the
land merely leased to the federal government, as was the
case with all the border forts. After the Indians stepped up
their attacks and the local sheriff was killed in one of their
raids, ranchers in the area began to move towards the fort
for protection. Some even tried to move into abandoned
fort buildings, but they quickly left after the absentee
owners threatened to take legal action. Nothing could stop
them from filching stones from the buildings, however,
and the early settlement in Mason was built with that
material.

Although the Indian atrocities increased with the
disbanding of the Frontier Guard in 1865, General Philip

Sheridan was reluctant to send federal troops out west again. It was not until Christmas Eve, 1866, that federal soldiers marched once again into Mason. They rebuilt the fort in the next several years, but never was there significant activity here again. The last troops rode west to Fort McKavett in 1869. With their departure, rocks from the rebuilt fort found their way down the hill to various buildings on or near the square.

Once again the hill was stripped. Nothing remained. Today there is little to show. You climb the hill and find a magnificent view, but then see only a rebuilt offiers' quarters, erected as part of a civic project in 1976.

For an idea of what was here, drive fifty miles out to Fort McKavett. The owner there lived in the commanding

Buffalo Soldier's Emblem

officer's quarters during the Civil War. When the troops came back this was said to be "the only habitable building." But Buffalo Soldiers (African-Americans) of the Ninth Cavalry under Colonel Ranald MacKenzie built extensively and well, and, after the final abandonment of the installation in 1883, the heirs of the owner sold off small pieces to individuals - a few acres to one, more to another, and so on. In this way the fort was preserved. The town was called Fort McKavett. Scabtown, a scrappy place across the river, dried up. A church and a school, built in the last years of the fort, continued in use. This version of Fort McKavett continued until 1968 when the state parks department started buying the site, bit by bit. Now the community of Fort McKavett is a ghost town, but the ruins there form one of the best preserved forts of the west.

ROBERT E. LEE AT FORT MASON

In the midst of my research on Mason I was called away to Washington, D.C. And there I had the opportunity to visit Lee's magnificent home, to stroll in the gardens, to observe the woods, the meadows, the stunning view back to the capital. I was well aware at that time that Lee came back to this home, Arlington House, after he left Fort Mason in February, 1861. That it was here that he paced the floor while making his momentous decisions. That it was from here that he crossed the river to speak with his mentor, General Winfield Scott, who was then Secretary of War and who offered him the position of commander of the Northern armies in the field. Scott knew Lee's potential from the Mexican War. But Lee turned down this offer, resigned his commission in the army, and, after the secession of Virginia, accepted the position of commander of its forces. He left Arlington for Richmond on April 21, 1861. He was opposed to secession - called it "revolution" in a letter to his son - and he was not in favor of the system of slavery. But he could not, in all good consciousness, forsake his state, "his country" as he called it, his neighbors, his friends, his cousins.

Robert E. Lee came from an old and distinguished family, the Lees of Virginia, who had settled and begun to prosper here in 1640. Each generation left landed estates and slaves for its descendants down through the decades. Lee men also tended to marry heiresses, women from neighboring plantations, even their own first or second cousins. But when this succession reached Lee's father, it met a stumbling block. His father, Light-Horse Harry Lee, a revolutionary war hero, was a wreckless gambler, a speculator, who went through all his money, fell deeply into debt, and shamed the family. His own father cut him out of his will in 1787. Then Light-Horse Harry even tried to pass a bad check on his mentor, George Washington, who, furious, told others to trust Lee in military affairs but not in financial matters.

Light-Horse Harry had married well - twice - but both families succeeded in blocking his access to their money. His first wife was his second cousin, Matilda Lee, and with her came the proud estate and family seat, Stratford, on the Potomac. When she died in 1790, however, she had left her assets in trust for her children. Stratford was to pass to her son Harry - called Black-Horse Harry - when he reached the age of 21 in 1807.

Light-Horse Harry's second wife was Ann Lee, daughter of the fabulously wealthy Charles Carter. The couple was married at Shirley, near Williamsburg. By the time Robert E. Lee was born in 1807, though, Carter had cut Light-Horse Harry out of all consideration, had restricted his bequests to Ann, had provided her with only enough to live modestly. Ann named the baby for two of her brothers, Robert and Edward Carter. A year later Light-Horse Harry languished in debtors' prison, and Ann was making plans to leave Stratford for Alexandria where several of Harry's brothers and sisters were already established. Young Robert grew up there in a townhouse that belonged to a cousin. Money was tight. His father fled to Barbados and died in exile in 1818. Ann was able to send her oldest son, Carter, to Harvard, because her brother, William Carter, paid the bills. The younger sons went to the free military academies, Smith to Annapolis and Robert to West Point.

Thus it was that Robert E. Lee was handsome, educated, and the descendant of a prominent family, when he asked the hand in marriage of his cousin, Mary Custis. He had no money, no estate of his own, but he was quickly accepted into the pleasant routine of life at Arlington. Mary Lee traveled with him to some of his assignments, but she bore all but one of their seven children at home and she spent long months at Arlington while he was away. By the 1850s she was severely crippled with arthritis. To travel to Texas was out of the question.

At Christmas, 1860, when Robert E. Lee was here, "up on the hill" as some remembered, his heart was heavy. Not only did he fret about the state of the Union and the possibility of impending war, but he thought also of Arlington House. George Washington Parke Custis, Mary's father, had died in 1857, leaving Lee as the executor of his will. He freed his slaves in his will as had his guardian George Washington, and he left numerous bequests, but he died in debt. He was the grandson of Martha Washington, the adopted child of Martha and

163

George, and the possessor of many "Washington relics," such as the great lantern from the front hall of Mount Vernon, the exquisite china from the Society of the Cincinnati, the bed on which George Washington died, clothes, books, silver, portraits, even the general's tent and camping equipment. Many things came down to Custis and he was happy to tell about them and to share them. At that time, Arlington was considered the second shrine to Washington, after Mount Vernon itself. And Mount Vernon had recently been acquired by an association of women who planned to open it as a museum.

Lee knew that fateful Christmas of 1860 that Arlington House would be among the first targets in the advent of a

Robert E. Lee

war between the North and the South. And so it was. After Robert Lee left for Richmond on April 21, Mary Lee started packing and sending away as much as she could. She left on May 15, reluctantly, but it was none too soon. By May 24th federal troops had occupied Arlington. They stayed throughout the war. At first the officers were respectful of Lee, a former comrade. But, as the war wore on, as casualties mounted, this respect turned to contempt. In 1864, when the military hospitals in Washington overflowed and the lone military cemetery there was filled, the federal government confiscated

Arlington plantation, set up tents for the wounded, and started burying the dead on the lawn in front of the house.

The Lees never went back to Arlington. General Lee saw it once from the windows of a train. Mary Lee returned for a sad, brief farewell after the death of her husband. The Lees had moved to Lexington, Virginia, where General Lee was President of Washington College. But neither lived many years longer. Robert Lee died in 1870, his wife three years later. After that, their eldest son sued for the return of Arlington, the only Southern plantation that had been confiscated by the government, but when it was returned to him, in 1883, he realized that the presence of thousands of graves in the front yard made it untenable.

Custis sold the plantation to the federal government for $150,000. Meanwhile, the Arlington National Cemetery was growing into the largest in the nation - an enormous gathering of tombstones. The house itself was neglected for decades, but, finally, in 1925 was refurbished and opened to the public. Some of the Washington relics can be found there today.

So Robert E. Lee's heart was weighed down during the Christmas of 1860 at Fort Mason. He fretted about the impending war, about Arlington, about his extended family. He participated in the festivities, in the traditional Christmas dance, but his thoughts inevitably slipped back to Arlington House, the scene of so many joyous Christmas reunions in the past, the place where his family had always rushed to greet him at the door.

HEY HOUSE (1903) *At the summit of Post Hill Road.*

Wilson Hey, the British cowboy, arrived in the United States in 1850 on his eighteenth birthday. He lived for a while in Tennessee, served four years in Forrest's Cavalry of the Confederate army, and then made his way out here - to the Wild West - in 1868. He went into ranching, but he found his true calling as county and district clerk, with one term as county judge at the end of his career. He served in these positions from 1872 until 1902. Just as he was undertaking these responsibilities, he married Hannah Korn, a member of a pioneer German family.

Hannah Korn Hey had her own tales to tell. Her half-brother had been captured by the Indians at the age of twelve and was not returned for four years. Hannah, herself, had been a 15-year-old guest at the party at the fort in late December, 1860. It was she who later told of attending this Christmas dance, of observing Colonel Lee, "who didn't dance with anyone, just sat and watched the rest of us, although he seemed to enjoy the fun."

This rock home, built late in their lives, in the very shadow of the former fort, is a good example of the late Queen Anne style. Fancy wooden panels in the front gables are the only adornment. A pair of cutaway bay windows balance the front. The original wooden front porch was replaced with concrete.

GAMEL HOUSE (1869) *104 San Antonio St.*

John Gamel's family had migrated from Ireland to Georgia in the 1790s, to Texas in the 1850s, and out to a point 10 miles west of Mason by July of 1860. He was then a lad of sixteen years and already an expert cowboy. Two years later he volunteered for the Confederate Army. On his return, he drove cattle to Kansas and started amassing his fortune.

Gamel bought property near the fort that included the community springs. Later, he donated these springs and part of the town square when the town was getting under way. In 1889, from his enormous holdings, he sold the Mill Creek Ranch south of Mason to George Littlefield and his nephew, J. W. White.

While still very young, only twenty, he married Kate Crosby and took her to live out on his ranch. In 1869, as the town of Mason was forming, he and Kate built a town house here. The house was not flashy, just a simple rock cottage with numerous outbuildings overlooking the southeast corner of the square.

After Kate died in 1880, Gamel married Alice Kettner, a young German woman from a prominent pioneer family. Alice made only a few changes at first, but later, after John Gamel's death in 1917, she replaced the wooden front porch with concrete, erected square posts in the Craftsman's style, and covered the rock walls with stucco. With these changes, the house does not look its age, but this one is among the oldest here.

Stage Stop

STAGE STOP (1850s) *307 San Antonio St.*

An even older dwelling stands a short distance away. This is a house from the 1850s, half-timbered in the manner of the early German settlers. Its origins are obscure, but later it is thought to have served as a stage stop between the time of the fort and the establishment of the Mason House on the square around 1876.

SMITH HOUSES (1872, 1884) *323 San Antonio St.*

One of John Gamel's contemporaries from Georgia, Caleb Cook Smith (C. C.), came out as a seventeen-year-old to work for the Gamel family, then to serve a stint in the Confederate Army, and finally to work for John Gamel himself until 1876.

In 1872, C. C. Smith had married Caroline Hoerster, a member of one of the earliest German families to migrate north from Fredericksburg. The young couple bought nine acres from John Gamel and built their first home, a picket house that still stands at the rear of the property here. (Covered with stucco now.) Later, they built the handsome stone house closer to the road, but the family spent as much time as possible on their ranch out near Blue Mountain.

ST. PAUL'S LUTHERAN CHURCH (1905) *Austin St. at Magnolia*

Richard Grosse, the German architect, designed three handsome sandstone churches in this area. The first was the Methodist Church at Art in 1890. The second was the Methodist Church at Hilda in 1902. And the third was the Lutheran Church in Mason two years later. His signature mark in all three was a circular window. Look for these in the gables above pointed windows.

The church at Art has the simplest design and is now remodeled inside. The church at Hilda is, by all calculations, a jewel - untouched inside or out, a sandstone church that gracefully incorporates limestone quoins and decorative yellow brick above lancet windows.

In Mason, Grosse used the same sandstone with decorative bricks around the windows and doors. But his design was expanded in 1953. The front half near the street is the newer section; his part is at the back near the altar.

FIRST CHRISTIAN CHURCH (1879, 1926) *Austin St. at Birch*

The Christian Church also underwent a facelift, this one a major change. It had been built as a simple, sandstone, pioneer church in 1879. Two doors at the front admitted the men and women separately. But, in 1926, a Philadelphia architect added a white portico with columns

White Barn

and an elliptical window in the front gable. This Neoclassical porch was in the same spirit as the red brick Bierschwale House (1914) across the street, which the same architect, Watkins Phillips, had also designed.

MORAN HOUSE (1884) AND BARN   *Austin Street*

Now we come to one of the most curious dwellings in Mason, a two-story house in the Italianate style that combines sandstone and limestone in fairly sizable blocks. The walls are formed of the dark sandstone, while the pale limestone runs up all the corners as quoins, outlines all the windows and surrounds the door. It also forms string courses between windows and doors. Since the house is not large and the openings are many, there seems to be as much limestone as sandstone. The effect is one of stripes, like a zebra pudding.

The house was built for the Leonard Light family. He was a wealthy rancher. His wife was part of the Ranck clan. Their barn and carriage house, with its great arched portal, is of the same vintage as the house.

WHITE HOUSE (1870s, 1890s) AND BARN   *323 Austin St.*

It is not hard to see the next two houses as the gems of Mason. Low, sprawling, built close to the ground, set in a glorious pocket of large trees and grassy lawns, with continuous low fences across the front of the properties, front porches at the ready, white wicker and rocking chairs and pots of caladiums on those porches.

The original part of the White House is old, nobody is sure quite how old. Although J. W. White and his bride,

White House

Cora Bridges, set up house-keeping here in 1891, the house dates back to sometime in the 1870s. They added rooms as the years passed, and the babies came. What probably started out as an L-shaped dwelling ended up as a T with a gable end facing the street and two porches flanking it. Some of the white gingerbread trim is very handsome, and the white trim and the dark green shutters look well against the reddish sandstone.

Among the outbuildings here is one of the extraordinary rock barns of the Hill Country. Very large, a combination of several buildings, the barn is right next to the street where you can easily see it. This was one of the attractions listed in Alexander's book, *Texas Homes of the Nineteenth Century.*

MIXON HOUSE (1891) *321 Austin St.*

The Mixon House shows the marks of Thomas Broad, a Methodist minister who also worked as a builder. Here you see tooled limestone blocks, carved flowers in the limestone trim, and stained-glass windows. You will also spot these in his Hamilton House on Bluebird Street.

SEAQUIST MANSION (1891) *400 Broad Street. Tours by appointment only. Ph: 915/347-6659.*

The Seaquist Mansion is one of the great houses of Texas. It ranks alongside the Littlefield Mansion in Austin, the Eddleman-McFarland House in Fort Worth, the Waggoner House in Decatur, and the Bishop's Palace in Galveston. All are late Victorian. All are masonry houses with contrasting trims, a variety of building materials within, and rich woodwork. All are shown together in D. B. Alexander's *Texas Homes of the Nineteenth Century.*

The Seaquist Mansion, a classic example of Queen Anne style, is built of the native sandstone, but here so much limestone and brick is incorporated that the facade is a veritable patchwork. While the contrasts in the Moran House emphasize the vertical, here there are horizontal bands of dark and light stone around the front bay of windows and around the front door. But these are interspersed with tooled or hand-carved limestone blocks. Around the front door alone, there are twenty-one of these hand-carved limestone blocks, each with a motif that

170

varies from simple geometric patterns to the elaborate carved grapes in the keystone.

On the south side of the house, in a marvelous patterned chimney that alternates bands of sandstone with bands of pale brick, another limestone keystone shows a likeness of the first owner of the house, E. M. Reynolds, at the top of a decorative arch - "head of the house." Below him, over a window at the left, his wife is shown with two lovebirds. At the right, his daughter is shown with birds about to fly off - soon she would be gone.

The original two-story dwelling here was erected before 1890 by Thomas Broad, the Methodist minister who built the Mixon House, the Hamilton House, and others. But soon, E. M. Reynolds, a New York banker, bought the original house, tore it down, and hired Richard Grosse to start from the ground up. Together they planned this Queen Anne mansion - no doubt consulting pattern books that were then readily available. They saved and reused the rock from Broad's house, placing most of the hand-carved sections around the front door.

Inside, the house has tall, narrow windows, some of which open as doors to the porches. The front staircase is walnut, constructed without a nail, but the rear stairs are cherry. Seemingly, no expense was spared. In all, there are seventeen rooms, including several alcoves, and fifteen fireplaces.

The most intriguing area is the third floor where various rooms were arranged for cards or billiards. A ballroom here has its own little balcony for the musicians. The stained-glass up here is the most striking of any in the house. Its colors fill windows and the top half of doors.

171

On the second level is a walkway out to a three-story tank house that contains the first shower in Mason. The cistern was above, the shower on the second level, and the milk house below. Both the Reynolds and the later owners, the Seaquists, rented out rooms and, undoubtedly, everyone partook in the pleasures of the shower.

The basement is so large that the Reynolds daughter and her friends skated here. You can see still the laundry room with its great black tub set in a kiln, as well as other wash pots for rinsing.

In 1919, the Reynolds sold their home to Oscar Seaquist, a bootmaker and rancher originally from Sweden. The Seaquist family substituted a concrete porch and concrete columns for the wooden ones on the first floor. This was a big change, of course, and it detracts from the authenticity of the design.

But this porch has held up well. Having seen the old Antler's Hotel (1901) in Kingsland the day before I toured here, and having viewed with alarm its rotting wooden porches on all sides, I could appreciate the value of a concrete substitution.

HAMILTON HOUSE (1890) *206 Bluebird.*

Around the corner is another house with a facade like a patchwork quilt, only this dwelling is small, unassuming. At the Hamilton House you see Thomas Broad's original ideas. Carved blocks similar to those at the Seaquist Mansion surround the doorway. The door here, as there, is narrow to accommodate these blocks. You see tooled limestone blocks in the quoins and above the windows. You see the same carved flower motif that is present in the Mixon House, but here the motif is repeated in the wooden balustrade of the porch.

This was the home of Erv Hamilton, a prominent rancher who hailed originally from Indiana. Next door was Cora White's sister, Lula, who married John Shaeg. That house, though another of Thomas Broad's, has only a tiny bit of decoration.

ST. JOSEPH'S CATHOLIC CHURCH (1876) *Ft. McKavett Rd. at Avenue B.*

The oldest church in town is that of the Catholics, financed by the Crosby brothers and sisters and two of their rancher husbands, John Gamel and W. E. Wheeler. On the exterior, it is a simple stone church with little adornment, a good example of building styles in the 1870s. But inside is another matter. A Hispanic member of the congregation, an artist trained by Spaniards in Mexico, painted angels and cherubs and garlands on a vivid blue sky across the vaulted ceiling. His name was Manuel Lopez, and the date was 1916. His work was a good example of the folk art in Mexican churches at that time.

In 1963, the artist's efforts were covered over. What a parishioner called "a hard-headed Dutch priest" extended the sanctuary and installed ceiling tiles that obscured the mural. He did not paint over it; he just covered it up.

Choir members could still see the cherubs, and members of the congregation did not forget. One old lady exclaimed: "Before I die I want to see my angels again!"

Then there they were all to see. A storm in 1989 blew in the roof and damaged the ceiling tiles. When the tiles were removed, there were the angels and the cherubs and the garlands against the vivid blue of the vaulted ceiling. Now they will stay in view for all to behold. Guardian angels in a church that is now eighty percent Hispanic.

RUNGE HOUSE (1924) *107 Avenue A*

The rock for this house came down originally from the fort. It was used in a store on the square in the 1880s. It then lay in piles after the store was razed around 1916. Eight years later, Carl Runge, the county judge, had the stone hauled off to the site of his new home, this twice-used stone. Here, in Mason, building stone seems to be like children's blocks. It is used and then reused. Sometimes in a house, sometimes in a store, maybe in a fence.

But the judge did not have long pieces for the lintels and window sills for the bands of windows in a bungalow, the popular style of the day. For these he went out to a quarry, and you can still see the discrepancy between the two kinds of stone - those from the fort and the newer ones he purchased at the quarry.

The house sits high above the street, with a front porch that wraps around it and provides inviting places to sit. The balustrade of the porch is made of blocks of the building stone. The house itself is a classic bungalow, a large one, with broad porch, large windows, and an upstairs section.

Carl Runge was the son of an old pioneer family. His father came to Texas from Germany in 1853 when he was four-years-old, served later as a carpenter's helper at Fort Concho, drove cattle to Kansas, became a lawyer and arrived here in 1876. He married Theresa Marschall von Beberstein, the only daughter of the esteemed von Marschalls who lived at Prairie Mountain.

The sons, Carl and Roscoe, born in 1892 and 1894, followed parallel paths. Both became lawyers, both served during World War I, both returned to practice in their father's office. Both married in 1921. Both young women were from Mason. Neither was German.

Carl Runge built this house in 1924, but, five years later, he was building the Fort Mason Hotel on the square with E. O. Kothmann. The hotel failed, and it took twenty years to pay off the debt, but Carl Runge moved on. He served in the Judge Advocate General's School during World War II, and later he moved to San Angelo. The stone bungalow had long since passed out of the family.

HARKEY HOUSE (1930s) *801 El Paso*

Take a minute to look around the neighborhood here. The banker Anna Martin lived across the street. Her house, from around the turn-of-the-century, is L-shaped and has a hipped roof. It is made of concrete blocks, the product of a backyard industry at that time. A concrete post near the street bears her name: ANNA.

About a block or so farther west you find "rocked" houses, of flagstone veneer, that were popular in the 1930s. Families gathered thin pieces of stone or chunks that could be split into narrow slabs, or "flags." These were ·laid up vertically in fanciful patterns, like crazy quilts. Small projecting stones were used as counterpoint. Usually brick was used to face windows and doors.

The Harkey House is a marvelous example. It is a bungalow with cream and red brick layered up like stripes edging all the openings and corners. It is very obvious that the original owner's rock collection decorates the walls. You see unusual shapes in abundance. Some protrude several inches from the wall. Clusters of crystals and pudding stones can be seen in several places. Near the door is an arrangement of fossils.

CAPPS HOUSE (1936)   *106 S. Avenue C*

Laverne Lee told me that constructing her family home was "like putting together a puzzle." Her father, a cattle trader, had picked up the rocks and brought them home, a few at a time. When it came time to build the house, he bought a load of Austin stone (cast stone) in big sheets, brought that back in a cattle truck, and handed it over to the workmen to saw into window sills and the cut stone around the front door. He used bricks to line the tops and sides of the windows, but Laverne says "bricks were expensive."

The Capps ordered the plans for a Tudor house, a small dwelling with a steep roof, a front-facing swooping gable, an arched portal, and a heavy door with little windows in it. There was no front porch. A side porch, which substituted for it, was later enclosed as a garden room.

But the reason to look carefully here is that this house - seemingly like many others - has extraordinary rockwork. In Dallas, such a house might have been built with a load of stone brought in, but here you see a family's rock collection. Lots of small stones with unusual shapes project out from the composition. Large boulders rest near the bottom. There is at least one pudding stone - those crazy looking shapes that remind you of the bubbly place in Yellowstone Park.

I queried Laverne as to how the family gathered these rocks. She said her father "would bring home a few at a time, would throw them into the back of his pick-up." She said friends would give them rocks, "two or three". She said the family would go out and "bring some back". All of this reminds me of Elizabeth Sasser's question in her architectural study of West Texas, *Dugout to Deco*: "Wouldn't it be fun to collect a house?"

COUNTRY COLLECTIBLES STORE *Hw. 87, 1 block N. of square.*

I asked the clerk at this rambling, cavernous antique store and junk shop about topaz hunting at area ranches.
"Have you ever gone topaz hunting?"
"Yes."
"And what did you get?"
"A sunburn."
Well, I thought, forget it. But then the clerk led me over to a huge safe, started fiddling with the dials, and drew out a special black box. Inside were three magnificent topazes - showpieces. One was round with a Texas star cut in the center. (I had seen a photograph of it in *Texas Highways*.) Another was oval and very large. The third was equally dazzling.

Dig, if you must. People have found impressive topazes on two ranches nearby. But I prefer to forego the sunburn and gape at the treasures here.

I poked around and found glassware, rock collections, twig furniture, and lots of old books. Books are kind of a specialty, I think. This is definitely the best place in Mason to find one of Fred Gipson's volumes.

Note: For serious topaz hunting, contact the Chamber of Commerce.

ANNUAL EVENT: BLUEBONNET COUNTRY LANES DRIVE *1st and 2nd weekends in April and May. Contact Chamber of Commerce, Ph: 915/347-5758.*

Wildflowers are amazing out here if there is sufficient rain. Bluebonnets can make a spectacular show, as can white poppies. Paintbrush ranges from pinks to bright red. Blue hills, granite outcroppings, stone fences, and live oaks form backgrounds for the displays.

Each year the Chamber of Commerce sponsors several drives in the country, out towards Art, down towards Hilda. Pick up maps and directions at the Chamber. April brings bluebonnets and paintbrush, but May brings coriopsis, Indian blanket, and Mexican Hats.

Mason is such that you can see wildflowers right in the middle of town. I have seen bluebonnets near the Catholic

Church, and, once in October, I saw a gorgeous wild bouquet just west of the square. October is mild, wonderful, some people's favorite time here. Flowers can be lovely during many months. The first time we saw the Hasse House, in early March, there were bright yellow flowers called Scrambled Eggs at the gate.

ANNUAL EVENT: CHRISTMAS HOME TOUR 2nd Sat. in Dec, 2-5. Contact Chamber of Commerce, Ph: 915/347-5758. Admission.

A special time of year to visit Mason. Efforts are made to show some of the attractions. One year it was the newly uncovered murals at the Catholic Church. Tours at the Seaquist Mansion are available.

LODGINGS: MASON SQUARE BED AND BREAKFAST (1900) *North side of square. Ph: 915/347-6398.*

An old commercial building with pressed-tin ceilings, Victorian woodwork, and oak floors is now an attractive inn on the square. This had formerly been a bank with living quarters above. Three rooms, each with a private bath, are available. All share the front sitting room, which has a balcony overlooking the square.

LODGINGS: HASSE HOUSE (1883) *7 miles west in Art on Hwy. 29. Ph: 915/347-6463.*

This old family home of Laverne Lee is out in the country on the 320 acres that have been in the family since 1860. Fully equipped, with two bedrooms, two baths, a Franklin stove in the living room, a complete kitchen, and a swing on the front porch. This has been my refuge in the Hill Country. (See more about the Hasse House under Art and Castell.)

RESTAURANT: COOPER'S OLD TIME PIT BAR-B-Q *Hwy. 87, 4 blocks S. of square.*

Choose your meat outside at the pit, then take it wrapped in butcher paper into a room with picnic tables, jalapeno peppers, onions, and white bread. This is rustic eating in West Texas style. The meats include not only brisket and ribs, but also cabrito, sausage, and an excellent barbecued chicken.

RESTAURANT: ZAVALA'S *Hwy. 87, 4 blocks N. of square. Open daily*

Zavala's will be open when you want to go there, at night, for instance. The food is not outstanding, but this place is the hang-out of local folks because it is large and can accommodate many and because it is open when you need it. The specialities include nachos, burritos, and fajitas.

Art and Castell

INTRODUCTION TO ART AND CASTELL

Art and Castell represent an extension of the German Llano River communities that we encountered north of Fredericksburg and south of Mason. It was at Castell that the Reverend Charles A. Grote settled after he moved north from Fredericksburg in 1855. He established the Llano River Valley Circuit of the Methodist Church that remains active to this day. The first permanent church was built at Art in 1858. A German Hymnfest that alternates between Castell, Art, Mason, and Hilda on the fourth Sunday in September was begun with the centennial of the first preaching up here in 1851.

ART (formerly Upper Willow Creek, then Plehweville) 7 miles E. of Mason on Hwy. 29.

When you arrive you don't see much because Art is a nineteenth-century ranching community with its houses, its church, and its store well spread out. "A scattering of buildings and houses" notes Gilbert Jordan in his book, *Yesterday in the Texas Hill Country*, a remarkable account of his early years here in the first quarter of the twentieth century.

The large Methodist church stands west of Willow Creek, the store is east of the creek, and the houses on the various ranches are tucked in here and there, but mostly well out of sight.

Gilbert's grandfather, Ernst Jordan, was one of the three pioneers who brought their families here in 1856. His family, along with those of Heinrich Hoerster and Heinrich Kothmann, made a caravan of ox-drawn wagons for the three day journey up from Fredericksburg. All the families were German, Methodists, and charter members of the Llano Valley Circuit. Two years later Ernst Jordan donated land for the first church, a log cabin that was burned in the Hoodoo War in the 1870s. This building was replaced with a simple stone version that doubled as the one-room school in the community. It still stands, due south of the store. Since school consolidation in 1946, which sent the children to Mason on buses, it has served as a community center.

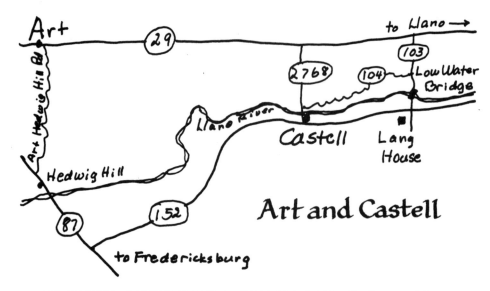

ART UNITED METHODIST CHURCH (1890) *Highway 29.*

In 1890, Ernst Jordan again donated land for a church building, this time on higher ground. You can't miss this large rock church as you drive along Highway 29. You wonder how they could have built this in 1890. The architect, Richard Grosse, then living in Mason., drew up the plans. You see his signature round window high under the front gable, but this church of 1890 is not as decorated as his later churches in Hilda and Mason.

Ernst Jordan donated rock from his property for the walls, and Gilbert's other grandfather, Anton Willman (a Catholic who converted to Methodism) gave the finer-textured sandstone for the corner quoins and the trim around the doors and windows. The stonemason August Brockman was in charge of construction, but the whole congregation helped, keeping the total costs down to a little over $3,000. Lumber was carted from the rail towns of Burnet and Waring, since this was two years before the rails reached Llano.

The double doors on the front separated the men from the women and children. In the early days the men sat on the south, the women on the north. All services were in German until 1927, and the change to English was very difficult. As Gilbert Jordan remembers, "It is one thing to learn to speak and understand a new language, but it is something else again to preach and pray in it." He recalls that the sermons could be delivered bilingually and the hymns were not an insurmountable problem, but to pray in English seemed out of the question. The pastors resorted to calling on members of the congregation to present the prayers, and of course they spoke in German. He says the

Art United Methodist Church

Lord spoke in German to the people, and they spoke in German to Him.

Behind the church is a wooden addition that looks like another church, and indeed it was. The Methodists here split into Southern and Northern branches after the Civil War and the Northern branch built down the road in 1893. After the reunification, in 1941, the Northern church was picked up and added on to the rear of this one for a Sunday School building.

In front of the church you find a tabernacle for revivals - the gatherings that replaced the old-time camp meetings in 1914 when automobiles made travel faster. Actually, to camp out at the church was not unusual because each family was accustomed to arriving for the day on Sunday, bringing food and preparing lunch at the family shed that each group maintained on the church grounds. For the camp meetings, families came for the week. They slept in tents, cooked at their shed, participated in family devotionals as well as the larger gatherings. Ervin Jordan, Gilbert Jordan's first cousin, who later became a minister at this church, recalls hearing five or six family groups singing different hymns at once. He said it was like being "on the very borderland of heaven."

HASSE HOUSE (1883) *Highway 29 . As a bed-and-breakfast, see under Mason.*

Across Highway 29 from the Methodist Church is the 1883 Hasse House, the home of pioneers that now serves as guest accommodations.

The Hasses, Henry and Fredericka (sister of Lizette, Ernst Jordan's wife) bought 200 acres from Heinrich Hoerster in 1860, built a log cabin and settled in as a ranching family. Henry served in the Confederate Army from 1864 to 1865. While he was gone, the family horses were stolen by Indians. There must have been many days that Fredericka was grateful that her sister lived across the road.

In 1883 the family hired a German rock mason to build a sandstone dwelling to replace the original log cabin. It had two rooms below, a loft above, and a front porch. This first section has cedar lintels above the doors, but in a later addition at the rear the windows are headed by segmental arches.

The Hasse's four children were Henry, Dan, John, and Lizette. Dan's sons were Ervin and Elgin, who started the Hasses Brothers store on Highway 29 in Llano. John was the son who remained here as a cattleman. It is his granddaughter, Laverne Lee, who owns and manages the house today. Lizette, the youngest, married Alwin Donop in 1896 in a ceremony and reception here that was long remembered. Her brother Henry wrote in his diary that it "took a week for Minnie Bickenbach and Minnie Jordan to bake all of the wedding cakes." The men of the family killed a beef to be barbequed on the wedding day. The couple were married at three o'clock on a Thursday in the Methodist Church, but the guests came here for the barbeque and the cakes. The family served nearly two hundred friends and relatives. People stayed late to visit, but, this being the Land of the Methodists, there was no dancing.

The Hasse House has been a favorite place for me, and I have wonderful memories of it: the soft crooning of an automobile from one end of Highway 29 to the other, the sun coming up and birds chirping everywhere, quails calling, breakfast on the patio in the back, and supper at the kitchen table. A cottontail rabbit drinking at the rear faucet, and a resident armadillo ambling through the edge of the front yard. Stars at night, the Big Dipper, and utter quiet.

CASTELL   *FM 2768, 3 miles S. of Hwy. 29.*

At Castell we dip down to the Llano River. Originally, the community was on the north side of the river, but later it moved. Now you find what there is of it just south of the bridge across the river. An old store remains from times past.

Behind the store is the Methodist Church. The rock section dates from the 1880s. The Methodist leader, the Reverend Charles A. Grote, had settled here in 1855.

The Lutheran Church stands about a mile east of town on FM 152. Not to be outdone by the Methodists, the Lutherans started here early, too. Their leader was Dietrich Rode of Cherry Spring, who rode up from his magnificent ranch to conduct services once a month. As a lay minister, he was authorized to perform all the rites. He invited young people to live on his ranch beginning each September to prepare for an Easter confirmation. He and his wife invited all others to stay with them when they traveled down to Fredericksburg.

With Rode's encouragement, the congregation built a sandstone church in 1893. The building still stands, and is, in its way, one of the unusual sights in the neighborhood. It stands in a field and is used as a hay barn now. To find it, go north across the bridge from Castell and turn immediately east on the dirt road there. You will pass through an old section of houses and barns and rock fences. At length you will see the former church. It is a small stone building with four windows on each side, double doors in front, and the date, 1893, carved above the entry.

THE ROAD TO LLANO

The prettiest drive to Llano from here is along FM 152. You stay close to the south bank of the river, dipping down to low-water bridges over small creeks, passing granite outcroppings in the fields, catching glimpses of the hills in the west, and finally pulling into the old-fashioned square at Llano.

Not far from Castell you will spot the ruins of the Hasse Ranch House overlooking the river. Don't miss the iron sign here. It is one of the best that we saw. "Hasse Ranch" is spelled out simply enough, but above is a cowboy with a lariat on his horse, several cows and calves, and a windmill, all executed in fine detail.

Then you come to another landmark, the extraordinary Lang House, a two-story sandstone dwelling, salt-box style, very early. It is one of those country houses in D.B. Alexander's *Texas Homes of the Nineteenth Century* that you think you won't find.

Just past the Lang House is a sign for FM 103. Take this a mile or so towards the river and find a long low-water bridge built in several sections, with water gushing out through spillways here, collecting in little eddies there, rushing around granite boulders along the edge. This exceptional low-water bridge is for exploring. Get out and scurry about if you can. But just to drive across it is a thrill.

ANNUAL EVENT: LLANO RIVER VALLEY GERMAN
HYMNFEST *4th Sunday in September. Alternates
between Castell, Art, Hilda, and Mason Methodist
Churches*

In 1951, the pastor at the Art United Methodist Church
was Ervin Jordan. His father before him had been pastor.
Ernst Jordan's son, Henry, had taken the job in 1906. He
had lived in his own house on his own ranch, but he was
the one who started the first parsonage.

But Ervin Jordan was pastor in 1951, an important
year. The German Methodists on the Llano River were
about to celebrate their first 100 years. Ervin was involved
in creating a pageant to help celebrate. But what seemed to
make the biggest impact was singing the old German
hymns. There was a move to meet annually to sing them
again, and the hymnfest continues to this day. Hundreds
come to join in. The festival includes members from the
four remaining churches of the Llano River Valley Circuit:
Castell, Art, Hilda, and Mason.

Llano

INTRODUCTION TO LLANO

Once when we were staying in Austin we took some friends up to Llano for the day. They wanted to take a jaunt into the Hill Country. Specifically, they wanted to see bluebonnets.

We drove up Highway 71 and saw some bluebonnets there, along with paintbrush and some fuscia phlox. Of course we had to get out of the car and look.

In Llano they were fascinated by the courthouse with its combination of brick and granite that has mellowed to exactly the same shade of pinky-beige. They especially liked the long bridge over the Llano River with its views back to the courthouse on one side and up to the North Side on the other. We walked across slowly, and they spied sturgeon, catfish, and even spotted gar. They peered for a long time at the low falls and at the piers of a low-water bridge that had been used to build the present one They marveled at the clean, spring-fed water.

On the other side, we tried the lemon squares at Jeannette's Homestyle Bakery and declared them "top notch." We looked at the Badu House, the old bank that is now an inn. Our friends thought its handsome exterior on one side and rubble construction on the other indicated that it had been a corner building.

For lunch we headed up to Highway 29 for barbeque at Brother's B-B-Que. We sat outside, the breeze in our faces. Jack Graham, the owner, came out to tend to the pits and stopped long enough to explain the style of the pitmasters in Llano. Barbequed chicken never tasted better.

After that we went down to Enchanted Rock, found it too crowded to stay there, and drove on to Willow City Loop. Over hill tops and down through vales and finally through fields of bluebonnets we sailed. Someone commented that it looked as though an artist had taken his blue paint and spread it from hill to hill. I never saw bluebonnets lovelier.

A perfect day: bluebonnets, bridge, bakery, brick and granite courthouse, barbeque. This is Llano in a nutshell. Come see granite in many variations, but also come to eat

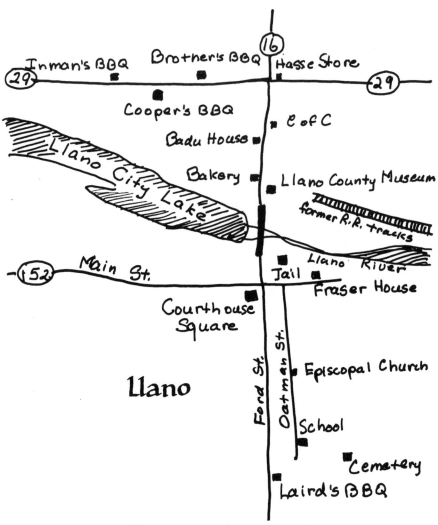

barbeque. *Texas Monthly Magazine* dubbed Llano the "Barbecue Capitol of Central Texas."

HISTORY

Llano is the story of granite - granite as used for the state capitol in the 1880s, granite sent out for innumerable county courthouses in the 1890s, granite as an industry. Llano is at the center of the Llano Uplift, ancient uplifted mountains, and there are eighteen different kinds and colors nearby. A railroad came from Burnet in 1892 to carry this granite out. The present courthouse went up in that year.

But first there were cattle. Llano was established by Anglo-American ranchers who were pushing west. They started the town as the county seat in 1856. The family that donated a large share of the land for the town was the Oatmans, a family that is still prominent today. John Oatman, from Kentucky, had bought two-thirds of a league and arrived here in 1853. His son, John Jr., built the first store and became the first postmaster after Llano was founded. He laid out the town in the next year or so, but then the Oatmans, as well as many others here left to fight for the Confederacy in the Civil War. This county voted for Secession, 134 to 72. It has remained southern to the core, got up its Civil War memorial in 1916, and then lined the square with other war memorials.

After the Civil War, Llano was primitive and backward for years. Indians roamed the area. The final engagement with them was not until 1875, at Pack Saddle Mountain nearby, and the last frontier cabin stayed on the square until 1883.

But meanwhile the cattle drives had started. In 1868 Damon Slator and Crockett Riley led the first. Many others followed. Not until the railroad reached Llano in 1892, did the trail drives taper off here, and cattle continued to be big business. As late as 1929, five train loads a day moved out of this county for months at a time.

After granite from nearby Granite Mountain was carted off to build the state capitol in 1885, prospectors came over here to look around. They found iron ore, but not in sufficient quantities nor with sufficient transportation to make it work. The brief flurry of the "iron ore boom," however, promoted the development of the north side of town. Only a few residences and some cow pens had been there before, but suddenly a whole new town was springing up. Developers came from out-of-town, some from Dallas, such as Henry Exall and J.S. Armstong. Prospects here did not pan out though, and before long this development withered. Fires destroyed one block in an enormous blaze. By 1892, when the railroad arrived from Burnet, the iron boom was over. The interests of the granite finishers had become paramount. The rails entered the north side, with the depots and attendant buildings there. Granite offices and finishing plants spread along the tracks for miles.

In the year the train arrived, the local pioneer of granite, J. K. Finlay, sent a carload of granite samples to

Fort Worth and Chicago. This load contained specimens of eighteen kinds and colors of granite. Each was the size of a brick. Each was polished on one side. Each was of fine quality, and the colors ranged from grays to pinks to blues to reds. Finlay's first big job came two years later when he sent up granite for the Kansas City Customs House.

Finlay had been working at a mill eight miles above Llano since 1888, but ten years later he moved in closer to Llano. By then, granite for county courthouses was popular, blue granite for the Dallas temple, polished pink granite for the steps and columns at La Grange, red columns for New Braunfels, eighty shafts of polished pink for Denton. Carloads of immense granite blocks for the monumental buildings at San Antonio, Fort Worth, Decatur, Waxahachie.

Finlay's company was bought by T. W. Norton in 1900. In the same year a German sculptor and granite man, Frank Teich, moved up from San Antonio. He established a large operation just east of town. Others went into the business as well. After World War I, trucks replaced the heavy wagons drawn by teams of oxen or mules. By the 1930s there were ten quarries and five finishing plants, making Llano what some called "the granite capital of Texas."

World War II, however, caused a slowing down. Railroad rates were unfavorable. F.M. Cassady, the granite dealer whose office is now Jeannette's Bakery, closed in 1942. T. W. Norton held out, but he died in 1948.

But by then there was another boom in the county. With the completion of Buchanan Dam in 1937, newcomers began to move in. A bank went up on the square in 1973. Earl and Ann Ruff took the old Badu House, formerly a bank on the North Side, and created an attractive country inn in 1980. The area around the courthouse square was entered into the National Register of Historic Places four years later.

And, from the first, it has been the Oatman family who have starred here. John Oatman was the first to arrive in 1853. His son developed the town. Another son, Hardin, was a country doctor. But it was Hardin's grandson, Wilburn, born in 1869, who practiced law here for many years, figured in all the local affairs, and wrote a county history that sums up most of them. His book was published after his death in 1967, but his son and grandaughter, Wilburn, Jr. and Sarah Oatman Franklin, have continued to be very active on behalf of the town and have also continued to reprint Wilburn's original manuscript and to add more material of their own. It is the Oatman family who are the torchbearers here.

ARCHITECTURE: SANDSTONE AND GRANITE

At first there were sandstone buildings here, similar to those in Mason, Art, and Castell. The sandstone was available four miles east and was brought in by oxcart. Also handmade bricks were manufactured, beginning in the early 1880s.

After use of granite in the state capitol, sparing use was made of it here in foundations and trims. The courthouse of 1892 is a fabulous combination of handmade brick and pink granite. The Badu House, formerly the First National Bank on the North Side, is red brick with a gray granite foundation and a checkerboard trim of polished and rough gray granite.

By 1900 some buildings were constructed of solid granite. The jail of 1895 is composed of huge blocks of granite, piled up. Likewise is the home of William Fraser, one of the Scots who came over to work on the State Capitol. The rock for Fraser's home came from the Granite Cliff Ranch, seven miles west on the Llano River. The ranch house there, also dating from around 1900, is a marvel of solid granite construction. William Fraser probably supervised the construction of these three buildings.

Nothing else went up to compare. By 1908 local builders had reverted to the local sandstone, much softer and easier to handle. The Masonic Lodge of that year has walls of golden sandstone, but it does show gray granite in its foundation and polished columns.

Llano flirted with other styles - a tiny Mission office in 1910, a Spanish Revival hotel in 1929 - but by the 1930s she was marching along with neighboring towns in the use of irregular chunks of local stones set like patchwork quilts in concrete. The Hasse Store of 1938 on Highway 29 shows this trend in its pink granite rubble set in pink mortar.

But it is in the WPA Library on the corner of the square that we find the astounding combination of all the principal building stones in the area. In its walls you see ruddy sandstone and white limestone, but also granite - and granite in the colors of a rainbow. If you look at the combinations on the north side of the building, you will see blue, black, and red, as well as speckled pink and gray. Only in this building, and in the new library of the 1990s that clones this effect, will you see all this together.

Solid granite slabs were used for a bank on the square in 1973. But truly extraordinary is a counter of llanite that Earl and Ann Ruff installed in the bar at the Badu House in the course of their restorations in the early 1980s. Llanite is a variety of granite unique to this area. It comes from a narrow strip just north of town. It cracks and crumbles easily and is not commercially valuable. But to have a counter top done in this granite - dark brown with rusty pink feldspar and light blue quartz - is indeed noteworthy.

LLANO COUNTY COURTHOUSE AND PUBLIC SQUARE

The new courthouse of 1892 reflected the times. It was of local, handmade brick with a marvelous trimming everywhere of pink granite, some smooth and some carved, and also a little white marble, which looks like frosting. Rough granite forms the foundation, outlines the string courses, decorates the windows, climbs the corners as quoins, and makes patterns in the gables. Polished granite provides columns at doors and windows. Granite is everywhere! But the amazing thing is that the bricks and the granite have mellowed to exactly the same color. I love to look at the combinations here. This courthouse is one of my favorites.

The style is Italian Renaissance. The architect was A. O. Watson of Austin. His firm, Larmour and Watson, designed the courthouses in Cameron, Comanche, and Cuero at about the same time. Buildings in this style were usually large, three-story edifices with classical orders at doors and windows, string courses, projecting wings, and hipped roofs. Openings were arched or straight-headed, or both in the same building - different window treatments on each floor, such as we see here.

The courthouse lawn is a large expanse of St. Augustine grass with trees arching overhead, old-fashioned benches, and a gazebo. It is a pleasant place to linger.

Many old stores gather around. The Acme Dry Goods Store has been in the same location for decades. Its building dates back to 1892.

Buttery Hardware Company on the northwest corner was the old Southern Hotel, built as a stagecoach inn in 1880. It continued as a hotel until the early 1950s. Its thick sandstone walls are covered now with stucco.

The Llano Uplift Rock Shop has a wide assortment of items. It was here that I bought a piece of llanite, the granite unique to this area. It was a small piece, polished on all sides. Later I went north to a highway cut on Highway 16 where I managed to find a small piece of rough llanite. This highway cut, nine miles north of Llano, is the only public access to this dark and strangely attractive stone.

At the WPA library on the southwest corner of the square we see a wonderful example of the rough stonework of the 1930s. At first you see limestone, then sandstone, then blue granite, red granite, pink granite - all colors.

Across the street is the bank of 1973 in sleekly polished slabs. The brick Hotel Llano (1929) is next door. It reflected the prosperity of the 20s. The cattle industry was strong and granite finishing plants were still flourishing. The hotel stayed open for decades. It is used now as an annex to the courthouse.

The Masonic Lodge (1908) at the southeast corner of the square held retail space below and meeting areas for the Masons upstairs. The facade shows a somewhat surprising combination of sandstone and gray granite.

WAR MONUMENTS *Northeast and southeast corners of the square*

An old Confederate soldier stands guard on the northeast corner of the square, a World War I doughboy on the southeast corner. In between are memorials to the fallen of other wars. Llano has done full honor to its men and women in uniform.

The statues are popular here. Somehow these men standing guard have a place in the affections of the townsfolk. I once saw a car full of teenagers stop by the World War I soldier, jump out, and pose to have their pictures made in front of him.

The largest crowd in the history of the town gathered in 1916 to dedicate the Civil War soldier. A long time had passed since that war, but Southerners still remembered, and, even fifty years later, wanted their memorial. The Daughters of the Confederacy commissioned the original

Confederate Soldier

pioneer of granite, James K. Finlay, and his sons, to make the monument. The sons, using their father as a model, carved a soldier of the local Confederate gray granite. Not the white granite that you see in Gettysburg - extremely fine-grained and with large sparkly crystals - but a wonderful gray granite, salt-and-pepper speckled, with tiny crystals scattered throughout. The statue was enthusiastically received, considered quite wonderful in its resemblance to the old pioneer. The citizens of the county turned out in record numbers for the dedication speech by Governor James Ferguson, who praised Southern women and spoke of his attachment to the song, "Dixie." Children were excused from school. Confederate veterans joined in the parade from the train station to the square.

This was the first time a Texas governor had made a speech in Llano, but before many years had passed, Governor Dan Moody came to dedicate the World War I doughboy. Standing on a mound of granite boulders, with knees moving forward, arm upraised, the bronze figure symbolizes "over the top." This time the commission had gone to a German sculptor and granite dealer, Frank Teich, who had arrived in Llano in 1900 and started a finishing plant and studio about a mile east of town. His design for this bronze doughboy is complete down to the last detail in his equipment. Teich received commissions to do monuments throughout the South. A marker about him is placed nearby.

A WALK ON OATMAN STREET

I walked down to the cemetery early one morning. I wondered if this wouldn't be a great place for granite tombstones.

I started off from Belle Laning's Fraser House and took up a route south on Oatman Street. The Episcopal church at 1200 Oatman is an early structure, sandstone, started for an academy in 1881 but taken over and finished by the Episcopal Church eight years later. It probably drew from a wide area. Episcopal churches did not fare well in the Hill Country. The nearest one of consequence was in Lampasas.

The modern public school complex at 1400 Oatman embraces an old structure that is worth some attention. The sandstone section in the rear, built in 1887, was the early school in Llano. It is similar to Richard Grosse's school house in Mason, but not as handsome or finely detailed as that one. An addition in granite was added to the front in 1902. It is impressive, but not of the same quality as other contemporary buildings here that are also of solid granite construction.

The cemetery lies due east of this modern school complex. Its entrance faces the back of the school stadium.

The view of the hills behind the cemetery was worth the walk down. I was not disappointed in the markers either. The "granite men" were here, the Finlays and Cassady, and it was fun to see what they would put up. The Mosses, ranchers from the south of the county, had a tombstone with a horse carved on the back side. Another that caught my fancy had a waving American flag, the stripes depicted in rough and smooth granite.

As I thought it might be, this is a marvelous place to see the various colors of the local granite and to observe what can be done with it. The granite here is coarse, and thus difficult to carve. Details for the state capitol were scaled down once the decision was made to use granite instead of limestone.

OLD LLANO JAIL (1895) *700 Oatman. Open during festivals.*

If you walk back up Oatman Street and head towards the river's edge, you see the old jail, a magnificent pile of granite: heavy, Romanesque in character, and probably supervised by the Scot, William Fraser, whose house is around the corner and looks much the same. The granite is in big blocks, laid in even courses. It took at least a year to build it.

LLANO COUNTY LIBRARY (1991) *102 Haynie.*

Adjacent is the new county library, set up in remodeled spaces taken from three old stores. What I found amazing here was that some of the ideas of the 1930s, specifically those of the WPA Library on the square, found their way here. The north wall is another patchwork of irregular chunks of limestone, sandstone, and granite. Who would have thought it? But then who would have thought we would see Tudor houses springing up again either?

LEONARD GRENWELGE PARK *Below bridge over Llano River. Entrance on south side.*

At first you'll see picnic tables overlooking the view. But then you'll see paths leading down. This is one of those special places where you go down to walk at the water's edge, to wade, to look for dikes in the granite bed, to see marshes, wildflowers, piles of sand, little pools of water here and there. Let the kids go down and see what they can find.

This was a favorite swimming hole in the old days. A bathhouse was here. In the county histories, there is even an old photograph showing a baptism here.

LLANO RIVER BRIDGE (1935)

The long bridge over the Llano river is huge, dramatic. It looms over the river and somehow over the town as well. An amble across yields a stunning view back to the courthouse and a number of buildings on the south side.

The town divides neatly here at the river, the southern half and the northern sector. Usually this division makes little difference, but it mattered a great deal in 1935 when the former bridge was torn away by an immense flood. Then, the south side had no lights. The north side, because of a broken water main, had no water. The courthouse, the post office, the doctors and undertakers were on the south side. The railroad was on the north.

The bridge that washed out had been built in 1892 when the railroad built to this point from Burnet. Its iron components came on the rails. But on June 14, 1935, when flood waters rose higher and higher threatening the bridge, townsfolk stood at either end to watch. Suddenly one of the four iron spans was torn off and washed downstream. Then another. And another. Finally, all four spans were gone, as well as two of the massive granite piers.

Everyone was aghast. But one in their number - Hazel Oatman Bowman, Wilburn's daughter, and a news correspondent - had thought to snap pictures as the bridge went down. In a remarkable series, her photographs show the bridge losing its parts. Afterwards she could not get her story out of Llano. She had to wait until the water receded enough for her to go to Fredericksburg by way of Castell.

People got out their boats. Boy Scouts sent hand signals. Buses went to either side and waited for passengers to cross over in a boat. It was months before a new bridge was ready. This time, put up by the Texas Highway Department, the new bridge was a good twelve feet above the flood level of 1935.

LLANO COUNTY MUSEUM *310 Bessemer. Sept-May: Wed to Sat, 10-12, 1:30-5:30. Sun 1:30-5:30. Summer, also open on Tues.*

An old drug store just on the other side of the bridge was converted into the local museum in the 1960s. Here you see a pink granite soda fountain and counter, other county relics, and samples of granites, talc, garnets, and graphite.

The museum also has a cache of books about the area. County chronicles by the Oatman family are here. Wilburn, Sr. spent his last years traveling throughout the county, talking to the old-timers, writing and typing up his findings. His own memories included riding the cattle trails north and, as a college student, rolling into town on the very first train. His son, Wilburn, Jr. and grandaughter, Sarah Oatman Franklin, published his book three years after his death in 1967. They later reprinted it, at the same time adding supplementary chapters.

JEANNETTE'S HOMESTYLE BAKERY *507 Bessemer.*

This little building is a jewel of the Mission Style. Built in 1910, at the height of the rage for Mission, it is stucco with tile decorations and has shaped gable ends on three sides. This was a one-room office for a granite company. The granite sign for the Cassady Grey Granite Company still rests in the yard.

In 1942, F. M. Cassady closed the business, and eventually the little building was converted into a bakery.

The carport in back, the room with the rounded windows, was closed in for more space. Another addition was made in the rear, but the front room remains the same. It now holds the display cases.

Today, Jeannette's Homestyle Bakery offers pigs-in-blanket (called "sausage wraps" here and gone by 10 a.m.) pecan pies, hummingbird cakes (banana, pineapple, pecans), fudge, brownies, fruit bars, apricot struesels, carrot cakes, chess pies. Needless to say, we never pass up a chance to sample the fare.

THE NORTH SIDE

The north side of Llano was put up as a business development in the late 1880s. A group of outsiders, including Henry Exall and J. S. Armstrong of Dallas, wanted to capitalize on the potential of the mining opportunities nearby. They planned a community, laid out streets, and promoted large buildings. Their company, the Llano Improvement and Furnace Company, built an enormous hotel in the middle of what was to be the public square. An elegant bank across the street (the present Badu House) opened in May, 1890.

But their plans did not work out. The projected iron boom failed, and the town of Llano could not support such a building program. The end came with a catastrophic fire in April, 1893. The blaze took almost everything in the Badu Block, the principal business location.

The big hotel went up in flames in 1923. It had been known as the Algona, the Franklin, and then the Don Carlos. The pile of ruins in the center of what had been envisioned as the public square remained until 1951. At that time the William Cameron Company built a lumber yard on the front part of the lot.

The Badu House (the First National Bank) was sold to N. J. Badu in 1898. The bank continued operations below, while Badu's family lived upstairs. The First National Bank closed in 1904, but the State Bank of Llano moved there in 1907. Later, after that bank closed, the family took over the whole house. They stayed until 1980, when they sold the house to Earl and Ann Ruff of Houston, who converted it into a country inn. Ann Ruff, a noted guidebook writer, described it in an article for *Texas Highways Magazine* as "a huge red brick and granite block that looked like a mausoleum with windows."

Several buildings behind the Badu House were reconstructed from the business block after the firestorm in 1893, but later they were leveled by a tornado. After that the North Side had little to show from the boom years.

One other spot deserves attention. The Dabbs Hotel was a boarding house for the rail men. They would climb off the train every afternoon at the end of the run from Giddings and Austin, stay overnight, and then board again the next morning. Its location at 112 E. Burnet is adjacent to the former tracks, the passenger and freight depots. The tracks were pulled up years ago, and both of the depots are now gone.

CHAMBER OF COMMERCE   *700 Bessemer, 915/247-5354.*

EVENT: LLANO COUNTY RODEO *1st full weekend in June. Robinson City Park, 2 miles W. on FM 152.*

Rodeo is a natural here in cattle country. The local event, with its bronc riding, roping, and steer riding, goes back to 1919. This is how rodeo was meant to be - in the open air.

EVENT: LLANO HERITAGE DAY *3rd Sat in Oct. Courthouse Square.*

Women spin, churn butter, and make cheese. Blacksmiths shoe horses. Buckskinners set up camp. Musicians strike up old-fashioned tunes. Food vendors ply their fare. On that day the square is full of activity.

LODGINGS: FRASER HOUSE INN (1900) *207 E. Main 915/247-5183.*

This is one of my favorite places, where I go to read, to write, to be alone. Belle Laning is a marvelous host. The house intrigues me. I settle into one of the big rooms

FraserHouse

upstairs, curl up in bed to read, look out at the lights on the other side of the river, wake up in the morning to coffee brewing and Belle's open doors to the front porch and the back terrace. She serves breakfast in her cozy dining room, and it is always something good, an omelet or French toast.

The house itself is one of the extraordinary structures in the Hill Country because it is granite of solid masonry construction. It was built by one of the master stone masons who came from Scotland to work on the state capitol in Austin, William Fraser from Aberdeen. He married a Llano native, Laura Griffin, and built this house for her around 1900.

He built with huge blocks of granite laid up in even courses, with wide and narrow bands alternating. In the lower front of the house are two bay windows, and the stonework seems especially precise around these.

Belle Laning has an interesting collection of country antiques. She decided to put floral fabrics on all the walls, and this provides a balance to the rather severe effect of the granite.

LODGINGS: BADU HOUSE (1890) *601 Bessemer*
915/247-4304.

The Badu House was of course the old First National
Bank on the North Side. The block here burned in 1893,
and six years later this building was sold to N. J. Badu. He
was a French immigrant to the United States who had
come to Llano as the manager of the Algona Hotel across
the street. After buying the house he settled into a long
career of promoting the minerals in the area. He died in
1936, his services held here at the house as was the
custom at the time.

Badu's daughter, Tillie, kept house for him after Mrs.
Badu died. Tillie was married to M. M. Moss of the
southern Llano County ranching family. At length, it was
Tillie's granddaughter who sold the house to Earl and Ann
Ruff of Houston in 1980. They appreciated the design of
the exterior with its handsome gray checkerboard of
granite set against red brick and its elegant doorways in
the style of the Italian Renaissance. Inside they used the
banking rooms in front for dining, retaining the white
marble floors and the shutters at the windows that roll up
and down. Ann put wallpapers here to soften the austerity
of the former bank. She arranged some of her family's
antiques upstairs. Earl put in his famous bar of llanite,
the rare granite found only in this area.

Earl died soon after the inn opened, and Ann sold the
property in 1985. Although it has continued under other
management, the inn still looks the way the Ruffs left it.
There are five bedrooms and a two-bedroom suite at the
front of the building. Breakfast is served in the dining
room, the main banking room. The white marble floor
remains, as well as a fireplace added by the Badus, and
Ann Ruff's coordinated wallpapers.

RESTAURANT: LAIRD'S BAR-B-Q *1600 Ford, closed Mon,
Tues.*

We have been enjoying Kenneth Laird's operation since
he was working out of his home across the street from the
Junior High School. We ate there several times in a little
house in the back yard. We remarked then on the superb
beans, the contribution of his Hispanic mother-in-law.

Then he moved to a larger house nearby, also on Ford Street, added a small deck in front, and set up his pits in the yard. We arrived on a Sunday noon and found people waiting in line. Some were taking out boxes of food for Sunday dinner at home. Others were eating there. We took our plate lunches out to a spot at a picnic table on the deck and soon Kenneth Laird's mother-in-law was coming around with a tray of delicious chocolate cake - a small piece for everyone, their treat, "a little something extra," she said. An old German woman there told us this was Mahagony Cake. She promised to send us the recipe.

Kenneth Laird came out to the pits from time to time to check on the meat. He explained how barbecue is cooked here - not smoked in the German style, but cooked directly over mesquite coals. These coals are prepared first in a fire-box and then moved over to the pit. The meat rests 30 inches above the coals, and the cover is 6 inches above the meat. This is the old cowboy method. The meat is unusually good. Laird says, "Everyone in Llano cooks this way, but no one in Austin."

RESTAURANT: BROTHER'S B-B-QUE *405 W. Young (Hwy. 29) Closed Wed.*

Everything is equally good at Brother's, but the setting is quite different. Jack Graham built his pits by the side of his brother's service station on Highway 29. When we first went it was a tiny operation, but later he had added a front room. He said the publicity in *Texas Monthly Magazine* had made it possible.

RESTAURANT: COOPERS OLD TIME PIT BAR-B-Q *604 W. Young (Hwy. 29) Open daily.*

Coopers is the old-time place where the others learned. It was started by Tommy Cooper in 1964. His father, George, ran Coopers Bar-B-Q in Mason. After Tommy Cooper was killed in a car wreck in 1979, Kenneth Laird was in charge here for a short time.

Expect superior meat here. You'll also find a large selection, including pork and goat. Just as in Mason, the folks here raise the lid of an enormous pit and you pick what you want.

RESTAURANT: INMAN'S KITCHEN *809 W. Young (Hwy. 29) Closed Sun, Mon.*

Inman's is not in the same league with the others. It is too plush - carpet on the floor, curtains at the windows, wallpaper. But the beans and vegetables are good, the brisket is tasty, and the bread is homemade. The main advantage to this place is that it is more apt to be open at night than the others.

Highland Lakes

I was driving along on Highway 29 with a friend when suddenly she exclaimed: "Let's go up and see the dam!" So up we went. Buchanan Dam is huge, overpowering, dramatic, one of the largest multiple-arch dams in the world, built in the 1930s with a great deal of manpower, impounding thousands of acres. You can walk across it for panoramic views, or you can drive down to the base for a different perspective.

But my friend and I contented ourselves that day with walking around the compound at the top of the hill, admiring the old granite administration building of the 1930s, and then seeing the photographs of the construction of the dam in a small museum.

The brief detour was a good introduction to the whole area. Of the government projects in this area, Buchanan Dam was first, in 1937. Others dams down the Colorado River followed, then Inks Lake State Park, the National Fish Hatchery, Longhorn Cavern. The federal government provided funds for all of these in the late 1930s.

In 1982, a private concern started boat tours up Lake Buchanan into the upper reaches of the Colorado River. Now what you can't see by land you can see by water. The *Vanishing Texas* cruises take you past inlets of the numerous spring-fed creeks that feed the river and past spectacular waterfalls. It is on these cruises that you look for eagles in the dead of winter. And, indeed, you may spot one.

In any case, the worst winter weather is fine for a trip down here. This is eagle-watching time. Longhorn Cave is a constant 64 degree, regardless of the temperature outside. When the weather's bad, the wildflowers are a long way off, plan to come here.

HIGHLAND LAKES: 1937 - 1951

In 1931, private interests were building a dam across the Colorado River thirteen miles west of Burnet. Electric lines had come up from a generator at a dam in Marble Falls, a branch railroad stretched up from the line between

205

Burnet and Llano, fifteen hundred men were employed.
The dam would provide flood control and make electricity,
both boons for the Hill Country. But with the economic
turndown in 1932, the Insull Company, which owned
controlling shares, slid into bankruptcy and this dam went
into receivership. It closed down at once. The men went
home, the dam forty per cent finished.

In the fall of that year the nation elected Franklin D.
Roosevelt as president. He supported the idea of cheap
electricity for the masses, and, soon after his
inauguration, he pushed through the establishment of the

Tennessee Valley Authority, a government sponsored complex of twenty-one dams near Muscle Shoals, Alabama, site of a World War I installation that had lain idle for 15 years because of disputes between public and private interests. Should water rights be reserved for private industry or were these rights within the public sector? FDR came down on the side of the latter.

In short order Texas followed suit with a Lower Colorado River Authority set up by the state legislature. Through the LCRA, PWA (Public Works Administration) grants could be channeled towards completing the dam on the Colorado River and other projects as well. By July 1936, the LCRA had bought out the Insull Company and work began again on the dam, which was eventually named Buchanan Dam for Representative James Buchanan, who was instrumental in getting the grant. For the dedication, in the fall of 1937, Secretary of the Interior Harold Ickes came to speak. He praised the use of the nation's natural resources to enhance the lives of all its citizens. He was followed on the stand by the new congressman from the area, the young Lyndon B. Johnson. After Buchanan's sudden death in February 1937, Johnson was elected to take his place.

Buchanan had succeeded in obtaining the second dam, Inks, in 1936, but later Johnson played a big role in the others dams down the river that made this area into a miniature TVA. The Highland Lakes, as they came to be known, included Mansfield Dam that formed Lake Travis (1936-1940), Tom Miller Dam that impounded Lake Austin (1938-1940), the Alvin Wirtz Dam for Lake LBJ (1949-1950), and the Max Starcke Dam (1949-1951) for Lake Marble Falls.

Only the huge Mansfield Dam and its long reservoir of 64 miles is designed primarily for flood control, but all the dams produce electricity, ranging from one to three generating units at each facility. The whole system is monitored very carefully, the generators operated from a central control at Buchanan Dam, waters allocated with great precision, balancing downstream users with upstream concerns. Cities and industries pay a higher price, but are guaranteed water in case of drought. Agricultural users pay less, but may be "interrupted."

The LCRA continues as a fifteen-member board appointed by the Governor. The Colorado River here is considered a "harnessed resource" supplying electrical power (now only about seven per cent of the demand), flood control, and water storage.

HYDROELECTRIC POWER

Getting the dams built was one thing, but getting electricity out to the people was another. For cities and towns, power was available almost at once. Electricity from Buchanan Dam went out to Austin in 1938. Burnet and Marble Falls made their applications in the same year.

In the countryside, however, it was considerably more difficult. Farm houses were not already wired, and farming families did not always understand the advantages of electrical appliances.

Roosevelt pushed through the REA (Rural Electrification Act) in 1935. Under this act, the utility companies were to make power available to farmers. As it became clear that this would not happen, the law was changed a year later to give preference to cooperatives of farmers. They could finance the wiring with self-liquidating loans. If they did not take advantage of this opportunity, though, the utililty companies could step in.

A major snag in this plan for the Hill Country was the low density of the population, the number of users within a linear mile. The requirement was three good users per mile. This was estimated to guarantee the repayment of the loan with 25 years.

Burnet had its lights, and Marble Falls, as indeed they had before Buchanan and Inks Dams. But not Johnson City and smaller places, not farms and remote corners of the counties.

It was with this project that young Congressman Lyndon Johnson became closely involved. The Pedernales Electric Cooperative (PEC) - representatives from Burnet, Blanco, Llano, Gillespie, and Hayes Counties - was formed in 1938, meetings were held, and a group was organized to sign up users. The fact that a five dollar bill had to accompany each signature slowed progress. Johnson came to the meetings, cajoled, pleaded, reminded the workers that if the cooperative failed then the Texas Power and Light Company would step in and offer rates that people could not afford. At a picnic on July 4th, he promised, "I'll get it for you." But how?

208

Through Thomas Corcoran he arranged an audience with FDR. Robert Caro in his *The Years of Lyndon Johnson: the Path to Power* relates that Roosevelt gave his permission to fudge the rule, adding, "Those folks will catch up to that density problem because they breed pretty fast".

With the loan from the REA approved, workers started to dig the posts and string the wires. The entire job had to be completed before anyone could turn on their electricity. And then someone shouted, "The lights are on!" It was a magical moment.

At an Appliance Fair in 1940 people learned more about the uses of electricity. More than light bulbs, it was pumps and indoor plumbing. It was milking machines and electric sheep-shearing equipment. It was radios, movies, and fans.

Texas Power and Light sold out their interests in ten counties to the LCRA in January 1939. Today the service area of the Authority is 58 counties. Only seven per cent of the electricity comes from thirteen generators at the dams; the rest is produced from natural gas and coal.

BUCHANAN DAM   *Hwy. 29, 13 miles W. of Burnet. LCRA Museum: Mon-Fri, 8-4:30, Sat, Sun 1-4. For guided tours of the powerhouse, Ph: 1-800/776-5272.*

Sometimes it's hard to park up by the dam because many visitors come. Some want to walk along the top of the dam for a glorious view of the thirty-mile lake. Others visit the LCRA Museum to see a gallery of photographs showing how the dam was constructed, the granite ridges in the river that formed part of the dam, the tents where the workers lived. Quotes from people who remember are sprinkled throughout the gallery, and, in an adjoining room, is a video presentation of interviews with people who were there: members of the LCRA commission, ranchers whose land was taken, construction workers, their wives.

A photograph of the dedication of the dam in 1937 shows the railroad spur twisting along beside the dam, a speakers' stand with copious patriotic bunting, and below it a sea of hats. It was an era when both men and women went out with their heads covered.

On a stroll around the grounds you will notice the administration building of the 1930s, granite with stone sills and lintels, exposed rafters. A peek inside reveals a huge fireplace in a large reception room. Doors open out to a long terrace overlooking the lake. A friend in Mason remembers neighborhood groups going there. She says, "It was a special place for people in the whole area to enjoy."

INKS LAKE STATE PARK *9 mi. E. of Burnet on Hwy. 29, 3 mi. S. on Pk. Rd. Admission. For reservations for camping, Ph: 512/389-8900 (M-F, 9-6).*

Inks Dam, Inks Lake, and Inks Lake State Park were named for Roy Inks, a dynamic young leader in the effort to get the dams built. He served as one of the original members of the first board of the LCRA. His death in 1935 was untimely - this young man of 46 years, Mayor of Llano, owner of a successful car dealership there. Immediately a move was made to name the second dam for him.

The LCRA donated 1200 acres on Inks Lake to the State Parks Department after the completion of the dam. In 1940 a unit of the CCC arrived to build roads, a boat dock, picnic facilities, but their efforts were cut short by the Second World War. The national focus was shifting towards the war. In 1942, Congress closed off the CCC.

This park is an utter delight, very beautiful and very popular. It is tucked into an area of gneiss, the metamorphosed rock that lies next to the granite of the Llano Uplift. Gneiss looks somewhat like granite; it is the same color as pink granite, but its texture is finer. The rough gneiss hills are weathered and carved by erosion. The trees, oaks and cedars, are low. Hiking trails fan off in several directions. The blue water of the lake is never far away.

I have friends who like to camp here. They find spots near the water where they can easily amble a short distance away for a swim. One of these friends once brought me here for a picnic and then showed me how to hike up past Devil's Waterhole in the northern part of the park. There are dikes in the gneiss there. Farther up, a waterfalls splashes in the creek that cuts down to form a cove in the lake.

NATIONAL FISH HATCHERY, INKS LAKE   *Off Pk. Rd. 4,*
just S. of state park. Mon-Fri 8-4. Closed on weekends
and holidays.

Close to Inks Dam is a fish hatchery built by the
National Youth Administration (NYA) in the late 1930s.
Fish for warm waters - black bass, bluegills, crappie, and
catfish - are propogated in large earthern pools, then used
to restock the lakes.

A glance up the hill at the structures of the 1930s
reveals an attractive compound of stone buildings,
probably of gneiss, with clean lines and good proportions.
The Dallas architect, David Williams, was chief architect
and assistant administrator of the NYA, and one likes to
think that people of his sort designed the government
buildings of that era.

LONGHORN CAVERN   *6 mi. S. of Burnet on Hwy. 281, 6*
mi. W. on Pk. Rd. 4. Open daily dawn to dusk. Tours on
the hour, 10-5. Call for winter schedule. No tours
Christmas Day, Christmas Eve. Ph: 512/756-6976.
Admission.

Efforts to develop Longhorn Cavern began about the
same time as the building program at Buchanan Dam. In
1931 the cave and 639 acres were acquired by the fledgling
state parks department. Very little money was available to
either buy or develop those first parks. This was only the
fourth in the system. Convict labor was brought in to
clear passages and ready the cave for visitors. It opened on
Thanksgiving Day, 1932.

Only the three large "rooms" in the cave were shown,
and these had been known for decades. Comanches had
used the spaces in the nineteenth century, and area
residents knew the Indians were there because they saw
smoke rising from a large crevice in the ground. In the
1920s a rancher laid a hardwood floor in one of the large
rooms and opened the Longhorn Ballroom on Saturday
nights. Nearby another space was filled with bleachers
and used for "air-conditioned" church services on Sunday
mornings. (Our guide said: "Binge and purge".)

But those three big rooms - the Indian Council Room,
the ballroom, and the area for church services - were all
that were ready for the dedication in 1932. Other passages

211

were filled with mud, and it was not until the CCC replaced the convicts (who had not been liked by the neighbors) that the present trails were made, tons of debris were excavated, and a lighting system was installed.

The CCC workers used the excavated dirt and stone to build park roads and administration buildings. They closed up four of the five existing entrances to the cave and provided instead a dramatic new entrance that passed under a natural bridge.

It is this entrance that you approach for a tour of the cave. It is set attractively in a garden of indigenous plants. You descend stone stairs, pass under the natural bridge, and then into the mouth of the cave, which itself is set in a limestone formation. Soon the guide points out a wall of calcite crystals: soft formations, some quite large, all extremely dirty before they were cleaned. A small bat may be shown. Only a few live in the cave.

After the three big rooms, and lively comments there, the tour moves through narrow passages to areas smoothed and polished by underground streams. Longhorn is a river cave formed by underground streams, not seepage. For this reason you see fantastic shapes formed by rushing water, but not many stalactites or stalagmites, the sometimes fantastic formations in those caves formed by dripping water. In a beautiful area, known as the Hall of Marble, where the walls and ceilings are polished smooth and tinted soft desert colors, the guide points out how far up the walls the mud and silt extended, the debris excavated by the CCC.

Up at the top again, visitors can see various kinds of rock from the cave in the administration building from the 1930s. Since a new headquarters was built in 1967, this structure now serves as a museum of the CCC in Texas.

Outside you will notice banded stonework of limestone and darker materials, some *palisado* (or picket) work, a terrace with a built-in bench, stone stairs climbing up to a viewing platform, and a wooden balcony on the other side.

Inside, you'll see broad cedar lintels above the openings, heavy wooden doors with exaggerated nailheads, and a corner fireplace with rounded hearth and a conical flue. But most unusual is the stonework here. At the base is a band of limestone, then another of granite, but above that are calcite crystals that had been brought out of the cave. Above that - masterfully crafted - is a row of dentils or brackets of a dark material, probably flint, again from the cave.

This very unusual building was designed by Sam Vosper, a New Jersey native, trained at the Pratt Institute in Brooklyn, who made his way down to Texas in the 1920s, became chief architect for the "new campus" at Texas A&M in the early 30s, but then got a job with the National Park Service. At A&M he was known for his gifts with ornamentation, and also for his travels to see old Texas buildings, especially those in the Spanish tradition. Here his interests undoubtedly merged. Instead of designing for ornaments then made of cast stone as he had at Texas A&M, he had a wealth of real stone to work with, and lots of different kinds. And he put to use his ideas from the Spanish tradition: outside stone stairs with contrasting coping, the whimsical viewing platform at the top of the stairs, the wooden balcony, the corner fireplace, and of course the studded wooden doors. The hand of a master was at work here.

ROCK SHOP *about 3.5 miles W. of Burnet on Hwy. 29. Ph: 512/756-6253.*

Another sort of experience awaits the visitor to the rock shop off Highway 29, a few miles west of Burnet. Dolph Planche displays many kinds of rocks and gemstones. He will tell you about them and may even offer to show you his shop in back. Once he talked to us about two big pieces of llanite in his front yard. He poured water on them so we could see the blue crystals. He said he thought llanite was not "true granite" because it weathered differently.

VANISHING TEXAS RIVER CRUISES *3 mi. W. of Burnet on Hwy. 29, 14 mi. N. on FM 2341. Daily at 11 A.M., if enough reservations. Reservations required. 3 hour tours. Admission. Ph: 512/756-6986 or 800/728-8735.*

American bald eagles coast down to Texas on the tail winds of cold fronts. The colder and rawer it is, the more apt you are to see them. They favor undeveloped areas like this where they can fish undisturbed for their food.

Maybe a thousand make it down to Texas every year, but along stretches of the Mississippi River, they are a

common sight. At Clarksville, north of St. Louis, they cluster close to a dam and catch the stunned shad that have passed through the gates. As many as eighty may be seen at once.

Here on Lake Buchanan a Llano County rancher started river cruises in 1982 to spur interest in the scenery and the wildlife. Eagles were not much of a consideration at first. But then a woman from the Austin Nature Center spotted one, and people began to take notice. When the rancher ordered a larger, partly enclosed boat for the trips, the new name for it was the *Texas Eagle*.

Our guide gave a running commentary about the lake and its history. He pointed out cliff wrens and red-tailed hawks, deer on the hillsides. He explained about the short, spring-fed creeks that empty into the river, and showed us some wonderful waterfalls. The boat went up 24 miles from its dock, 8 miles into the river. I would have liked to have seen Gorman Falls, but the boat turned around 6.5 miles short of that point.

ANNUAL EVENT: MIDWINTER BALD EAGLE SURVEY
2nd Sat in January. Sponsored by the Texas Parks and Wildlife Dept. Call to volunteer. Ph: 903/566-1626.

Texas bird watchers participate in the annual tally of eagles throughout the nation. The sites in Texas range from the Llano Estacado to the Gulf of Mexico. Buchanan Lake is divided into seven zones with a counting boat in each. The count lasts a little over an hour, then the participants gather to compare maps and determine the count. A count of 24 would be high for Buchanan Lake.

LODGINGS: LAST CHANCE RESORT *Off Park Road 4, 3 mi. S. of entrance to Inks Lake State Park. Ph: 512/756-7766.*

A few years ago a young journalist for the the *Dallas Morning News* ventured out for a New Year's celebration in the Hill Country. She wanted to see the vaunted eagles on Lake Buchanan, and her group found rooms here at new condominiums overlooking the upper reaches of Lake LBJ, just below Inks Dam. They saw eagles, quite a few of them, on a *Vanishing Texas* cruise. On New Year's Day they toured Longhorn Cavern and found "a roaring fire and free coffee" when they emerged.
We followed her lead and found the new condominiums at the Last Chance Resort just as she said - clean and attractive, with wide decks looking out into old pecans and over a pleasant view of the lake.
Snow Birds come down from wintry Michigan or Iowa to spend the cold months in one of the units. Monthly rates are available.

LODGINGS: THE ANTLER'S, KINGSLAND *1001 King St. Ph: 915/388-4411 or 800/388-0007.*

Just as this book was finished, word came that the old railroad hotel at Kingsland was open for business. The Antlers Hotel has long held a place in the imaginations of its neighbors. It was first opened as a hotel on the Austin and Northwestern Railroad in 1901. Its location was near the spot on the Colorado River where the railroad bridge crossed.

In 1923 a family bought the hotel for a vacation headquarters, but by the early1990s they were gone and the place was for sale. Now new owners have restored the wooden porches that encircle the building. They have arranged the little rooms upstairs into suites. Downstairs, in the big lobby and dining room, they have retained the pot-bellied stoves.

Burnet

INTRODUCTION TO BURNET

Burnet is the ultimate place of revivals. Again and again the town has risen up and fallen back, only to rise again. The most recent change of this sort came in the early 1990s. At that time Burnet was a sleepy little town, but in July 1992, an excursion train from Austin came roaring into town on weekends. Passengers spilled out of its cars and fanned out in all directions. Burnet suddenly came alive.

Restaurants sprouted near the depot. Shops opened around the square. Even a park with delightful trails along Hamilton Creek was developed a few blocks west of the square.

All this is within easy walking distance of the depot. Passengers, alighting at noon and reassembling around three o'clock, have ample time to look about. They soon notice a handsome stone Masonic Lodge built in 1854 just south of the square. They also quickly spot the 1884 jail, northeast of the square. Some even pause for a moment to study the courthouse, a severely angular granite box of the 1930s.

This courthouse rose during another period of high activity. Burnet had languished during the early years of the Depression, but federal programs provided a bonanza

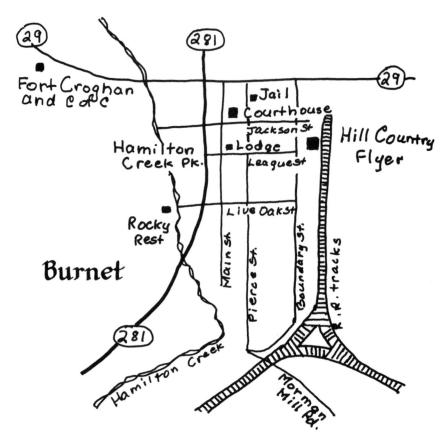

here. Dams on the Highland Lakes, electric lines, and highways meant work for every able-bodied man in the county. There were also WPA grants for a water system, sewers, paved streets, and this courthouse.

HISTORY

Just fifty miles from Austin, this was the frontier after that town was founded in 1839. Settlers moved west along the Colorado River, some coming to claim headrights they were granted as veterans of the Texas War for Independence from Mexico in 1836, others buying or negotiating for those claims. Land was cheap - $.50 per acre. Indians were an ever present danger, and many were killed out here as they had been east of Austin. But new land beckoned.

By 1848, claims had been settled, lands surveyed, and a Texas Ranger station established three miles south of the present Burnet. Since the leader of the Rangers, Henry McCulloch, was also the administrator of the claim, he was in a position to sell it when a young man came out to visit his brother-in-law who was stationed there. Samuel Holland, twenty-two years old and a recent arrival in Texas from Georgia, liked what he saw and arranged to buy the grant of John P. Rozier of Bastrop County. He paid fifty cents an acre for the spread. 1280 acres. Then out he came with his few possessions, the first settler in the future county.

Not long after this the federal government moved to establish a chain of forts along the Indian frontier as part of its responsibility in accepting Texas into the Union. Holland balked at a fort here, three miles south of the present Burnet on Hamilton Creek, so scouts selected a site farther north on the creek, on land that belonged to John Hamilton of Travis County. About this time the Hamilton grant was leased to Peter Kerr to graze cattle. Kerr, a native of Pennsylvania who had come to Texas in 1824, soon arranged to buy the claim (2,250 acres at $.50 an acre). He leased the western portion to the government and encouraged the growth of a town on the east side of Hamilton Creek. By the time the fort was abandoned in 1853, as part of the general movement westward, Burnet County was organized, the town of Burnet was the county seat, and Peter Kerr had realized considerable funds from the sale of lots. He made more money a year or two later by selling off parts of the fort. In his agreement with the government, all government buildings and improvements that were not removed would revert to him.

Two young men from Kentucky were instrumental in forming the town. Logan Vandeveer and William Magill had come as suppliers to the fort and they stayed on as leaders in the fledgling community. They had ridden their horses down to Texas as young men and fought together in the Texas Revolution. They remained close friends, even naming children after each other. Vandeveer built the stone lodge, the first substantial building in town, in 1854. His store was on the first floor, and he served as postmaster. He also started the first school.

It was Logan Vandeveer and William Magill and their families who went down early to make arrangements for a Fourth of July picnic at "the great falls" in 1855. (The site of the present Marble Falls.) They built a large brush arbor and arranged seats and a speakers' stand beneath it. The picnic was one of those wonderful occasions when everyone in the county was invited, when men barbequed great hunks of beef and pork, when millers gave flour and women made up big loaves of bread, when farmers brought loads of roasting ears or watermelons, and when those who made pies excelled with dewberries, wild grapes, or plums.

This description of the picnic comes from Noah Smithwick's *The Evolution of a State* (1900). Smithwick was living at the Mormon Mill south of Samuel Holland's property. He had come out to Burnet County to work as an armorer at the fort, but later he bought the mill from a colony of Mormons when they decided to move farther west. His recollections, gathered by his daughter at the time of his death, remain a classic in Texas literature.

Smithwick goes on to call the 1855 Fourth of July Picnic "the greatest event the country had ever enjoyed." His fourteen-year-old son read the Declaration of Independence. A band consisting of a "lone fiddle" played "Yankee Doodle" and "Hail Columbia." Then Dr. Thomas Moore, who hailed from Kentucky as did Smithwick himself, was "orator of the day." Smithwick said of Moore's speech: "the doctor's sonorous voice rang out the paean of liberty above the nodding heads of the weary audience, mingling with the roar of the water and reverberating among the distant hills." Then, it was dinner and dancing under the arbor on a thick layer of sawdust. The reels were called out until dawn.

Another talented writer in this area, Ottilie Fuchs Goeth, remembers that her family floated down the river on a raft, with loud cheering upon their arrival. She recalled "everyone was in high spirits." But then she adds, "No one was aware of the cloud forming on the political horizon; all were still true to the Union." Her opinion was that this was "still was the Texas of old."

But the passions of the Civil War were to change that Texas forever, to shatter that early sense of community. Dark suspicions, ugly accusations, and threats ensued. Some fled, some were ambushed and killed.

By 1861, Dr. Moore, the long-winded orator at the picnic, was down in Austin as a member of the Secessionist Convention. Smithwick, strongly anti-Secessionist, pulled out early for California, leaving Burnet on April 14, 1861, the day Union forces evacuated Fort Sumter. Adam Johnson, a man who would figure prominently later on, was off to volunteer for Confederate forces in Kentucky. Logan Vandeveer died during a cattle drive in 1855, but William Magill, Samuel Holland, and the Germans south of the Colorado River served in the border guard to protect against Indian raids. Magill did lose a son during the war. Fifteen-year-old John was out looking for stock with several companions. They were surprised by an Indian attack and John was shot from the saddle. Samuel Holland also lost his nephew and namesake when he was killed as he and a group of others took a load of corn and wheat to the Mormon Mill to be ground.

Later, the situation became tighter when conscription was instituted. Some of the Germans volunteered then. Ottilie Fuchs Goeth's brothers moved away after receiving the message from a friend that they were no longer safe. One hid in a safe haven in East Texas. The other volunteered for an artillery unit in the Confederate Army. Her husband, Carl Goeth, worked in the Quartermaster's Corps, making saddles. They might be Unionist at heart, but the Germans here hid that fact and helped the Confederate cause in one way or another. Some were teamsters. Some supplied horses and mules. And, of course, some hid.

In general, it was too late to leave. Vigilantes saw to that. They had told Smithwick they would "get him" when they could get organized and get around to it. Smithwick did not stick around to find out, but others were not so fortunate. John Scott, the county's first judge, was threatened anonymously with the message that he was no longer safe. He was killed as he crossed the county line on the way to Mexico. Though a Yankee, he had helped supply the Confederate effort and he had four sons serving in the Confederate Army.

Scott's body, like those of others, was thrown down into "Dead Man's Hole," a sinkhole that went straight down at least 300 feet, from which the remains were not exhumed until after the end of the war. Scott's widow recognized his remains from his "peculiar jaw bone and teeth."

Scott, from New York and New Jersey, had owned no slaves. Others - Smithwick, Moore, Holland, and Kerr - had owned one or two. Magill had five. In 1860, there had been 235 slaves in the county, divided among 70 owners.

The county voted solidly against Secession, 248 - 159. This was not prime territory for plantations, or a slave economy. But after the war started, anyone not "for the South" was suspect and was in danger of being killed by the "bushwhackers," those who shot from the bush, or ambushed. Ottilie Fuchs Goeth speaks of them as "Fire Eaters."

When the war was finally over, Adam Johnson came back, blinded, and started a store with John Moore, the twenty-five-year old son of Dr. Moore. Johnson traveled to Austin for supplies, taking along a small boy for "eyes." But before long Federal troops arrested Dr. Moore, his son, and a group of others. They were accused of activities on behalf of the Confederacy and taken off to prison in Austin for seventy-eight days. After they returned, the Moores packed up and left Burnet for good. Off they went to Waco.

Adam Johnson, now frightened, fled out to the wilds of eastern Llano County. He and his family stayed there for three years, long enough for things to cool down. He felt safer out there than he had in Burnet, stating, "I much preferred to face the dangers of Indian raids rather then the meanness and rapacity of the reconstructionists." He herded cattle to market, always taking along someone as "eyes". He tells us in a memorable passage, "I never went out without my shotgun, which, loaded with buckshot, could do full execution even in the hands of a blind man who was practiced in its use."

Johnson's two-story house in Burnet, built for his bride Josephine Eastland in 1860, was at this time used for the "Burnet Male and Female Academy," a private school he and and others had organized in 1866. When the Johnson family returned to Burnet in 1871 they moved back into their home, "Rocky Rest" on Hamilton Creek just west of the square, and the school moved to another location. Johnson opened another store and operated as a land agent, relying on his remarkable memory for the places involved.

It was at this time that he began to gather the circle of relatives and friends who were to play instrumental roles in Johnson's later endeavors. Among these were T. E. Hammond and Emanuel Sampson. Hammond, from South Carolina, arrived in 1871, went to work for Johnson, married Josephine Johnson's sister, and later became a leading lawyer. Sampson, the former sutler at the fort, married Josephine's widowed mother and was serving at the time the Johnsons moved back as the Chief Justice (or county judge).

With the 1880s came a railroad from Austin, the narrow-gauge Austin and Northwestern, the extension of a line from Giddings. There was a flurry of excitement. A bank went up on the square. Merchants tore down their wooden buildings and erected two-story stone structures. But the railroad faltered, faced foreclosure, and was auctioned off in front of the Travis County Courthouse in Austin. Cow country could not support it.

Not long after that, however, the Capitol Commission decided to use the granite at Granite Mountain for the new state capitol. The railroad to Burnet was reinstated, and a link was built down to Granite Mountain. Everything in Burnet was suddenly in high gear. A granite cutting and shaping yard was set up just south of town. Convict labor that had been used for the railroad extension was now ready to work on this granite. Then the international union of granite cutters boycotted the job, sent out notices to cutters not to come, and caused a complete halt in the operations. Some months later, sixty-two Scots were induced to come to Texas to continue the work. The Scots and the convict labor finished the job in 1888.

Adam Johnson had donated seven miles of the right-of-way for the extension to Granite Mountain, and he had guaranteed arranging for the rest of it. The granite itself was given free. The owners of the mountain had despaired of ever being able to do anything with it. As they said: "You couldn't run a single cow on it. Why, you couldn't even trade it for a good saddle horse." Little did they realize that building with granite would become the fashion for government buildings after the completion of the capitol in 1888. Self-respecting courthouses at places like Dallas, Fort Worth, and San Antonio had to have a little, at least a few columns, maybe the foundation, or maybe the whole building of the big blocks, just like the capitol. Needless to say, the owners of Granite Mountain sold out for a fortune in the 1890s, $90,000 for the 640 acres.

But then Burnet fell back. Adam Johnson and his circle directed their energies towards developing Marble Falls. The railroad interests continued the rails from Granite Mountain over to Llano, which became another major granite center. The population of Burnet dropped off.

The next revival came with the 1930s. Two major highways were passing through town, Highway 281 and Highway 29. Dams were going up on the Colorado River. Stumps were coming down in the flood plain. Electric lines were stretching across the land. The CCC was developing Longhorn Caverns nearby. In town, WPA grants were boosting a water system and sewers, paved streets, and a new courthouse. People said that "any able-bodied man" who wanted a job could get one.

A slump followed in the forties. Many people left with the war efforts and never came back. Agricultural efforts lagged. But in the fifties some of the descendants of the pioneers formed an historical society and then bought part of the grounds of the former fort, a hundred years after it was disbanded. They moved in early cabins, including one that had belonged to the Vandeveer family. They even found a desk that had been made at the Mormon Mill.

And so it has been with Burnet, rising up and falling back. It was a great moment in 1992 when an excursion train arrived from Cedar Park, just north of Austin. Back came a train along the same tracks that been built in 1882. And, just as then, folks spruced up around the square, opened shops and restaurants.

We were there once on a Sunday when the train was pulling out. Bells were clanging, passengers were hopping on board, townsfolk were lining the tracks to wave, the locomotive was backing up with a jerk and a jolt. A new spirit was abroad in the land.

BURNET COUNTY COURTHOUSE (1936) *Jackson and Pierce Streets.*

When the citizens of Burnet County had a chance to replace their 1874 stone courthouse, they grabbed the opportunity. A PWA grant smoothed the way in 1935. The owners of Granite Mountain, the Darraghs, gave an exceedingly low bid on the stone - in fact, they lost money on the deal. But they were glad to see the new county courthouse in the local stone, the same pink granite as the state capitol.

The granite here was put up in huge sawn panels. These look as though they were just sliced off the side of

the mountain. My husband said it looked as though
someone had a bar of ice cream and cut down through it.

The roof is flat. Tall piers at the front doors replace
columns. The windows are aluminum. Everything is
perfectly symmetrical. This was the style of the PWA in
those years. Some called it "starved classic." In any case,
it was economical, and it utilized the materials at hand.

Of decoration, there is some, though very little and
quite rustic. Two stylized panels of low relief embellish the
doorways, the larger one at the front door on the eastern
facade. Cowboys and Indians tell the story of the frontier
in angular, hard-edged, incised carvings, the kind of
carving you see on a tombstone. You see only side views of
all the figures. Jan Morris, writing for *Texas Monthly*,

called these "bas-reliefs of pioneering scenes in the
Assyrian mode."

But, inside and out, the building is of a piece. Great
slabs of pink granite without and marble wainscoting and
terrazzo floors within. Aluminum windows, plain doors,
and plain furnishings. A wonderful example of PWA style.
It looks bereft on the Burnet square because nothing in
the surrounding area complements it. The courthouse
would like more trees and some bushes. In fact, I think it
would like to move altogether. I can picture it in Boulder,
Colorado, with wide green lawns and mountains behind.

225

In regard to the floors, I fell for terrazzo after I saw the red and yellow and gray patterns here. A friend calls it "poor man's marble," but no matter. I found the marvelous terrazzo floors in the State Capitol in Austin, installed in the same year as the floors here. I went to see the whimsical patterns in the new section of the Dallas Convention Center. (The new is chipped stone set in an epoxy glue. The older method was chipped stone mixed with cement.)

Then I began to see terrazzo everywhere. It was in schools, office buildings, hospitals. After that I saw the "real thing" in Europe - marble floors, old and worn in the old sections of the Louvre in Paris, new and shiny in the I. M. Pei addition to the Louvre and in the Barcelona airport. But I noticed that in Europe, too, most new floorings are terrazzo. It is practical, it is attractive, it provides lots of color.

THE SQUARE, THE JAIL, THE LODGE *Washington and Pierce Streets*

The buildings around the square don't have much to say to the courthouse. Either they are old, two-story limestone storefronts from the 1880s, or they are postwar buildings such as a library and a bank from 1964. In either case, they can't communicate with a brash granite box from the 1930s.

The best of the buildings from the 1880s is the jail of 1884 at the northeast corner of the square. It was designed by F.E. Ruffini of Austin. It is very similar to the Second Empire courthouse at Blanco. Some say this is a miniature of the other. Both are among the finest of the stone buildings in Texas of that era.

South of the courthouse, at 309 S. Main, is the stone lodge and store of 1854. Built by Logan Vandeveer, one of the town's founders, it was the first substantial stone building in town. It still is a landmark. Not many stone buildings of this caliber remain from the early days in the Hill Country.

Close by, at 108 E. League, is one of the original houses of the early period. The rear section, the rock part, dates from 1856.

"HILL COUNTRY FLYER", AUSTIN AND TEXAS CENTRAL RR *Depot in Burnet, 3 blocks E. of square on Jackson. Sat, Sun, leaves from Cedar Park, north of Austin (Hw. 183 at FM 1431) at 10 A.M. Returns 5:30. Free shuttle buses in Burnet. Ph: 512/477-8464. Admission.*

The "Hill Country Flyer" swoops into town and comes to a stop at its depot three blocks from the square. It comes every Saturday and Sunday at noon. It will stay in Burnet for three hours before the passengers reboard, the whistle blows, and the Flyer is gone again.

Since July 1992, this excursion train has wended its way up the tracks from Cedar Park, north of Austin, on weekends and holidays. A group of volunteers had formed the Austin Steam Train Association and acquired some coach cars and a 1916 locomotive from Southern Pacific. (The engine, retired in 1956, burns waste oil picked up from service stations.)

Since the beginning this train has been met with amazement - and delight - in the Hill Country. Folks come out to wave at the railroad crossings. At least one couple has been married while riding along. A bicycle race in the summertime pit cyclists against the train - 35 miles for the cyclists along Highways 183 and 29, and 33 miles for the train. All speedy cyclists win since it takes two hours for the train.

We tried to see it pass in Bertram one Saturday morning, and storekeepers knew when it came through, around 11:30. We missed it somehow, but that night when we were driving back on Highway 29 we saw some steam rising and then dimly lighted windows rolling along. We realized, with a start, that it was the train! We rushed on to Bertram where we stopped and waited by the tracks. A huge headlight bore down on us. There was a mighty roar as the locomotive passed, whistles screaming. What a thrill!

We found out later there were night runs, Twilight Flyers, on the first and third Saturday nights of the month. (Call for information.)

HAMILTON CREEK PARK *Jackson Street, 2 blocks west of the square*

The path in front of "Rocky Rest" is part of a new development along Hamilton Creek. A park has been created here in a place that no one seems to have considered before. It is quite lovely. Now the local residents come out for a stroll every evening. This is a prime example of how the new excursion train has helped people see the potential here.

ROCKY REST (1860) *404 S. Water Street.*

Along the path through the park, you catch a glimpse of the original home of Adam Johnson. He built it for his bride, Josephine Eastland, in 1860. During the Reconstruction Era he leased it out as a school. The family returned to this home in 1871, but soon their attention was directed towards a new house on a hill east of Burnet, "Airy Mount." (See under Lodgings.)

The house looked different in the Johnsons' day. At that time there was a one-story wooden porch at the door, shutters at the windows. The modern changes are such that you wonder about the antiquity of the house. A tall porch with two-story columns looks like the work of the 1940s. The ungainly second-story window over the door reflects a former doorway to the balcony over the original porch.

FORT CROGHAN MUSEUM *Hwy. 29 W. April 1 to 2nd weekend in October, Mon, Thurs, Fri, Sat 8-5, Sun 1-5. Ph: 512/756-4297.* CHAMBER OF COMMERCE *here as well.*

Fort Croghan was built in the first chain of forts west of Austin, in a line that went from the Rio Grande up to Fort Worth. Like the others, like Fort Worth in fact, it was built of logs. And, again, like Fort Worth, people moved into the buildings after the fort was abandoned.

The federal government leased the land for this and other forts in the west. As noted above, the cattleman Peter Kerr bought the claim here, leased part of it to the government and established a town east of the creek. Later he sold off parcels of the fort grounds with attendant buildings for handsome profits.

And so it was that the larger buildings, the officers' quarters and the hospital, were sold off with a few acres. People lived in them for years. An early school was held here. A stone powder house was built here during the Civil War. But, eventually, the life of the town shifted east. The log buildings of the fort disintegrated. Soon all were gone, except the big hospital, which lasted until 1922. Its logs were sold off as fence posts.

It was not until the 1950s that the descendants of the pioneers in Burnet rallied to buy a portion of the former fort. Of course, they could not recover all of it - properties extending all the way down to the creek - but they developed almost two acres on Highway 29, spruced up the old powder house from the Civil War era (the only old building remaining), and then moved in structures from around the county. They found a stone cottage that Logan Vandeveer had built for his father in the 1850s. This cottage resembles the rear portion of the Galloway House south of the square, which remains in its original location. They found log houses out in the country. They even were able to procure a desk made at the Mormon Mill in the 1850s.

ANNUAL EVENT: FORT CROGHAN DAY *2nd weekend, October.*

A wonderful time to visit the fort is during these special days when costumed guides demonstrate soap-making, weaving, spinning, and the arts of the blacksmith. Children can try their luck on old-fashioned stilts.

ANNUAL EVENT: CHRISTMAS PAST AT FORT CROGHAN *1st and 2nd Sats in Dec, Hwy. 29 W.*

Come in the early evening for a candlelight tour of the fort. The cabins are ablaze with candles and lanterns and fires in the old hearths. Cedar wreaths hang on the gates. Carollers serenade.

ANNUAL EVENT: MAIN STREET BETHLEHEM *1st and 2nd weekends in December, 6-9 P. M. One block S. of Hwy. 29 at Vandeveer St.*

Burnet was early to join its neighbors in the regional lighting project. The special focus here is on a live nativity scene with camels, donkeys, and chickens. Actors play the parts of townsfolk in Jesus's time. They bake bread, pay taxes, or fail to pay taxes and get thrown into jail.

Adam Johnson moved his family up here on the hill in
the early 1880s. The time had come to move away from
what he and Josephine considered an unhealthy spot
down by the creek. The only problem was that Johnson
was too busy with his other projects to get the house
completed. So the family lived in a large stone barn for
several years. Finally, Josephine put her foot down and
Adam finished the house. The last child was born in the
new house. But, Johnson in a hurry did not get up a
second story, as had been his intention. The handsome
stone dwelling is today as he left it - one story only.

The house faces the valley, the site of the new railroad. You don't see much of it from the highway. But the barn sits prominently up on the hill and it is the barn that provides the accommodations for guests today. Three attractive rooms with private baths are available. There's a full kitchen and a large living room, which all the guests share. Breakfast is included. This would be a good place for a family reunion in the Hill Country.

RESTAURANT: RIVERWALK *635 Hwy. 29 W.*

Home of country cooking, waffles for breakfast, a luncheon buffet. Rolls, pies, and cobblers.

MORMON MILL ROAD *South on Boundary Street. Pass under the railroad trestle. Follow signs for FM 340, then Mormon Mill Road to Hwy. 281 in Marble Falls.*

Getting off the main road here may remind you of jaunts on Willow City Loop near Enchanted Rock. The route is paved, though some of it is single-lane. It passes over low-water bridges and through some scenic spots.

This back route takes you past the sites of the pioneers in the area. Three miles south is the farmstead of Samuel Holland, the first permanent settler here. There's a marker at the side of the road.

Eight miles south is the location of the old Mormon Mill. Noah Smithwick owned this property in the 1850s.

Marble Falls

INTRODUCTION TO MARBLE FALLS

You never feel far from the Granite Mountain here. You can look up and see it from many points in town. And you can spot building materials made from it everywhere. You see them in old buildings and new, bungalows with the familiar tapered columns in solid granite and a modern city hall of enormous pink slabs that would be at home in downtown Dallas. One large house was made of rubble left from shaping the blocks of the Texas State Capitol. There's a granite school, banks, churches. Even the popular Blue Bonnet Cafe has its share. The table tops and counters are large pieces of polished granite.

MARBLE FALLS: COMPANY TOWN

After Adam Johnson acquired the land here, he formed a company with relatives and a few friends and began to develop Marble Falls. (See Burnet for the first part of this

Adam Johnson

story.) The principal claim here had been awarded to a Texas patriot killed at the Alamo, and Johnson encountered many obstacles before he was able to obtain the deed for half of it in 1885. The other half was acquired by his business partners in 1886. Johnson then received power of attorney for all of it the following year.

Only a short time elapsed before Johnson formed the Texas Mining and Improvement Company. His partners were his brother-in-law T. E. Hammond, his son Robert, his sons-in-law George Christian and W. H. Badger, Badger's father, and four friends. The charter for the company was filed in Burnet County on July 6, 1887. Within the month the town was surveyed and lots were sold. In 1889, Johnson's company promoted the final spur of the railroad from Granite Mountain, and, in 1891, gave lots as a donation towards a bridge across the Colorado River. His group was also involved in establishing a school up on a hill overlooking the town.

But his dream, a flourishing mill on the river, eluded Johnson. In 1892 he formed the Marble Falls Cotton and Woolen Mills Company and began the construction of a large building, 315 feet by 100 feet, two stories with a basement. He had to go to the East to get money to finish this structure, but then there were no funds for machinery. The spacious and handsome building down by the river's edge stood empty. Johnson had overreached himself. How familiar all this sounds today.

Johnson lost control of the water rights on the Colorado River in 1907. He sold out to C. H. Alexander of Dallas. Four years later second-hand machinery was installed in the mill building, but again insufficient financing caused the venture to fizzle. It was not until 1925 that a working mill was in place at the site. And it was only four years after that, in 1929, that the Insull interests of Chicago bought this mill and its dam to generate the electricity needed at the Buchanan Dam project. As part of a deal with the Lower Colorado River Authority in 1935, the Marble Falls dam was sold again. A factory once again operated here after World War II. But fire destroyed the building in 1964, and ten years later its ruins were removed. Not even the falls in the river remain now. In 1951, "the great falls" were submerged with the fifth dam.

The end of Johnson's company town was in sight when he sold the water rights in 1907. Soon the town voted to incorporate, with Robert Johnson, Adam's son, elected the first mayor. After that the newly incorporated town voted

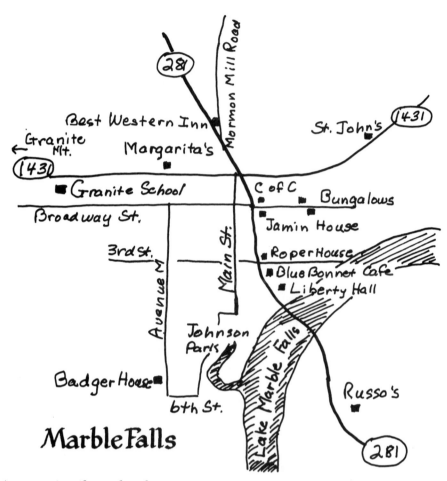

The following text labels appear on the map:

281

Mormon Mill Road

Best Western Inn

St. John's

1431

Granite Mt.

Margarita's

1431

Granite School

C of C

Bungalows

Broadway St.

Jamin House

3rd St.

Main St.

Roper House

Avenue M

Blue Bonnet Cafe

Liberty Hall

Johnson Park

Lake Marble Falls

Badger House

Russo's

6th St.

281

Marble Falls

to acquire the school system. Two years passed before legal matters were settled and a bond issue was passed, but in May, 1909, Marble Falls owned the school on the hill.

Robert Johnson had chosen to live here in Marble Falls in a large wooden house that still stands at Second Avenue and Highway 281, but his father never moved his place of residence from "Airy Mount" in Burnet. By this time, Adam Johnson was old and past his prime. Clearly the momentum shifted to the younger generation after 1907.

But one of his monuments still remains up on the hill above town. The granite school remains open and in use, though it is now surrounded by a modern complex. We went up once to see the old building, walked into the main hallway and studied the class pictures on the walls. We were intrigued with this display. Some of the classes were

235

tiny, others larger. Our class - 1954 - was minute. Marble Falls was just entering its period of growth and expansion then. The last dam on the lakes was completed in 1951, ranchers were selling out to developers, home sites on the Highland Lakes were becoming popular. We could see that the graduating classes increased after that. But this old school stayed as it was, and it is now one of the finest of the old school buildings that survives in this region. I like to think of it as a monument to Adam Johnson, the Confederate general blinded in battle who never let that handicap stand in his way, the aggressive developer and dreamer who founded Marble Falls as a company town.

MAIN STREET

Main Street is in reality Highway 281. That ribbon of concrete built in the 1930s cuts a broad swath through the middle of town and most places of interest are located on or near it.

But another street lies nearby. A block west. A narrower street, shorter, less pretentious. This was the Main Street of old, and it still bears that name. A granite bank building from the 1890s is there. (Second and Main). Venture in today for a look at a modern art gallery.

The bank is in the old style of solid construction, while other buildings up the street are veneered with granite rubble. The police station has a remarkable facade of large granite pieces fitted together like a crazy quilt. In Llano the same technique was employed in the old library (1940), and in the new library remodeling of the 1990s, but there different colors of granite were used together. Here, there are only the pinks and beiges from Granite Mountain.

The fire station is quite plain, done in panels of rough and smooth granite, while the city hall, around the corner at Third and Highway 281, shows something else altogether. The sides of the building look like long thin bricks, but upon closer inspection you realize this is granite. (You'll see these long thin pieces in houses all over town.) The front has the smooth granite panels that you see in downtown Dallas or in the buildings around the state capitol in Austin. But interspersed here are narrow bands of black granite used as a trim.

ROPER HOUSE (1888) *707 E. Third St.*

The Roper House, across Highway 281, was built during the early years of beige handmade bricks. But here you find granite again. Large pieces of granite were used for lintels and sills for the doorways and windows. As in the Llano courthouse, where bricks and granite make a beautiful blend, the effect here is very attractive.

George and Elizabeth Roper had come to Burnet County from Georgia after the Civil War. He was the brother of W. H. Roper, who had ranched in this area since 1859 and who was one of Adam Johnson's partners. Elizabeth, born in England, had inherited enough money from her father to put up this large dwelling.

With twelve rooms upstairs and a large dining hall below, the Roper House opened as a hotel. It was very popular, ideally situated, and it stayed in operation until after World War II. George died in 1910, Elizabeth in 1922, a grandaughter ran it for a few years, and then others outside the family took over. Today it is used as offices.

BUNGALOWS (1920s) *501 and 418 E. Broadway Street.*

By the 1920s styles had shifted to the bungalow. It was in favor everywhere. But here, in granite territory, the bungalow takes a delightful turn. The distinctive squared and tapered porch support is hewn here of solid granite. The big chunky base is also a solid piece of granite, as well as the small capital above.

These two cottages have other surprises. At 501, there is a wall of rough granite with smooth pieces forming coping stones at the top. At 418, sections of the sidewalk are polished granite. These are probably slabs salvaged from some other building site.

ST. JOHN THE EVANGELIST CATHOLIC CHURCH (1961) *205 E. 10th Street.*

The Catholic Church of 1961 is a masterpiece of rough and smooth granite pieces fitted together. Around the doorway are polished panels. The coping and cross at the top of the front gable are polished, but the walls are a mixture of both smooth and rough finishes.

The church was a community effort. After the plans were donated, a contractor gave his services and the electrical company followed suit. The owners of the Granite Mountain quarry gave the stone and even sent workers out to help. The whole endeavor was like a church-raising in the old days, like building the first Catholic Church in Fredericksburg or the Methodist Church in Hilda.

THE CHAMBER OF COMMERCE AT THE OLD DEPOT
Hwy. 281 at Broadway St.

The depot for the Granite Mountain and Marble Falls Railroad was built in 1893 on Avenue N. It was built of box-and-strip construction (board-and-batten) with the lumber no doubt arriving on the rails. The depot housed both passenger and freight operations. In recent years, moved to Highway 281, the building serves as the offices of the Chamber of Commerce.

GRANITE SCHOOL BUILDING (1891) *2005 W. Broadway.*

Nothing much was altered after the city bought the private school that had formerly belonged to the Texas Mining and Improvement Company. Some repairs were made, the outhouses were moved, new ball fields laid out, but no new buildings joined the old one until the last years of the Depression. Then a high school built with a PWA grant extended the campus. After World War II, some surplus buildings were moved in from Camp Wallace. Later, an elementary school and a newer high school augmented the cluster. But, throughout the changes, Adam Johnson's granite schoolhouse remained the centerpiece of the campus.

There it stands today, proudly facing the river valley, a monument to the early days of this town. Its granite is worn now, but the building is not defaced. It stands as one of the most distinctive of the large schoolhouses remaining in the Hill Country from the nineteenth century.

GRANITE MOUNTAIN *1 mile W. on FM 1431.*

A short side trip takes you out to see the quarry at Granite Mountain. Huge slabs of granite lie about, cranes stick up in various directions, loaded trucks wait to pull out. You see this, but not much more from behind the fence.

Across the road, however, is a small roadside park. Here you can enjoy the glorious view up here. You also find tables made of slabs of granite. But, best, here you can make a further expedition. Cross over one of two stiles in the park and find on the other side a wonderful area to explore. Great cuts in the granite suggest this area was once quarried. Paths lead off into the woods and down to a small pond. Dikes in the granite are reminescent of Enchanted Rock. In fact, this place would be a good substitute for those who can't make it up to the top of the Rock.

BADGER HOUSE (1888) *404 South Avenue M. (Hard to find. Go south on Ave N, past RR tracks to stop sign, house is on the left.)*

The Badger House faced the river as did all the principal buildings at first - the Roper Hotel, the school, Robert Johnson's house. You can catch a glimpse of this one from the cliffs on the other side of the lake because of its size and because of its position on the west side of town.

Brandt Badger was one of the main partners of Adam Johnson, and, like Johnson, he was an Confederate Army veteran. His family lived in Gonzales, Texas, but after his son married Johnson's eldest daughter in 1883, business interests drew him closer to this region. He opened a store in Burnet in 1885, but only a year or so later he was attracted to the fledging Marble Falls. His big house, one of the first, was constructed from the "shapings" left from forming the blocks for the Texas Capitol. It is remarkable for its fine details around the windows, and especially for the incised patterns around the front door. No where else do we encounter pilasters of polished granite with designs of potted flowers. "B. Badger, 1888" is found in the lintel over the doorway.

JOHNSON PARK *S. Avenue J between 1st and S. 5th Streets.*

Around the corner from the Badger House is Johnson Park, nestled in an inlet of Lake Marble Falls. This is an attractive place, a peaceful spot on a quiet stretch of the water. Bring a picnic here. It is an easy walk back to Main Street, as the latter peters out just above this point.

ANNUAL EVENT: WALKWAY OF LIGHTS *Late November to January 1.*

Marble Falls was quick to jump on the bandwagon when the Johnson City Garden Club proposed Christmas lighting for area towns in 1990. Without a courthouse square to illuminate, the city leaders endorsed the idea of a fantasy land along the banks of Lake Marble Falls. Tall Christmas trees, Santas in sleds, and herds of reindeer are portrayed in thousands of tiny lights.

LODGINGS: LIBERTY HALL *119 Avenue G (Hwy. 281 at 2nd St.) Ph: 210/693-4518.*

Robert Johnson's large wooden house down by the lake is now a country inn. The space has been divided into four 2-room suites. Some sitting rooms overlook the lake. Breakfast is served in the rooms. Also a separate kitchen with a breakfast room is available to the guests.

Photographs of the Johnsons - Robert, his father Adam, and others - line the walls.

LODGINGS: BEST WESTERN INN *1403 Hwy. 281 N. (at Mormon Mill Road) Ph: 210/693-5122 or 800/528-1234.*

This is a traditional inn that could be any place, but the Best Western here has a fabulous view of the hills. Breakfast in the lobby is included in the room price. There's a swimming pool and hot tub. Some rooms have refrigerators and microwave ovens.

RESTAURANT: BLUE BONNET CAFE *Hwy. 281 at 2nd St. Ph: 210/693-2344. Open all meals except Sunday night.*

The old standby here is the Blue Bonnet Cafe, haven of good food since 1931, first on Main Street and then at this location since 1946. It is home to fork-tender pot roast, potatoes au gratin, fresh vegetables, and pie. Lots of pies - peanut butter meringue, German chocolate, and coconut cream - all lined up in a case at the rear.

Sunday is an amazing day. First, there's breakfast with oatmeal, omelets, homemade donuts, sweetrolls, and toast made of homemade bread or "Texas toast". Then there's Sunday noon dinner, and this with all the traditional

Blue Bonnet Cafe

things and always pie for dessert. Try the peanut butter meringue. Chances are the waitress will bring a little cup of chocolate to dribble over the top.

The table tops here are another treat. All are slabs of polished granite, and each is a different color and texture. One is a fine-textured, salt and pepper gray, the same light gray as the the Confederate soldier on the courthouse square in Llano. Another is dark gray with brilliant accents of mica. A third is dark brownish llanite, with rusts and subtle hints of blue. The most spectacular table is an enormous round one in the back room. It is, appropriately enough, of the Granite Mountain pinks and grays.

RESTAURANT: JAMIN HOUSE CAFE *701 Hwy. 281 N. (at Broadway) Daily: 11-9. Ph: 210/693-3979.*

This is a restaurant to settle into for a relaxed stay. There's a glassed-in porch at the back with comfortable cushioned metal furniture, ceiling fans, potted plants that creep up and around, and lattices at the windows that shield the view outside. It is an oasis on a hot day.

The food comes quickly by the basket and the plateful. First, a basket of cornbread that is sweet and dense. Then a plateful of fried shrimp or wood-fired salmon with spicy beans and rice, well-seasoned greens, slaw, and corn fritters.

It is a big meal, but, nonetheless, we always save room for dessert. I spied my favorite on my first visit. I asked the waiter "What is that?" and motioned to something at the next table. Key Lime Mousse Pie turned out to be a "fallen souffle," a delicate lime souffle smothered with whipped cream and then topped with a thick lime custard. I now find it impossible to pass this by.

Jamin House is Caribbean: the furnishings on the porch, the dense and sweet cornbread, the key lime souffle. Its owners lived long enough in the islands to learn about the food. They specialize in "jerk," a seasoning of hot and sweet peppers, onions, thyme, cinnamon, and nutmeg, which they rub on chicken or beef before grilling over an open flame. They even mix jerk with mayonnaise to serve with fried oysters or broiled red snapper.

RESTAURANT: MARGARITA'S MEXICAN RESTAURANT
1205 FM 1431 W., daily 11-9, Ph: 210/693-7434.

Margarita's is a very popular Mexican restaurant. This is a place for seafood enchiladas or fajitas. We especially enjoyed the barraco beans in little pots. The guacamole was excellent. Desserts included flan, cheesecake and sopapillas.

RESTAURANT: RUSSO'S *South of Colorado River on Hwy. 281, turn up hill due east of roadside park. Follow signs.*

Russo's is an amazing place on a hill south of town. The food is not exceptional, but the view is extraordinary. You look out across a wide expanse of the Colorado River valley to the west and north across Marble Falls. You see Main Street, the Badger House. Some people come here to view the Walkway of Lights by the side of the lake in December.

Tables are arranged next to big plate glass windows. Outside there's a wraparound balcony.

Hamilton Pool

INTRODUCTION TO HAMILTON POOL

One of my friends in the Hill Country received an offer for a free night at a bed-and-breakfast on Lake Travis. She and her husband went on Christmas Eve and made a pilgrimage out to Hamilton Pool and Pedernales Falls State Park. They took food in an ice chest, nibbled as they went along. "It was glorious," she said, "so peaceful."

It would be hard to think of two more splendid spots for a quiet holiday than Hamilton Pool Preserve and Pedernales Falls State Park. Both are tucked away into folds of truly spectacular scenery. Many have thought that looking at Hamilton Pool, now protected as a county park, was an exalting experience. Some have even called this spot "the most beautiful one hundred acres in Texas." Pedernales State Park, with its seven successive waterfalls, is equally thrilling.

Water falling fifty feet from the lip of a creek into a crystal clear pool that invites swimmers, tall cypresses lining a creek, waterfalls dashing down rough stretches in a river, temperatures dropping ten degrees with the descent into a grotto , wild ferns everywhere - these are the treasures of this pocket of the Hill Country.

ROUND MOUNTAIN

This is the jumping off place for a jaunt into the hills. Leave Highway 281 behind and head east on RR 962.

About a half mile along you will spot on the south side of the road an old stagecoach inn and a large, handsome barn. Both were made of locally quarried stone. This was the home of a widow, Elizabeth Martin, back in the 1870s and 1880s. She ran a stagecoach inn for the routes that crossed here.

GOETH HOUSE (1882), CYPRESS MILL   *1 mi. N. of RR 962 on RR 304, E. of road.*

Finding this house in the hills meant a great deal to me. It was the home of Ottilie Fuchs Goeth, whose book *Memoirs of a Texas Pioneer Grandmother* (1915, 1982) was the most intriguing of any I read about the Hill Country. The book vividly illustrates the area's rich German heritage.

Ottilie came as a nine-year-old from Germany in 1845, just as Texas was becoming a state in the Union. Her family lived first at Cat Spring near Houston, but they moved west to Burnet County in 1853 when her father was able to secure a claim that had been granted to a German killed in the Texas Revolutionary War. The Fuchs family place was south of the Colorado River (just west of Highway 281), but later Ottilie moved to this large sheep ranch with her husband, Carl Goeth.

The Fuchs (as well as the Goeths) were educated and cultured people, even though Ottilie's generation had to forego formal education in this country. Her father, a Lutheran minister in Germany, gave her lessons at home. She learned to appreciate the classics in German literature and music.

In her memoirs written towards the end of her life, Ottilie writes not only about what people did but also

244

Hamilton Pool

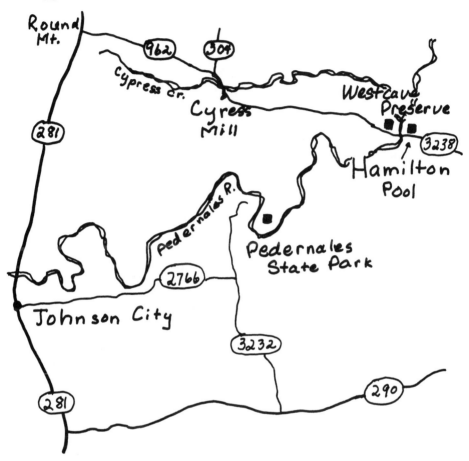

about what they thought. She tells of Northern Germany in the years before they left, her father's life as a Lutheran minister, his dissatisfaction with the established church there. She describes the preparations to come to America, the hardships here, the move to Burnet County. She writes of the horrors of the Civil War and also of the effects on the community of German reunification in 1871. She tells of a visit she and Carl made to Germany in 1892, of their encounters on her relatives' landed estates.

Her first stories were printed in a German newspaper in Austin. She finished the chronicle and published it in German in 1915. After her death, her youngest son, Max, and his wife, Marie, lived here and managed the ranch. Their daughter, Elsie Goeth Youngblood took over after that. In 1969, Elsie sold the ranch outside the family. And also in that year, another grandaughter, Irma Goeth Guenther, translated Ottilie's memoir into English. Finally, in 1982, a larger printing was made available.

You can't see much of the house from the road, but at least you can glimpse Ottilie's "chain of hills smiling above the liveoaks." Memories of this location will stay with me, and her book will remain on my shelf. Knowing Ottilie through her recollections was one of the unexpected pleasures of the research on this book.

ST. LUKE'S EPISCOPAL CHURCH (1956), CYPRESS MILL
Services at 9 a.m. on Sundays.

When a friend was called away to a funeral at St. Luke's Church in Cypress Mill, she discovered that Becky Crouch Patterson, the artist who designed the windows at St. Barnabas in Fredericksburg, had done a beautiful set for the tiny church here. If anything, these are more stunning than those in town because the light catches them in a different way. Also the gorgeous setting here can be glimpsed through clear sections of the windows. There's a wonderful interaction between inside and out.

Without this message from my friend, I would have passed by this church. St. Luke's is an unpretentious A-frame built in the 1950s. But now, since December 1995, it has become one of the special places in the Hill Country. Becky Patterson, daughter of Hondo Crouch of Luckenbach, has designed windows with religious symbolism in abundance but also has built her themes around Texas wildflowers, birds, and beasts.

The large window at the back has eastern exposure, and with the morning light shows hills, cactus, sheep, and running water. This represents Psalm 122: "I will lift up my eyes to the hills." The colors are soft purples, browns, golds, reds, turquoise. Some of the glass has a wavy texture. There are even some glass roundels, "jewels" - as you find in turn-of-the-century art glass.

Along the sides are narrow panels that show thistles, bluebonnets, sunflowers, cactus, mountain laurel, as well as fish, birds, and butterflies. I once sat next to a small rabbit. In the brochure about the windows, this rabbit represents humility.

Outside, on one of the braces of the A-frame, is a tiny marker to William and Luisa Fuchs, grandparents, and

Frederick and Dora Fuchs Reiner, parents of Herman Reiner, who donated the land for the church. William Fuchs was the brother of Ottilie Fuchs Goeth, whose house is mentioned above, and also one of the sons of Pastor Fuchs, who made his way to Burnet County from Germany. William and Luisa came to Cypress Mill at the time of the Civil War. They eventually owned vast acres down to the Pedernales River. It was some of this land that Herman Reiner, the grandson, donated for the church.

In the old days, the German community celebrated holidays and special occasions at a dance hall. They did not build a church or participate in organized religion. By the 1950s, their group had disintegrated. The dance hall was sold to outsiders and then razed.

At that time ranchers in the area wanted another community center; specifically they wanted a church. Herman Reiner gave a parcel of land, and then neighbors brought an interesting assortment of rocks for the walls. The Episcopal Church agreed to sponsor the congregation, although the spirit is still that of a community church where all are welcome.

WESTCAVE PRESERVE *RR 962 at the Pedernales River. Open weekends. Tours: 10,12,2, 4. Or by appointment. Ph: 512/825-3442.*

At Westcave Preserve tours are offered down into a collapsed grotto, a depression in a creek with a cresent-shaped ledge above. Moisture is held in below by the ledge and a canopy of trees. While above you see liveoaks, cedars, and cactus, you descend to a level of Spanish oaks, willows, and box elders. Then you drop farther down to the floor of the grotto where you observe cypresses, maidenhair ferns, and red columbines. Orchids may be growing there. The temperature will likely be lower by ten degrees than at ground level.

The grotto was formed by the collapse of a cavern ceiling under a stream bed. The stream then chewed away soft layers of shale and sand under a thick limestone ledge, thus forming a shelf. There are many such collapsed areas in the Hill Country, but most are dry. Here spring-fed water pours over the ledge, forming an oasis of coolness and beauty in an otherwise parched terrain.

Under the ledge at the Westcave Preserve, seeping water
has caused a large flowstone to develop. This obscures
part of the natural opening under the ledge. If you walk
behind this flowstone, it is like being inside a cave.

While this place was privately owned, it attracted
trespassers who compacted the soil and left lots of litter.
Then, in 1974, a conservation group hired John Ahrns, a
student of horticulture, to direct volunteers to carry out
the trash and construct paths. Ahrns than began to lead
groups down to the grotto. Still leading the groups today,
Ahrns gives a fascinating description of the natural forces
at work. He points out the various kinds of plants. He also
takes visitors to a viewing platform where they can see the
Pedernales River, including Hammett's Crossing, the only
way to get across the river for many years.

HAMILTON POOL PRESERVE *3 mi. E. of Westcave
Preserve on same road. (RR 962 becomes RR 3238 at
Pedernales River. Daily 9-6. (Closed on some holidays).
Admission. Ph: 512/264-2740. Guided tours: Sat at 10
A.M. No drinking water in park.*

Hamilton Pool is one of the extraordinary places in
Texas. It is another collapsed grotto like the one in
Westcave Preserve, exactly the same formation, but here
the spaces are large, there is no flowstone blocking the
area under the curved ledge, and sprays of water fall like
diamonds from fifty feet above. The pool below beckons
swimmers.

A short walk from the parking lot takes you to the
pool. You hear its splashing water even before you glimpse
its loveliness. You can walk entirely around it, passing
ferns under the ledge, and admiring the waterfalls
bouncing off the surface of the pool. You can also hike
from here down to the Pedernales River. Lush stands of
cypress trees line the creek down to the river. At first the
stream forms small pools, with little rapids between them.
These reminded me, though in miniature scale, of the
waterfalls among the giant boulders in Pedernales Falls
State Park.

Hamilton Pool has been cherished for generations. One
of the Texas governors, A. J. Hamilton, came out here to
relax. His relatives owned the property then, around the
time of the Civil War. Later, the B.J. Reimers bought it

and opened the pool to swimmers and picnickers. William O. Douglas and many other naturalists came and remarked on its beauty. Hamilton Pool became almost a hallowed place, held in the same rank as Enchanted Rock.

Finally, in 1985, Travis County bought the property from the Reimers. Now some areas are closed off for rehabilitation. Access is more carefully controlled. After the parking lot is filled, the next car will have to wait for an empty spot.

PEDERNALES FALLS STATE PARK *9 mi. E. of Johnson city on RR 2766 or 7 mi. N. of Hw. 290 or RR 3232. Admission. Call for camping. Ph: 512/389-8900. Bring drinking water.*

At Pedernales Falls State Park, with nearly 5,000 acres, there's room to spread out. No limit on cars here. No access limited by numbers on a tour. You won't have the same explanation as you would with a guide, but you will be able to find plenty on your own. You can swim in an attractive area of the Pedernales River, fish, camp, and hike on rugged trails. You may even be able to find small collapsed grottoes on some of the remote trails.

The premier sight, of course, is the spectacular falls in the Pedernales River. These falls descend in seven stages, from one plateau to the next, carving intricate passages as they proceed. From top to bottom, the water drops thousands of feet. If you look at the bank on the far side of the river, you can see that the earth tilts in the area of the falls. This tilting causes the series of plateaus.

The river snakes down through a maze of rocks, polishing stone, piercing boulders, carving rills and grooves in the limestone. Near the bottom there are white streaks in the darker limestone. These are white calcite veins, fossils of crinoid stems. There are potholes also. If you look carefully at these you see several little stones in each one. These move around in the turbulence of a storm and make the holes larger.

For a good view of the falls, go first to the overlook. All paths lead in that direction. Then, to see the head of the falls, follow a path to your left. Stay with the trail at the top of the cliff at first and then pick your way down.

For the trail to the lower reaches of the falls, turn to your right from the overlook. Steps lead to a trail that takes you down.

From 1937 to 1970 the ranch belonged the C. A. Wheatley family. After the state parks system bought it in 1970, park officials began to develop an extensive system of trails throughout the vast territory. You can still see some evidence of the ranch in remote areas.

Across the river from a section of the park is the land of Herman Reiner, the donor of the small tract for the church at Cypress Mill. If you look at the map, you can see how close Cypress Mill is to this park. Close perhaps, but a long drive away, because the only bridges across the Pedernales River are at Highway 281 and Hammett's Crossing, which lies between Westcave Preserve and Hamilton Pool.

Johnson City and Stonewall

INTRODUCTION TO JOHNSON CITY AND STONEWALL

The really special time to see Johnson City is at night in the Christmas season. The Saturday after Thanksgiving it is transformed by thousands of tiny lights. The square, the park, the central areas become a fairyland. Then it is that a procession comes down by the square. The Lighted Hooves and Wagon Wheels Parade features bands and trucks and floats - the only qualification being that each must have lights. There are twinkly flickers on the bugles of the band, thin neon tubes on horses hooves, basic flashlights twirled by the Girl Scouts. Anything goes!

On another evening, several weeks later, the Boyhood Home of Lyndon Johnson and the Johnson Settlement (the early log cabin of his grandparents) are open for a "lamplight tour." Lanterns and candles make this a magical moment.

Closer to Christmas, Lady Bird Johnson and her family come out to light an immense tree at the LBJ State Park in Stonewall, fifteen miles west. This is a tradition that now goes back nearly thirty years. Local churches - Lutheran, Catholic, and Baptist - participate in a short program. Then bus tours head off to see the decorations at the LBJ Ranch and finally proceed to the Sauer-Beckmann Farm where handmade garlands are strung along the fence, and lanterns light the way. A tree glows with real candles, and a table is laid with cookies and cakes and homemade bread from a wood-burning oven, and sausages made right there on the farm. Since this is a "living farm," recreating the era of 1915 to 1918, there is no electricity. To be there on a night like this is indeed special.

THE JOHNSONS

You can't mention this town without discussing Lyndon Baines Johnson and his relatives. They go together like hand and glove. His grandparents, his great uncle, his father's first cousin, his parents: all were here. They came early, settled the place, lingered, surged forward again in the twentieth century. LBJ picks up the trail then. His efforts as a young Congressman in the 1930s made telling effect in this and other places in the Hill Country.

Finally, his purchase of his aunt's ranch 15 miles west of here in 1951 reinforced the trend of the gentleman rancher in the Hill Country. Wealthy from the

Lyndon Baines Johnson

communications industry by then, he poured huge sums into the ranch, and it became a model in the region.

Johnson City was named for a cousin, the town builder, James Polk Johnson, but truly the name stands for all of them.

Great Grandfather Jesse Johnson came to Texas from Tennessee in 1846. He had six children, and meant to leave each of them an inheritance, but at his death in 1856, his children found his accounts in the red instead of the black.

Two of his sons, Sam and Tom, came to Blanco County as very young men around the same time as their father's death. After the Civil War, in which they fought for the

252

South, the brothers bought property here at the future site of Johnson City and then started a large cattle operation. They drove thousands of cattle to the railheads in Kansas, enjoying huge successes in the drives of 1867, 1868, 1869, and 1870. In the drive of 1871, they met failure, and they went down with this one bad year. They had not held money in reserve, had invested in property across the Hill Country, and had borrowed to the hilt. It was the old story of speculation. Sam Johnson, Sr. was never able to repay his creditors.

Sam and Tom Johnson sold their property here to their nephew, James Polk Johnson, who had been part of their cattle operation. It was James Polk who laid out Johnson City in 1878 and gave it the Johnson name. He built a new home on the old Johnson place, a stone barn, and also the bank and the hotel on the square. He dreamed of Johnson City as the county seat and rooted for his town during the courthouse fights in 1879 and 1885. But James Polk died, five years before the county seat was moved here in 1891. His bank then served temporarily as the new courthouse.

Johnson City felt less of the Johnson energy until 1913 when Sam, Jr., his wife Rebekah, and their eldest children, Lyndon, Rebekah, and Josepha, moved into town from the farm in Stonewall, 15 miles west. Sam, Jr. had taught school and farmed as well as representing this area in the state legislature. Now, he was successful in real estate. Until 1920, his family was comfortable.

After Sam ran again, successfully, for the State Legislature in 1917, he became the most prominent citizen in Johnson City. Once again, the Johnsons owned the bank and the hotel. But, in 1919, after the deaths of his parents, he bought out his brothers and sisters in the purchase of the family farm, 433 acres in Stonewall that had been bought with his grandmother's inheritance in the 1880s. This was money Sam didn't have. He borrowed it. He borrowed more to buy equipment. When the farm failed to produce, almost immediately, Sam went under. By 1922, Sam had lost everything. He moved back to his former home in Johnson City, now mortgaged, only with the help of his brothers, Tom and George.

But Sam, Jr.'s debts were repaid. Twenty-five years later, in 1937, after Lyndon Johnson had finished college in San Marcos, had worked for Congressman Richard

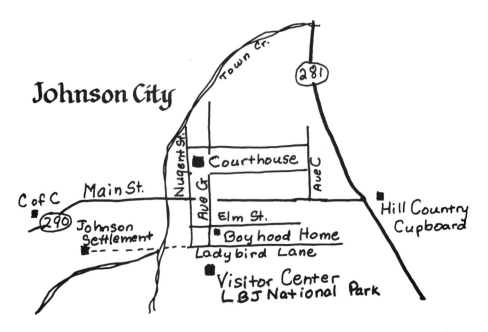

Johnson City

Town Cr.

281

Courthouse

Nugent St.

Ave G

Ave C

C of C

Main St.

290

Johnson Settlement

Elm St.

Boyhood Home

Ladybird Lane

Hill Country Cupboard

Visitor Center
LBJ National Park

Kleberg, and had just run for his first term as Congressman, his father died - $5,000 in debt. Lyndon Johnson made good on those debts, though it took years to do it. A story is told in Merle Miller's *Lyndon: An Oral Biography* of a German farmer who received Lyndon when he came one day, hat in hand, offering to pay on his father's debt. He offered half of what his father owed. The farmer accepted it and thought well of the young Congressman.

It was another three decades before President Johnson began to acquire the various sites of his childhood and form them into an extraordinary Presidential complex. He and Lady Bird had bought his aunt's ranch at Stonewall in 1951. His aging aunt had then gone to live in Johnson's boyhood home in Johnson City, a house that the Johnson family had not relinquished. Lyndon and Lady Bird had spruced up the aunt's large house at the ranch and entertained many friends and relatives there before he became the 36th President in 1963. Then, between 1963 and 1969, the ranch house at Stonewall was known as the Texas White House. It was during those years of his presidency that Lyndon and Lady Bird Johnson took further interest in the other sites of his childhood.

In 1972, two month before Johnson died, the package was completed and presented to the National Parks

System: a portion of the LBJ Ranch (to be continued as a working ranch), the ranch house, the replica of his birthplace, the country school he attended, the family cemetery, his boyhood home in Johnson City, and the log house there where his grandparents had lived around 1870. The family cemetery contains the graves of three generations going back. The houses represent the same. Seeing the places here is like visiting Washington's Mount Vernon or Lincoln's New Salem and Springfield if you could add the original homes of Washington's and Lincoln's fathers and grandfathers.

A further point is that the Johnson story, over a hundred years of it, from cattle drives to the modern presidency, touches on most of the major issues in the Hill Country. They came early, they fought in the Civil War, they led cattle to Kansas. Eliza, Sam's wife, hid from the Indians under the floor boards of her log cabin. James Polk Johnson, the cousin, was the town builder - like many another of his era in the Hill Country. Sam, Jr., tried to raise cotton around 1920. The land was worn out. He failed. Young Lyndon fled to California in the 1920s - as did so many others. Lyndon Johnson, a young Congressman, brought a measure of hope by encouraging the chopping of cedar and the restoration of the grasslands, badgering the citizens of five counties to band together to form the Pedernales Electric Cooperative. With electricity came the modern age.

Lyndon's buying his aunt's ranch in 1951, only six years after the war, encouraged the trend towards the gentleman rancher, towards investing outside money in dams and irrigation, new fences, and registered Herefords.

Lady Bird Johnson's influence extended to other natural sites in this area. As First Lady she had led forty-seven "Discover America" tours throughout the United States. Not only did she focus on rehabilitating cities, appreciating smaller towns and villages, but also on preserving unique national sites. She led groups to the redwood forests in California, to Padre Island in Texas. Because of this emphasis, this new wave of environmental awareness, steps were taken in this area to protect certain special places. The State Parks system bought Pedernales State Park from a ranching family in 1970. The Westcave Preservation Corporation was formed in 1974. Enchanted Rock passed from the Moss family to the state park system in 1978, and Travis County bought Hamilton Pool in 1985.

While other ranching compounds in the Hill Country may be more fascinating from ·an architectural point of view, no other family. saga encompasses so much of the rich history of the area, from early to late, or reflects so closely economic and political developments. With the Johnsons, most of the threads come together.

BLANCO COUNTY COURTHOUSE AND PUBLIC SQUARE
N. off Hwy. 290 on Nugent St.

When you drive into Johnson City you see the signs for the LBJ School and the Pedernales Electric Cooperative. This is without doubt Lyndon Johnson's town, but it was Jame Polk Johnson's, too. He was the cousin who bought out Lyndon's grandfather and great uncle in 1871. He laid out a town here eight years later, and he led subsequent fights to get the courthouse here. He built the gristmill and cotton gin on Highway 290 (now the Feed Mill Complex), the wooden hotel on the square (still standing), and a fine stone building that is now the bank on the square. This stone building served as the first courthouse after the county seat was moved here in 1890, but by then James Polk Johnson was dead.

Lyndon's family moved into town in 1913, when he was five, and he must have watched with fascination while the present courthouse was erected in 1916. Of large limestone blocks, with smooth trim, the structure rose in the center of the square. The architect, Henry T. Phelps, was from San Antonio, and the contractor, James Waterston, was a stonemason from Scotland who came over to help with the state capitol in Austin.

The tall, stately courthouse with two-story Doric columns and classical details dominates the square. Across from it stands a nineteenth-century stone jail and James Polk Johnson's stone bank. But there's not much else. For shopping turn back to Highway 290 and find the Johnson City Antiques Emporium in an old gas station with a cutaway corner.

LYNDON JOHNSON NATIONAL HISTORICAL PARK
VISITORS' CENTER *S. of Hwy. 290 on Avenue G. Open daily: 8:45 - 5 (except Christmas Day and New Year's Day). Ph: 830/868-7128, ext. 231.*

The Visitors' Center is a handsome structure that was built as a hospital in 1969. It now houses exhibits and films on the Johnsons and an excellent bookstore. I found a tape there of President Johnson's humor that has enlivened many an hour on the road. My favorite joke is this: "I'm getting my book out. It will be ready next year. And I've already received *seven* unfavorable reviews! "

From here you take off for your tour to the Boyhood Home, just north, or to the Johnson Settlement, a short walk to the west. (If you need to ride, speak to the guides at the Visitors' Center.)

The rest of the tour is at Stonewall, 15 miles west on Highway 290. Stop at the LBJ State Historical Park Visitors' Center there to make arrangements for a bus tour.

LBJ BOYHOOD HOME   *S. from Hwy. 290 on Avenue G. Open daily: 9-5 (except Christmas Day and New Year's Day) Tours every 30 minutes.*

The Johnsons moved into this house in 1913, when they came into town from the family ranch at Stonewall. A T-shaped Victorian dwelling, it had been built by the local sheriff in 1901. Almost two acres came with it. The Johnsons kept chickens and a cow. The outbuildings are still there.

Lyndon, five years old, arrived with his parents and his sisters, Rebekah and Josepha. Sam Houston and Lucia were born here in Johnson City.

His parents wanted regular schools for their children. Also Sam was now involved with real estate.

When you enter the front door you find yourself in Sam's office - the front hall - with a roll-top desk, an office chair, and a bookcass. To the left is the girls' bedroom, while to the right is the dining room, the heart of the house. Here the family gathered for meals, lengthy discussions, debates, spelling bees, and to listen to the radio. And it was here, after Sam's death, that the family convened to divide up his possessions and make an account of his debts.

A formal parlor in the front holds some of Rebekah's furniture, but mostly her furnishings were placed at the Birthplace on the LBJ Ranch.

More bedrooms and a "tub room" lead off from the dining room to the west. Then immediately behind the dining room is the kitchen. Here the linoleum on the floor, the wood-burning stove and open shelves remind some visitors of their grandmothers' houses. Rebekah did have running water here. You see a small sink under the kitchen window.

Porches in the corners lead off from all these rooms. One in back was for sleeping, and one in front for debates. Lyndon is said to have hidden under the bed next to a nearby window so he could hear the political conversations his father held with guests on the second of the front porches.

In 1937, Lyndon Johnson gave his first political speech as a candidate on the porch where he had listened to debates as a child. His father roused himself for the last speech of his career. He introduced his son in what must have been a remarkable address.

When Lyndon ran for Senator, in 1941, he spoke again on the porch, on election morning. There is a widely reproduced photograph of him at the microphone, his mother at his side, and Lady Bird next to her.

The house was then rented out, though it still belonged to the Johnsons. After Sam's death in 1937, Rebekah had stayed here for a few years, but in 1940 she moved to Austin. Then, when Lyndon and Lady Bird bought his aunt's ranch, Aunt Frank moved into town to live here. She lived another ten years or so, and after that the house was used as a community center. Lady Bird Johnson writes in her diary of hanging family photographs here at that time.

In 1969, the Boyhood Home became part of the LBJ National Historical Site. It was then taken back to the era before electricity, around 1920. The furnishings, though largely not family pieces, are representative of the period. National Park Service guides give excellent tours. They don't hesitate either to say that things never looked this spiffed up when the Johnsons were here.

JOHNSON SETTLEMENT *South of Hwy. 290. Self-guided walking tour from Visitors' Center. Daily 9-4:30, except Christmas Day and New Year's Day.*

The log cabin here has a certain mystique. It is a wonder it survived as it did through the decades, not touched or disfigured by modern civilization. This was the home of Lyndon's grandparents in the late 1860s, the headquarters of their cattle operation, the nucleus of Johnson City. After they sold out to their nephew, James Polk Johnson, in 1871, they moved away from the area and James Polk built a large frame house closer to the highway. (That house was destroyed in 1918.) He also built a barn close by.

Before James Polk Johnson died, in 1885, he sold the southern portion of his property to John Bruckner. His family remained here a long time. Whether or not they lived in the Johnson log cabin is not clear, but in any case they did not add plumbing or electricity. It was the

Johnson Settlement

Bruckners who built the handsome stone barn near the cabin.

When Lyndon Johnson was president he brought visitors here to see the log house and the barns. He told the story of grandmother, Eliza, hiding under the floor boards of the house when there was an Indian attack around 1869. She grabbed up her baby, stuffed something in her mouth, and fled down a trap door.

After Johnson came back to Texas in 1969 and began acquiring all the Johnson sites, this one was added to the collection. At first it was a "living farm museum" and I was fortunate to find the house open one day with someone cooking biscuits and soup at the hearth in the kitchen. Since then funds were cut off and the only time the house is open is during the Christmas celebration on the second Saturday in December. On a regular tour, you have to content yourself with looking through the windows.

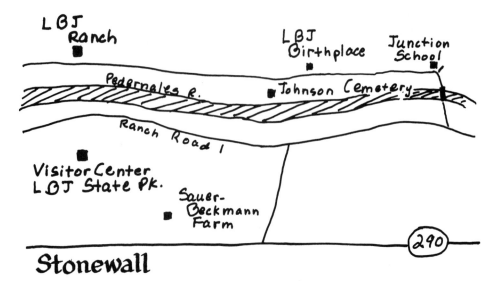

Stonewall

LBJ RANCH. *Bus tours available at LBJ State Historical Park, Hwy. 290 at Stonewall.*

On probably the first of the newspaper interviews here, Elise and Art Kowert of Fredericksburg drove out to see Lady Bird and Lyndon Johnson in 1951. The Johnsons had just bought his aunt's ranch and were busy making plans for it. LBJ had to learn about ranching. He planned to build a dam across the river at the front of the house and begin an irrigation system. Lady Bird was making plans for landscaping. Eventually there would be wide lawns between the house and the river, hedges, a swimming pool, and a paling fence set on a stone foundation at the road. Huge trees arched overhead. This lovely setting would help her forget that Lyndon had not bought property in her part of the state, deep East Texas.

Lyndon's aunt was Frank Johnson Martin, wife of Clarence Martin, district judge for many years, local leader, and mentor to Lyndon himself. The Martins had bought this house and some of the surrounding property in 1909, the year after LBJ was born just up the road. They added a large frame section to the original rock dwelling, creating an impressive ranch house, and one that Lyndon knew well.

After Clarence Martin died in 1936, his son was the heir apparent. But Tom, an only child, also died in 1948. It was after that that Aunt Frank wanted to sell.

Several years passed before the ranch was ready for company. A severe flood in 1952 caused damage inside and took down some of the large trees in the front yard. But, at length, all was ready and the Johnsons made frequent trips down from Washington where he was Minority Leader and then Majority Leader of the Senate. They began to welcome a long parade of visitors. By the time Johnson was Vice-President, and then President, this Texas home had become a refuge. It was called the Texas White House.

Lady Bird tells in her *White House Diary* of the Christmas visit in 1964. It was the first time LBJ came back as president, and she writes of her shock at the changes. There were little white guard houses at the gates, searchlights outside, Secret Service men everywhere. But then the huge extended family gathered around and they had a merry time.

Several days later they entertained their first state visitor, Chancellor Ludwig Erhard of Germany. They took him to Fredericksburg to see the sights there. They attended a service (largely in German) at the Lutheran Church, where they heard a men's choir sing "Silent Night" in German. Back at the ranch it was time for barbecue and folk dancing and another choir and music by Van Cliburn. At the end Lady Bird thought it a success. The German visitors had been in a place where there were "ties of kinship."

After Lyndon and Lady Bird Johnson came back permanently to Texas in 1969, they acquired the rest of the

Lady Bird Johnson

package they finally donated to the National Park Service in November, 1972. This included the Junction School and the Johnson Settlement, as well as the Birthplace, the Boyhood Home, the cemetery, and a chunk of the LBJ Ranch. They also supervised the opening of the LBJ State Historical Park across the road, which included the Sauer-Beckmann Living Farm.

LBJ meanwhile had taken an interest in ranching, built up herds of Hereford cattle, improved the soil, rotated crops, put in terracing and cross fencing, hired capable foremen - in short, made this a model ranch.

He wanted future visitors to be able to see a working ranch, and that's just how it is today. After driving by the house, the bus tours proceed slowly to the rear, allowing passengers to glimpse the LBJ white Lincoln Continental convertibles (in a garage behind plexiglass) and then back to the foreman's house, the coastal Bermuda grass, the horses, the barns in the rear. You also see the airplane strip, a helicopter pad, and hangars.

You catch the excitement of a president living here, but you also can sense how immensely pleasurable and relaxing this place was for the weary Johnsons who fled the hectic pace in Washington as often as they could.

LBJ BIRTHPLACE *Bus tours available at the LBJ State Historical Park, Hwy. 290 at Stonewall.*

Lyndon Johnson was born here August 27, 1908. His parents had married in Fredericksburg the previous year and were living here at the family ranch. Lyndon's grandparents had moved back to this area from Buda, Texas, in the 1880s. This had been their home, but by 1908 they lived a half mile up the road, and Sam and Rebekah were here. There were Johnsons everywhere: Sam's parents, Sam and Eliza; his sister Ava and her husband John Harvey, his brother Tom and his wife Kitty. And during the following year his sister and her husband, the Clarence Martins, bought what would become the centerpiece of the LBJ Ranch.

Sam and Rebekah moved to Johnson City in 1913, but they were back out here in 1919 after the deaths of his parents and Sam's decision to farm the old family property. Sam did not succeed in this, ended up in debt, and sold the family land in 1922 to O.J. Striegler. The house where Lyndon was born was used by tenants. By 1935 it had deteriorated and was torn down.

In the 1960s, Lyndon Johnson acquired this property and then rebuilt his birthplace on the old foundation. Though it is only a replica, and maybe not worthy of much note, the little house was of great interest to the Johnsons and they put the family treasures here. A cousin in Johnson City sent a wood-burning stove for the kitchen. One of Eliza's trunks and her kitchen table are here. Rebekah's furniture is in several of the rooms. Also here is her mother's crocheted bedspread, which was a wedding present to Lyndon and Lady Bird, as well as her grandmother Baines's green and white calico quilt.

JOHNSON CEMETERY *On the bus tours. Available to the public after 5 p.m.*

There are wonderful stories about the gatherings here at the various funerals.

Lyndon himself spoke of his grandfather's funeral to Doris Kearns, the author of *Lyndon Johnson and the American Dream.* He told her of standing near one of the large oak trees and watching the coffin being lowered into the ground. He said a "light rain had started to fall" and his grandfather would have been pleased. Then he saw his father crying - the first time he'd seen this. He went to his father after the ceremony and walked away with him.

When his father Sam Jr. died in 1937, there was a great outpouring of mourners, which extended down the banks of the river. People came from great distances to say goodbye to a state legislator who had done something for them, such as small stipends or pensions. Men stood in the uniforms of the First World War, the Spanish American War, even five in the gray garb of the Confederates. Ava Johnson Cox, Lyndon's cousin, told the biographer Robert Caro (*The Years of Lyndon Johnson: the Path to Power*) that she was amazed by all this. She hardly recognized the uniforms of 1898 and she could hardly believe that there were still five Confederate veterans who could come.

Lyndon's funeral in January ,1973, followed days of lying in state in Austin and Washington and a state funeral at the National City Christian Church in Washington. Presiding here was Father Wunibald Schneider from the local St. Francis Xavier Catholic

Church. Leontyne Price sang "Take my hand, Precious Lord." Billy Graham spoke. John Connally gave the main address. There were all kinds of people at this funeral, "plain people" Connally called them. And there were African-Americans. Merle Miller in his *Lyndon, An Oral Biography* tells of an old black man who said to Luci Johnson Nugent: "Ma'am, you don't have to tell me he loved me. He showed me he loved me. A tree would have had to fall over me to keep me from being here today."

Aunt Jessie was there. Eighty-nine years old and the last surviving sibling of Sam, Jr. She wouldn't stay away, even though it was bitterly cold. Two weeks later she died and was buried here with the rest of the Johnson kin.

There they are, lined up, plain red granite stones in a row, Frank and Clarence Martin in the front, huge trees arching overhead, the Pedernales River very close. A beautiful spot.

JUNCTION SCHOOL (1910) *On the bus tours. See above.*

Lyndon Johnson's first school was just a few hundred yards from his birthplace. A country school at a crossroads, it had been built in 1910, the land conveyed by John Pehl with the understanding it would revert back to his family if the school closed. The teacher and most of the pupils were German. LBJ attended briefly as a four-year-old in 1912. The next year his family moved to Johnson City.

In 1947, when enrollment had dropped to seven pupils, the school closed and the land reverted back to the family. Then the building began a second life as a private home.

People were still living here in 1965 when the Johnsons used the front yard as the setting for the signing of the Elementary and Secondary Educational Act. LBJ's old teacher came back, but also busloads of his former students in Cotulla and Houston. It was a kind of homecoming. "A gold-star day," Lady Bird called it in her diary.

In 1972, the owners at that time donated the old schoolhouse to the National Park Service, making it the final piece of the complex.

LBJ STATE HISTORICAL PARK *Main Entrance on Hwy. 290, Stonewall Open daily 8-5, day use only. (Except*

*Christmas Day and New Year's Day Ph: 830/644-2252.
Buses for tours of LBJ Ranch: 10-4, Admission.*

Along the south bank of the Pedernales River, across
from the LBJ Ranch, is a beautiful state park that
encompasses attractive picnic spots along the river, a
swimming pool and ball courts. A large Visitors' Center in
the middle is the gathering spot. Here buses take off for
tours of the LBJ Ranch. Here are photographs of the
Johnsons, their grandchildren, and important visitors, as
well as other exhibits and an old log cabin from the 1840s
that was built by Johannes Behrens, a German
immigrant.

The land for this park was bought by friends of
President Johnson in 1967. Plans were laid over the next
several years, but the formal dedication did not occur until
August of 1970. Four months later Lady Bird Johnson
gave the first of her Christmas parties here, a tradition
that continues to the present. (See below.) And, in the
same year, she inaugurated barbecues and awards for
maintenance workers in the state highway department.
Those parties were held here, too - and still are. The
beautiful park has almost become an adjunct to the
Johnson home.

SAUER-BECKMANN FARMSTEAD   *LBJ State Historical
Park. Open daily: 8-4:30 except Christmas Day and New
Year's Day.*

The state parks system bought this farm in 1966 and
eventually reopened it as a timepiece showing the years
1915 to 1918. A staff or "family" do the daily chores of
baking and cooking lunch, sweeping the yard, tending to
the animals, planting a garden, butchering. There is no
electricity, no plumbing, no refrigerator. School children
are entranced by all this.

We were there once when the chickens had to be
gathered into the hen house for the night. Otherwise,
some of the varmints in the woods would get them.

Another time a woman was sweeping the yard. This
was the old-fashioned way of keeping fires away, ticks out,
and so forth. This swept yard is kind of a shock to modern
eyes. There are flower beds, however, next to the wire
fence, and these neatly edged with bricks.

The rambling house of rooms strung out in single file is interesting in itself. Started by a German family, the Johan Sauers, in 1869. with simple log structures, it grew to the east to encompass a stone house in 1895. After the Sauers sold to the Beckmann family in 1900, the latter added a separate frame, L-shaped Victorian house, again directly to the east. It is connected to the older structures by a breezeway. After this last addition, the family set up their kitchen in the stone house and had bedrooms and a formal parlor in the Victorian house. This is the way you see it today.

The house from 1915 has a front porch with gingerbread trim, a front entry with long narrow ovals in the woodwork facing the door, pressed tin siding, hardwood floors, and high ceilings. The bedrooms look inviting, but the parlor is stiff and forbidding in the fashion of the period. It is here that the Christmas tree was set up. This was a room that the family used only for special occasions and that could easily be shut off before the moment Christmas arrived.

In the breezeway is what served as a refrigerator. It is a tiered arrangement of shelves with white gauze draped over them and water oozing gently from a container above to a trough below. The wet sheets of gauze kept food cooler than it would have been otherwise.

The kitchen is a marvelous room with a blue-enameled, wood-burning stove in one corner, a hutch at the far end, and a big wooden table and benches in the center.

It is here at the kitchen table that you can sample the sausages made on the farm and the freshly baked breads and cakes from an old recipe book. But all this only on one special night close to Christmas. Open house at the Sauer-Beckmann Farmstead follows the annual Tree Lighting Ceremony at the LBJ State Historical Park. Lit by lanterns and candles, graced by homemade garlands on the fences and in the windows, it is a night to remember.

ANNUAL EVENT: PEACH JAMBOREE *Stonewall, 3rd weekend in June.*

The peach crop in this area is duly celebrated. There is something in the soil here that makes the peaches especially good. Fruit stands line the road between Stonewall and Fredericksburg. There are at least three

stands in Fredericksburg itself and a big distribution center in Stonewall. Tourists come out for the peach season, and there is great disappointment for everyone when the peaches are ruined by a late freeze, when the crop fails.

The festival here is a focal point of the season. There's a parade on Saturday morning, and then lots of pie judging and cobbler sampling.

ANNUAL EVENT: LIGHTS SPECTACULAR *Johnson City. From the day after Thanksgiving to Jan 1. Lighted Hooves and Wagon Wheels Parade on Sat after Thanksgiving, 6:p.m.. on courthouse square.*

In 1990, the garden club in Johnson City was inspired by the spectacular Christmas lights at Marshall, Texas, and asked why not here? They got busy making plans for their decorations, spoke to neighboring towns, and soon a regional lighting tour was underway.

They dropped a curtain of tiny white lights from the second story cornice of the courthouse, wrapped more

around the chimneys, put finishing touches on the dome.
Then the courthouse at Johnson City was transformed.

We were there on a balmy evening that felt more like
San Antonio than the Hill Country. Lights were
everywhere. In the trees, on all the buildings. The entire
square was gently lit. We had never seen Johnson City
look like this.

Soon it was time for the Lighted Hooves and Wagon
Wheels Parade. We watched the participants gather at the
east end of the square. Every entry had lights. They were
strung around the grills of pickups, tied to saddle blankets,
wrapped around wheels, strung along the tops of covered
wagons. Horns and flutes in the band twinkled with lights.
Horses hooves had neon bands. A few floats came from
out-of-town, but mostly this parade was homemade and
wonderful.

Afterwards we went into the courthouse to see the
lighted tree upstairs and then we found Santa waiting in
the small public park on Highway 290. Adjacent was the
Chuckwagon Food Court where we ate turkey legs ("the
best ever") corn-on-the-cob, and drank hot cider. At
another booth the tamales were gone very soon. We said:
"They must have been good." "The best" said a woman
standing close by.

ANNUAL EVENT: LAMPLIGHT TOUR   *Johnson City, 2nd
Sat in Dec, LBJ National Historical Park, 6:30-9:30 p.m..*

Lanterns at the LBJ Boyhood Home suggest his
youth, the era before electricity. But a block away, at the
headquarters of the Pedernales Electric Cooperative, there
is a blaze of lights from 150,000 tiny bulbs in all the trees
around the building. It is a beautiful sight. The boyhood
home and the headquarters, together, symbolize the
changes in the twentieth century.

Over at the Johnson Settlement, the doors are open at
the old log cabin, a fire is burning at the hearth, and there
is merriment, but this house shows the austerity of the
earliest era here. Gifts were simple. Decorations were few.
Christmas on the rugged frontier was far from lavish.

ANNUAL EVENT: TREE LIGHTING CEREMONY AND

EVENING TOURS Stonewall, 3rd Sunday in December, LBJ State Historical Park. 6 p.m.

In December 1970, not long after the park was dedicated, Lady Bird Johnson and her family came to flip on the lights on a huge cedar tree in the courtyard of the Visitors' Center. Thus began a charming Christmas custom of welcoming the neighbors from surrounding communities. She continues to come, now with grandchildren, and many in the communities volunteer to help. A short program includes representatives from all the churches here - Lutheran, Catholic, Baptist.

Cookies and punch are served and then visitors begin to load on to buses for a night viewing of the LBJ Ranch House with its gorgeous display of lights in the bushes and on the balcony railing, a look at the birthplace, and then a drive across the river again to the Sauer-Beckmann Farm for the special evening the volunteers have been planning for weeks. They have wound cedar and yaupon holly through the top of the wire fence, spread a garland of it over the archway, placed wreaths in the windows. They have made sausages and head cheese, baked cookies and cakes.

And, now, there it is. The house and yard lit with lanterns. Swags of greenery everywhere. The Christmas tree on a table in the formal parlor. It is lit with real candles, just as in the old days. (And there are plenty of people around to keep watch!) The other decorations are gaily colored sugar cookies, popcorn garlands, apples and oranges, the traditional Christmas treats.

And then to the kitchen and a glorious array of homemade bread and sausages and headcheese, cookies, pies, cakes. What they have to eat here always looks so good, and this is your chance to try some.

Soon you are back on the bus. It's an abbreviated tour on what a state park employee called "this one magical night."

LODGINGS

For guest cottages in Johnson City, contact Bed and Breakfast of Johnson City at 830/868-4548. At least five are available.

For accommodations in the country, contact the Chamber of Commerce in Johnson City. Ph: 830/868-7684.

RESTAURANT: HILL COUNTRY CUPBOARD *Johnson City, Hwy. 281.*

The Hill Country Cupboard is the kind of place where you go in and order chicken fried steak and fried okra and corn bread and blackberry cobbler. It is old-timey with ceiling fans and blue and white oil cloths on the tables. There are also hamburgers, soups, and vegetable plates.

Index